# Reach for the Stars

## S U C C E S S   S E C R E T S

From Top Trainers, Speakers, & Consultants So You Can Soar!

D1188602

*Compiled by* Doug Smart

James &
Brookfield
J&B
Publishers

*Atlanta, Georgia*

# Reach for the Stars
compiled by **Doug Smart**

Cover Design: Paula Chance
Editing: Kathy Meyer
Book Layout: Darlene Nicholas

For more information, contact:
James & Brookfield Publishers
P.O. Box 768024
Roswell, GA 30076
(770) 587-9784

Library of Congress Catalog Number 97-75590

ISBN: 0-9658893-0-0

10 9 8 7 6 5 4 3 2 1

# Dedication

*To grow, we must have the gift of dissatisfaction.*
*We must want circumstances to*
*be better than they are now.*
*If we are completely satisfied with our present state*
*in life and with everything that surrounds us, the*
*pilgrimage has ended for us, and we've already*
*settled in our little city of compromise.*
*We're bogged down in the quicksands of*
*complacency, lost in the sterile valleys of inertia,*
*and frozen in the ices of status quo.*
*It is only through divine discontent*
*that we keep moving forward.*
*Remember, you gotta wanta.*

**Cavett Robert**
**(1907-1997)**

# ★ Table of Contents ★

# ★ Introduction ★

Glance at a nickel and you know what the house looks like. I thrilled at the opportunity to see Thomas Jefferson's Monticello first hand. I ended my seminar at 3:45 and wheeled my rental car out of the hotel parking lot at 4:00. Good timing. Charlottesville, Virginia, being a small city from colonial times, would logically have its historic buildings in a convenient central age spot, I reasoned.

I knowingly aimed my car toward the oldest part of town. "It's got to be around here somewhere," I optimistically whispered. I saw old houses, old business buildings and a glorious old university. "It's got to be around here somewhere." I circled like a crow hoping to glean corn in February. "There has got to be an old street marked by a old sign that I'm not seeing. I'm not a quitter. Keep trying," I resolutely murmured. At 4:25 the frustration level choked the logic of my brain cells and I betrayed my gender by stopping for directions. Back in the car I muttered, "How was I suppose to know it's a *farm* 10 miles out of town." At 4:40 I swung into the tree shaded parking lot a half mile from Moticello and felt a surging wave of relief as I read the "open until 5" sign but felt marooned on the rocks of despair at "last tour leaves at 4:30." Bad timing. Success denied. (It would be 3 years before I could get back there *early*.)

"I did this to myself," I thought "I knew what I wanted and cruised to find it. I thought I'd just stumble onto success once again." I reached for a star and failed. Do you do that? Do you keep pushing forward looking to stumble onto success? Do you also feel frustrated when it doesn't happen the way it *should?*

My dad always says, "If you want to be successful at something real fast, be around people who are already successful at it." His love of that chestnut inspired this book. The trainers, speakers, and consultants in <u>Reach for the Stars</u> don't purport to have all the answers. It's just that we have spent quality time with a few hundred thousand people over a few years and we have learned a few things. And each of us is motivated by a desire to share what we've learned with you so that you have an easier journey as you reach for your success stars.

Don't be surprised to find contradictions in the advice shared here. Just as Presidents and royalty rely on cabinets of advisors to help guide them with a richness of opinions, so too, we present you with a variety of workable solutions. Choose the ones that best fit your style and situation. Call us mentors. We hope the messages in these pages inspire and guide you to new heights of achievement. If you would like to *literally* call on us, phone numbers are included. I personally selected each author and can unequivocally state that each will welcome a call from you to discuss a particular challenge you face.

Thank you for choosing to read <u>Reach for the Stars</u> to help you succeed in reaching *your* stars.

Doug Smart

# ★ 1 ★
# The Compelling Persona

by **Karla Brandau**

*Great men are meteors designed to burn*
*so that earth may be lighted.*

NAPOLEON

I grew up in Idaho where as a teenager, I spent long summer days under clear, hot skies raking hay on our farm. I thought it was mindless work to drive the tractor up and down the fields raking the hay into rows for the bailer to gobble up and make into tight bales.

So I used to dream… dream of becoming someone. I didn't know where I would go or what I would do when I grew up, but I knew I would use every fiber of my being to become "somebody."

Now that I have left the family farm behind, I relate to comedian, Lily Tomlin, when she said, "I always dreamed of becoming somebody… I guess I should have been more specific."

As I started into the work world and set out to become "somebody," I observed people who had compelling auras around them. I noticed people who had certain qualities to which I was magnetically drawn. I analyzed them, trying to identify what the magnetism was and decided there were several factors.

Today, after spending many years in corporate America, I have synthesized four main characteristics individuals with compelling personas possess. These characteristics are present in various mixes, and normally an individual will be stronger in one than the others. The four characteristics are:

- Purpose
- Integrity
- Charisma
- Collaboration

When you find people with huge doses of any one of these qualities, you want to sit next to them in meetings and listen carefully to the advice they give you. You want to get *tied to their coattails* and *hitch your wagon to their star* for you know they are the movers and *shapers* of the next decade.

I affectionately call these character groups the:

- Purpose People
- Integrity-based Bunch
- Charismatic Crowd
- Collaborative Collection

## Compelling Characteristics of Purpose People
*There can only be one winner. Do you still want to play?*

## Purpose
Purpose is a stimulating element of life. It includes goal setting but is much larger. A purpose remains constant over several years and has great benefit for the human psyche: it tranquilizes the mind and becomes a point on which the soul may fix its intellectual eye.

As the mind is focused and purpose crystallizes, purpose acts as a catalytic force, an organizing principle, for everything that is done. It directs daily effort and jumpstarts each morning.

## Purpose People Ignite Fires
The Purpose People are intense workers and aggressively pursue life. Purpose People know how to focus and they play to win.
I grew up playing the piano and trying to be fine and refined. When I fell in love, I fell in love with a quarterback and a pitcher. He introduced me to a different world, the rough and tough world of athletics. One night we were watching a TV movie about Vince Lombardi, the legendary coach of the Green Bay Packers. I will never forget one scene.

Lombardi had just taken over as the coach of the downtrodden Packers and was in a press conference. The reporters were anything but kind. They were making jokes about Lombardi's purpose: to win!

One reporter, with a sneer in his voice, said, "Oh, when you say you will win, does that mean you will win two games this year?"

In controlled rage, Lombardi said, "Let me tell you about winning, mister. Winning means that you are willing to give more and play harder than anyone else. If you're smaller, you better run faster. If you're slower, you better hit harder. If you'd put that to practice in your life, you'd be winning Pulitzer Prizes instead of sitting here in a snowstorm asking stupid questions."

Lombardi ignited fires inside the Green Bay Packers and they became the dominant team of the 60's and won Super Bowls I and II.

**Purpose People Direct Organizations**

In organizations, with true Vince Lombardi style, Purpose People typically have roles where they manage and direct others because they are excellent at making decisions, are assertive, and are producers with everything they touch having a bottom-line, results-oriented urgency.

**How To Develop More Purpose**

If you want to develop more purpose in your life, do these things:

1. *Decide why you exist and what your purpose is.*

Buy books or attend seminars designed to help you clarify your values, write mission statements, and set goals. Take some down time. Get away from the frenetic pace. Go to a quiet place and think. Decide who you are, what defines who you are and what you want to achieve.

When your purpose as an individual is clear, it will be easier to translate the process to your organization. Organizations with clear purposes are those that consistently win in the world marketplace.

2. *Take responsibility and offer no excuses.*

Mike Krzyzewski is the coach of the Duke Blue Devils. He led them to back-to-back national championships in 1991 and 1992. However, the most important story may be about the year before when they were humiliated in front of a 30 million television audience by the University of Nevada, Las Vegas in the NCAA championship game. The final score was 103-73.

In Season on the Brink, sports writer, John Feinstein tells that Krzyzewski attended West Point where as a plebe, only three answers to any questions were allowed: "Yes-sir!" "No-sir!" and "No-excuse-sir!" Many times Krzyzewski heard himself saying, "No-excuse-sir!"

That night as he faced a sea of reporters, he could have offered excuses. However, his West Point experience had taught him that when he failed, in the big things or the small ones, it was his responsibility — no one else's. He would not only accept that he failed; he would remember and learn from it.

So looking squarely into the cameras that night, he said: "They beat us in every way possible. If I had a hat, I would take it off to them." To himself, he said, "Wait until next season." The next season they won their first of the two national championships.

### 3. Dump emotional baggage.

This example of Krzyzewski also illustrates that people with purpose don't hang onto failure, disappointment, or the irritations of the day. They take responsibility, deal with it, learn what they can and move onto greater achievements. They know that nothing we attempt is ever without error and they see life in terms of what they learned from the experience, not in terms of failures.

Krzyzewski tells his players, "Never forget a defeat because that is the key to victory."

### 4. Practice finding answers and being decisive.

Visualize a sign on your manager's desk with the letters: BA. This sign does not mean bad attitude or born again, but it means *Bring Answers!* It is a reminder to do the research, analyze the options, and choose the best route *before* you approach the purposeful manager.

### 5. Let Purpose People mentor you.

Peter Swet in *Parade* magazine reports that when Jay Leno first met Johnny Carson, Johnny said, "You seem like a very funny young man. But you don't have enough jokes."

Leno was devastated. Then Leno watched the Carson show and saw him do 15 to 20 jokes in the time Jay took to do three. Leno filled the time with clowning and gestures, not jokes. Even though Leno resented what Johnny had said, he took it to heart and began honing his material. Leno said, "I'll always be grateful to him for giving me real advice — hard as it seemed at the time."

Sometimes our egos get in the way but if you lack direction, purpose, or can't decide what to do, find one of the Purpose

People and ask for advice. Your learning curve will be cut in half, and your floundering will take a vacation.

## Compelling Characteristics of the Integrity-based Bunch

*Resolve to perform what ye ought,*
*and perform without fail what you resolve.*
BENJAMIN FRANKLIN

### Integrity

Integrity is the core principle that keeps business in business. Can you imagine a world where vendors don't deliver and customers don't pay for product?

To meet someone and feel from her aura that she is a person of integrity is a compelling reason to do business with that person.

### The Integrity-Based Bunch and Conscience

The Integrity-based Bunch is the moral conscience of us all, much like the little boy in the grocery store who wanted some grapes. His mother tasted a grape, found them to be sweet, put two big bunches in her cart and continued her shopping.

They reached the checkout counter and after the mother had written a check for the groceries, her young son tugged on her jacket and in anything but a timid voice said, "But Mommy, you didn't pay for the grape you ate." The mother looked at him for a few seconds, dug through her purse, found a penny, laid it on the counter and said, "And that is for the grape I ate."

### The Integrity-based Bunch Do Quality Work

In your organization, the Integrity-based Bunch insure that work is done to a high ten and that quality standards are met. They insure that the rules, policies, and procedures are followed. They add intellectual thinking to discussions and are good at weighing the pros and cons of decisions. They are tenacious people who stick to a project until it is finished.

The Integrity-based Bunch is honest and obedient. They obey such commands as: Under penalty of the law — do not remove this tag — notices on pillows, mattresses, or hair dryer cords. They never go "in" when the sign says "exit only" and they return wallets — with all the money still inside.

## How to Develop More Integrity

If you want to develop more of the compelling attributes of integrity, do the following:

### 1. Keep your word.

An old story told about a professor, Dr. Karl G. Maeser, illustrates this point. In an address to the student body, Dr. Maeser gave a definition of what he meant by honor. "My young friends," he said, "I have been asked what I mean by 'word of honor.' I will tell you. Place me behind prison walls — walls of stone ever so high, ever so thick, reaching ever so far into the ground — there is a possibility that in some way or another I may be able to escape; but stand me on the floor and draw a chalk line around me and have me give my word of honor never to cross it. Can I get out of that circle? No, never! I'd die first."

When you promise work done by the 1st, make sure it is completed by the 1st. When you say, "I'll handle that," make sure you handle it. You will become known as someone who can be trusted.

### 2. Volunteer for worthwhile causes.

Philip Smith is one of the world's finest classical trumpeters. He plays for the New York Philharmonic. Thomas Hartman in <u>Just a Moment</u> says that Smith feels two things helped him achieve success: his love and dedication to music and his volunteer work with the Salvation Army. Some of Smith's first public performances were with the Salvation Army where his father was a bandmaster of the Army staff band.

Each Christmas Philip Smith volunteers and can be found in his Salvation Army uniform outside a department store or a supermarket playing carols. His cap will be pulled down tight. Many will pass by without dropping their change in the kettle and some may tease him. No one will recognize him as the man "they wanted to hear at the concert, but the tickets were sold out." However, "Joy to the World" and "Silent Night" will be mysteriously articulate and inspiring.

### 3. Go the extra mile.

The founder of the popular chain of discount-muffler shops, Sam Meineke, grew up as a sharecropper's son in Oklahoma.

When the family moved to Pasadena, Texas, he mowed lawns for 50 cents and by the time he was 21 he had scraped up $600 for a down payment on a service station. He recalls that for six months he was working from 6 a.m. until 10 p.m. but wasn't making any money. Then one day a man came in for a dollar's worth of gas. Since business was slow, Meineke wiped his windshield, then said, "Sir, I'll do the inside too."

"Tell you what, son," the customer replied, "fill'er up. I've never had this kind of service."

Suddenly Meineke had found his business-success formula: "Treat the customers right and give them extra service." Soon cars were lined up around the block.

Give this same attention to detail as you service the customer both inside and outside of the organization and you will make huge advances toward achieving the compelling personality.

### 3. Develop self-discipline.

The Integrity-based Bunch finds the success that comes with discipline and practice. We are all familiar with the self-discipline it takes to be a great athlete or musician. It is reported that after a stunning performance, the pianist Paderewski was enthusiastically approached by a woman who said, "I would give my life to play like that." Paderewski replied, "That is exactly what I have done."

Let's look to another realm: acting. Michael Richards makes us all laugh so effortlessly as Kramer on *Seinfeld*.

Effortlessly? Maybe not. He is a perfectionist and doesn't hang around after the show to hobnob and pose for photographs, but retreats to his dressing room to go over his pickups (scenes that will be reshot with the cast after the audience has gone) and additional scenes he will insist on reshooting (in close-up) with a skeleton crew till 2 o'clock in the morning.

Seinfeld says that Richards is completely committed to go to any length to make a comedic moment work, up to and including killing himself.

You don't want to kill yourself over a project, but success does take daily discipline and effort.

### 5. Be a finisher.

Henry Wadsworth Longfellow once wrote: "Great is the art of beginning, but greater is the art of ending."

In October of 1982, Linda Down, a 25-year-old woman, finished the New York City Marathon 11 hours after she started. Why even report this finisher? Because she had cerebral palsy and was the first woman ever to complete the 26.2-mile race on crutches. Even though she fell half a dozen times, she kept going. Her handicap limited her speed but not her determination.

You don't have a genie to finish your work. If you want to have a compelling persona, use discipline and determination to be a finisher.

## Compelling Characteristics of the Charismatic Crowd —
*Dance with the sunbeams of life.*
KARLA BRANDAU

### Charisma

A young lady in a seminar recently asked me, "How can I develop more charisma?" That question made me stop and think. How do you define it? What is it? How *do* you get more of it? Why do you want it?

Charisma is a powerful quality that draws people to you. It is flashy and flamboyant. It is warm and friendly. It is showy and animated. It is humorous and fun.

One sales professional, with tons of charisma and consistently a top performer, told me, "I love selling. I just get up every morning and go out and talk to my friends." He did intuitively what corporations spend millions of dollars trying to teach.

### The Charismatic Crowd Animate Life

Susanna Clark said,

> "You've got to sing
> Like you don't need the money.
> You've got to love
> Like you'll never get hurt.
> You've got to dance
> Like there's nobody watching.
> You've got to come from the heart
> If you want it to work."

Susanna Clark has just described how the Charismatic Crowd lives life. They give life 110%. They smile; they laugh; they tell jokes. They enjoy friendships and take time for relationships.

Their attitude about life can be summarized by a friend who told me what she wanted at her funeral:

"I want the church to be brimming. I want glorious obituaries lightly spiced with some irreverent anecdotes about my life. I want laughter along with the tears. I want everyone to know that I had a whale of a time walking about God's earth."

### The Charismatic Crowd Energizes Organizations

In organizations, the Charismatic Crowd creates an environment of optimism and excitement. They are great at planning promotions, jump-starting projects, and ensuring the annual awards dinner is lively.

They provide relief from the intensity of the work day.

### How to develop more Charisma

If you want more charisma in order to have a more compelling persona, work on these points:

*1. Have lively body language.*

When you walk, walk with spryness and spirit.

When you shake hands, pass on something of yourself, much like Mark Twain did when he met Helen Keller. Helen Keller, though both deaf and blind, commented, "I can feel the twinkle of his eye in his handshake."

When you greet people, look them directly in the eyes. Let your eyes show them that your heart is home.

Laugh with people. Let your smiles cover your whole face. Remember, it takes 45 muscles to frown, and 17 to smile. How hard do you want to work?

When you are asked, "How are you today?" Reply, "Terrrrific!"

*2. Treat everyone like a VIP.*

When a person from the Charismatic Crowd talks to you, he can make you feel as if you are his best friend and that he has all the time in the world just for you.

Mary Kay Ash, founder of Mary Kay Cosmetics, attributes her success to the ability to make every single person she meets feel special. She teaches her sales professionals to pretend everyone has a sign around the neck that says: *Make me feel important.*

Next time someone makes a magical connection to you, observe what the person did to make you feel your worth. Try the techniques on the next person you meet.

*3. Develop your conversation skills.*

To members of the Charismatic Crowd, friendly chitchat comes easily and serves them well in social situations.

They use conversation techniques such as:

… oh. It was the best movie?

… you're kidding. Tell me more.

… uh huh. I see.

Intuitively they draw you into conversations about your kids, your pets, your last vacation, your favorite sit-com, or your favorite baseball club. Their techniques are so subtle that when you are done talking about yourself, you walk away and say, "My, we had a great conversation. I really like him."

*4. Develop your optimism.*

As M. Scott Peck stated in *A Road Less Traveled*: "Life is difficult. Once you accept that, it no longer matters." Internalize this concept and you can get on with developing your optimism.

Comedian Joan Rivers developed the optimism of the Charismatic Crowd when she had a tough time coming back after the suicide of her husband and manager, Edgar Roseberg. In her book Still Talking, she writes, "Even if things go badly, the bottom I might hit would be nowhere near as deep as what I have been through. I have become my version of an optimist. If I can't get through one door, I'll go through another — or I'll *make* a door. Something *terrific* will come no matter how dark the present."

The Charismatic Crowd sees the silver lining. They expect success every day and know that attitude is everything.

*5. Develop your humor.*

Humor endears you to people. For instance, a friend of British actor Michael Caine invited him to come along when he had a dinner engagement with the great boxing champ Muhammad Ali, who billed himself as the fastest man in boxing.

Caine described Ali as "ebullient" (saucy and high-spirited) and was a bit apprehensive when Ali asked Caine, "Do you want to see my right hook?" Caine said, "Yes," hoping Ali would miss his chin in the demonstration. Ali stood absolutely still for a second or two and then said, "Do you want to see it again?"

Caine became a fan.

Humor also helps you out of tight situations much like the waitress who came out of the kitchen with a tray of food held confidently above her head on one hand. The tray of food was brimming with succulent steaks and mashed potatoes smothered with gravy. At the last minute the tray started to tip. It tipped and tipped until a plate slid off and landed in a lady's partially opened purse. The waitress looked down and said, "You wanted that to go, didn't you?"

## Compelling Characteristics of the Collaborative Collection

*Never doubt that a small group of thoughtful,*
*committed people can change the world.*
*Indeed, it is the only thing that ever has.*
SUCCESSORIES

### Collaboration

A Kikuyu proverb states: "When elephants fight, it is the grass that suffers."

Human nature makes us territorial animals. We stake out what is ours and go to war if our turf is threatened. A certain amount of this is necessary for self-preservation, but it must be harnessed if we are going to develop this fourth characteristic of the compelling persona, collaboration.

The Collaborative Collection seeks to mediate, to bring people together, and to build win-win solutions for everyone so the grass, or the organization, does not suffer.

### The Collaborative Collection's Gentle Touch

The Collaborative Collection has a gentle touch about them, much like Clint Eastwood developed as a director. John Balzar in the Los Angeles *Times* reports that Eastwood doesn't yell, "ACTION" when he is ready to start a scene. Instead he says a casual "Okay." Eastwood explains he learned when filming *Rawhide* that when you yell "ACTION," it sends adrenalin not only through the actors, but through the horses as well who end up jumping out of the shot, making you start over again.

## The Collaborative Collection Are Team Players

Mary, a human resource director, shook my hand then looked me straight in the eye and with an intense tone of voice said, "Your programs on team building are the most critical programs I will offer this year because this company does not fire people due to technical incompetence, they are let go because they can't get along with other team members. I am constantly looking for ways to help them build their team player skills."

Today's work environment demands more teamwork and collaboration for organizational success. The reward for teamwork is a certain exhilaration that comes from winning by overcoming obstacles together. It does not matter whether you are part of a surgical team, an opera cast, or the sales team for a new product.

## How To Develop Collaboration Skills

If you would like to develop the skills of collaboration, try these suggestions:

*1. Listen carefully.*

When you listen to people, do you listen as carefully as Baltimore Oriole Cal Ripken, Jr. did a few years ago?

Steve Wulf writes in *Time* that Ripken, the man who broke Lou Gehrig's "Iron Man" record for the most consecutive games played, doesn't just sign autographs–he engages people in conversation. One day a woman asked for an autograph for her daughter, Kelly. Ripken wrote: "If you look like your mother, I'm sorry I missed you. Cal Ripken." The mother then described her eligible daughter.

Several months later, the daughter, Kelly, was in a restaurant and Ripken was signing autographs again. Kelly walked over to Cal and thanked him for being so nice to her mother. Ripken said, "You must be Kelly. You're six feet tall, blond, you have green eyes, you went to the University of Maryland, and you work for the airlines." They were married four years later.

*2. Be diplomatic and tactful.*

I was shopping for a new suit and found one that was a perfect color and had great style. The coat fit wonderfully well, but the skirt was a little too tight around the waistline. I sadly took it off and as I walked out of the dressing room, I noticed a sign that said, "Alterations —skirts, $7.50." I could afford that, so with a big smile I asked the clerk who had been helping me to see if the skirt could be altered. She called her competent Chinese tailor who measured my waist, measured the skirt and then said, "So sorry. So sorry. The skirt can come out 1 inch. You need two." "I'll buy you a can of slimfast," the clerk quipped.

Ouch!

People in the Collaborative Collection are very tactful. They don't say, "That suit looks bad on you." They say, "This suit might look better." They don't say, "He is brash and rude." They say, "He has the potential to be rude in certain situations."

You will make great progress in developing a compelling persona if you practice tact.

*3. Accept people "AS IS."*

One day in Chicago at Marshall Fields, I saw a young woman eyeing the clothes on the bargain rack. She pulled out a lovely dress. When she looked at the price tag her faced showed disbelief — the price was so low. However, the dress was marked, "AS IS." She anxiously checked the dress for flaws and found that it only had a couple of buttons missing which she knew she could easily replace. She purchased the dress and got great value for her money.

The same principle applies in the *scratch and dent* section of appliances stores. My neighbor bought a washer with a dent on the side that went against the wall. She also got great value for her money.

The point? Everyone has a scratch or a dent or a button off somewhere. The Collaborative Collection understands this human fact and in a nonjudgmental, patient way, they accept people "AS IS." Being accepted "AS IS" permits individuals to build self-esteem and improve performance.

*4. Be supportive.*

Barbara Bush gives us an example of the people support offered by the Collaborative Collection. Carl Sferrazza Anthony in his book *First Ladies*, reports that at a celebration for the bicentennial of the Constitution, Barbara Bush was to appear on an ABC-TV special filmed before a live audience of 800,000. Earlier that day, Bush had met a 62-year-old retired construction worker, who was scheduled to read the Constitution's Preamble. The man had only recently learned to read and was so nervous about appearing that he wanted to cancel just hours before the show. Bush drew his fears out of him. When he explained there were words he didn't understand, she said she ran into words like that as well and suggested they read the Preamble together.

On stage that night, the duo began, but, as the man's confidence grew, Barbara Bush lowered her voice. A class act indeed.

*5. Be authentic.*

Bob Greene in *Hang Time*, his book about Michael Jordan, tells of Carmen Villafane, a little girl with cerebral palsy. She had been a quadriplegic all her life. Her face would often twitch uncontrollably and her arms and legs were subject to violent spasms so she was strapped into a wheelchair.

One year during the week of Valentine's Day her parents bought tickets to the Bulls' game. Her wheelchair was on the main floor when the teams came out before introductions. She tried to steer herself up close to the Bulls' bench. When stopped by a security guard, she said, "I want to give a valentine to Michael Jordan." The security guard allowed her to move closer. She gave the card to Jordan. He said, "Is this for me?" Carmen was too excited to say anything. She nodded. He opened it, read it right there and thanked the little girl.

She never dreamed she would get that close again until unexpectedly a thick envelope came in the mail. It was filled with tickets to every home game for the season with a note that said, "I hope you enjoy the season ahead. I'm looking forward to seeing you at every game, Michael."

Now she sits right behind the Bulls' bench.

Take time out of your busy life to be human and real. It will add to your compelling persona.

### *Developing all Facets of the Compelling Persona*

The marketplace is changing. Management is changing. This was brought home to me in a conversation I had with a human resource executive from McDonalds. He told me that managers with only a purpose orientation were not being promoted. Those getting the nod were a blend of purpose, collaboration, and charisma. Integrity was assumed.

Most individuals have one area that is stronger than the other three. If this is true of you, I challenge you to develop all facets of the compelling persona. To do this, I suggest you:

1. Reread these pages and decide your strengths. Enjoy them.

2. Next, pick a point in one of your weak areas and write down a few things you can do to make this attribute a strong factor in your personality.

3. Act consciously on what you have written.

Now, write me a letter and tell me your success story. Tell me how you developed a compelling persona. Send the letter to:

Life Power Dynamics, P.O. Box 450802, Atlanta, GA 31145-0802  E-mail: **Karla@kbrandau.com**

When you have developed a compelling persona, your influence will be extraordinary and you will be one of those who shape the future.

# Karla Brandau

Karla Brandau is the President of Life Power Dynamics, a company she founded in 1985 to assist corporations and their employees to increase profits through improved leadership, interpersonal relationships, and personal competence. Her client list includes Coca-Cola, Motorola, Lucent Technologies, BellSouth, and Digital Equipment Corporation.

Karla graduated cum laude from Brigham Young University, has been an instructor for the American Management Association, and is a past president of Georgia Speakers Association. She is a member of the American Society for Training and Development, a member of Meeting Professionals International, and is listed in "Who's Who of Executive Women." In addition, she is a member of National Speakers Association and is a candidate to earn the Certified Speaking Professional designation.

She has written the book, <u>Winning Calisthenics, *Mental Exercises for Success*</u>, and produced a tape series, Time For Results.

You can reach Karla at Life Power Dynamics, PO Box 450802, Atlanta, GA 31145-0802 Phone (770) 923-0883, Fax (770) 931-2530, or E-mail: <u>Karla@kbrandau.com.</u>

# ★ 2 ★
# Health, Wealth, Happiness... and a Pothole

by **June Cline**

The ground flew up and smacked my face so fast; I didn't even have time to blink. So, that's what those tiny pebbles in the pavement look like at ground zero. I felt like a dropped camera in a Steven Spielberg film. The shock, surprise, and suddenness of my fall played over and over in slow motion in my mind. I had successfully stepped into a pothole, a hole in the road.

My right ankle was dying with a pain that made me sweat. I knew I was really hurt. Huddled in the fetal position at a three-way stop in the road, I grabbed for my ankle. My hands didn't make it past my bleeding knees, which were screaming for attention since plowing themselves into the pavement in a last ditch effort to save my face — successfully. I hung onto my knees, rocking myself like I needed to be in a home. I had been walking and talking with a nice woman that I didn't know — to quote a Southern saying from "Adam's house cat." We had just met — when I dropped out of her sight.

People at the stop signs were getting out of their cars to help me. Well, it is the South. It was after all Chastain Park, one of the nicest parks in the Buckhead area of Atlanta, Georgia. The woman I was talking with exclaimed, "I heard something pop! I heard something pop!"

Until that moment, I had been in a state of shock. But, with those words, from a woman I did not know, I let the whimpering begin. Wailing soon followed. I was just about to break into some good old writhing with pain when a distinguished looking middle-aged man knelt down beside me.

"May I touch your leg?" he asked gently. Frankly, he was cute. And even if he was some kind of pervert passing by the park in the wee hours of a Saturday morning, I was in need of attention.

"It hurts; it hurts" I remember whimpering. "We just need to see if it's broken." Someone else was repeating, "Do we need to call an ambulance?" I was thinking "Life Flight! Send in the helicopter!" The man kneeling beside me said calmly "Let's give her a moment."

"Are you a doctor?" someone asked. "No, but I play one on TV," would have been okay with me. "Yes, I am," he replied. YES! My angels at work. They always come through. A doctor happens by Chastain Park at 8:00 a.m. — just at the moment when I sink my foot into an 8-inch pothole. Now that's my idea of success! I love how my life works! I am the most blessed person I know. Can you think of times you thought you were really in trouble or had a specific need and from out of the blue came an answer or just the inspiration that you needed? I believe that's how our angels work. Sometimes, I get goose bumps when it happens. I call those "angel hugs." They love to give 'em, if we are just willing to receive 'em.

I was still lying in the fetal position, staring at his "Bruno Tamales" and thinking… "nice Dockers's." Within five minutes, this guardian angel doctor had me up and limping to a nearby bench. "It's not broken," he said, "but it's gonna hurt and you need to get it elevated and iced." I must have hit my head because I actually heard myself ask, "Then, you don't recommend that I do my ten miles today?" "Uh, no," he replied with a gentle but stern smile. He turned to leave. I asked him his name. He told me. "Thank you, Dr.____," I repeated his name — which for the life of me, I cannot remember. I held his gaze for a sincere moment and silently thanked him again from my heart to his soul. With the connection made, he turned and walked away. I hope he knew how successful he was that day.

By noon, I was back home telling my long "sore-ded" tale to my husband, the light-of-my-life-the-flame-of-my-eternal-being, Jerry E. Cline. I completed the details of how I painfully drove myself back to Kennesaw and headed straight to my chiropractor's office, who took a tuning fork, whacked it against a bench, and touched several areas on my right ankle and foot while asking, "Does this hurt?" It didn't hurt, and he, too, announced that my foot was not broken explaining that had it been, I would have wanted to whack him at the first tuning touch. He then confirmed the same corrective action given by that nice doctor with the "Bruno Tamales." Jerry listened. Looking somewhat perplexed and concerned for me, he repeated "Chiropractor? Tuning fork?" "Did the chiropractor then sacrifice a chicken? Did he have a bone in his nose?" he asked. We have a fundamental difference about the value of chiropractic care, and I can always count on him to lighten the moment I playfully said "Where are those tuning forks!"

## Lessons From Life's Potholes

There's a lot you can learn from a pothole. Sometimes, you gotta fall down before you can climb up. I realize this is a very deep and philosophical kind of statement, much like "Success is a journey, not a destination." But, who really knows what that means either? Whose journey is it? And aren't we all wondering where the heck the destination is? If you have seen Billy Crystal's movie <u>City Slickers</u> you know the answer… "It's this one thing." You and I get to figure out what that one thing is for us.

I do know that fear jumped all over me on that perfect day when my journey was to successfully race-walk 10 miles in preparation for a later destination in the Honolulu Marathon. In order for me to allow myself to commit to the time, energy, and money that it would take for me to complete this 26.2 mile event, I had tied it mentally to my health, business, spirituality, and happiness. And, in a split second — a date with a pothole — my mental picture of what each of those looked like was gone.

Have you ever linked your goals, actions, or dreams to something precious and allowed that linkage to pull you out of a pothole? Have you allowed yourself to work through the pain of feelings, inaction, inadequacy, boredom, or despair? Have you given yourself permission to experience the joy and the pain of commitment, dedication, determination, and dependability? I had linked everything to this upcoming event. I knew that my physical health and energy would improve by dedicating myself to exercising, sleeping, and eating right. I quickly figured out that I couldn't *wing* 26.2 miles. I've spent a lot of my life *winging it*. And, frankly, I am pretty darn good at it. But this event would require true dedication — the kind of dedication I needed in my business.

From that thought, I realized that this event could have a positive impact on my business. I identified some specific *steps* I wanted to take and determined what I needed to focus on in my business. My time management skills would definitely have to improve to incorporate 15 - 40 hours per week of race walking. To paraphrase a workshop I recently attended, "Time management is a choice. And the reality is, in today's environment you and I do not have the time not to manage our time. There is no 'time out' with time." Each day that I had the courage to take the time to *go the distance* physically, I equated with having the courage to *go the distance* fiscally in my speaking and training business. To my surprise the quality time devoted to me began to generate new material and ideas. Ten miles out is a long way. I carried a small tape recorder to capture the creative flow of ideas that often were overwhelmingly exciting.

This is when I made the spiritual connection. While going the distance, I decided to listen to my angels and to look for ways they would show up in my life. I received incredible gifts from the Universe during my walks. Sometimes… I could hear God smile. One of the greatest gifts I have ever received while on my race walking journey was hearing the sound of bagpipes one day coming from the woods of Kennesaw. For a moment, I was concerned about my mental health. But, sure enough, I followed the sound and found a kilt-less man, wearing denim shorts, playing bagpipes in the middle of an open field. The sun had almost set into the blue evening of the night, and the echo of the music hung in the trees like a light fog. It was beautiful and surreal. Beneath the glow of a gas street lamp, I gave him a standing ovation and a double thumbs-up. He nodded without missing a note.

I thought, "Man, is this perfect or what! The only way it could be better is if there were a full moon." I walked out of the woods… into the view of the biggest, pumpkin orange, full harvest moon I have ever seen. YES! Angels at work… I could hear God smiling. Now, that was a moment. It was one of those moments that will make me smile when I am old and happy, rocking in my chair — remembering when I had the strength, courage, and determination to go for my dreams. And isn't that what life is truly about? It's just a series of moments. I call them *memory makin' moments*. The good and bad news is we get to assign the feelings that we attach to all of our moments. Talk about feeling connected! I was that day, and on many other walks, in the woods of Kennesaw, Georgia.

## Mental Potholes and How to Go Around Them

I was connected to a different picture as I lay there hurting by that pothole. I allowed pain, fear, and the words of a stranger, "I heard something pop," to send me into a whirlwind of emotional panic. In a heartbeat, I saw myself on crutches, catching a plane for Indianapolis where I would be speaking for the National Rural Water Association Monday morning. I already knew I would use my sore armpits (from the crutches) as new material. I saw six months of training go down the drain. With only two and a half months left before the Honolulu Marathon, would I have time to recover and be prepared? I wanted to see Honolulu from a view that few will ever experience and to complete an event that less than 1% of the population is even willing to try. How often and how quickly are we willing to let our plans and dreams go out the window due to a set-back? The bigger question is why do we do that? Extreme pain seemed a good enough reason for me. I knew that the way I handled this situation would determine not only the future of my foot, but also my future — period. Dr. Vern Morgan, a friend and leading authority in the area of Human Potential, has a saying: "How you do anything is how you do everything." Now, that's deep — almost as deep as that 8-inch pothole. How would I handle this?

"Every challenge is an opportunity to become more than you currently are." I heard this once in a tape. I loved it, and I believe it. That is exactly why I had taken on the challenge of a marathon. One of my success strategies is to always be involved in something that is bigger than I am — something that takes me outside of myself. The Georgia Leukemia Society Team-in-Training was the perfect opportunity. Talk about a win/win situation. Professional speaker, marathoner, and soul mate friend, Steve Moroski, introduced this organization to me. Not only would I be forced (notice I did say "forced") to make myself stay in shape, but I would also be raising money for a wonderful cause. I would also have the honor of meeting and sponsoring a child who had the biggest challenge of all—fighting leukemia. Now that's a big pothole.

## Torey's Pothole

I will never forget the day I met my honoree. Picture me nervous as I knocked on the door of young Torey McKnight's house in Monroe, Georgia. What does a humorist say to a seven-year-old boy with leukemia? Add being kid-less to the scenario, and you've got a pretty speechless professional speaker staring into the face of a mother with two darling kids wrapped around her knees.

"Hi, I'm June Cline with the Leukemia Team-in-Training. I'm a little early—by about three hours, I hope that's okay." "Sure it is" she replied. "We've been excited to meet you." "Whew," I thought, "my mouth still works." I had made it to first base. "And, you must be Torey," I said to the older child. "No, I'm 'T'." he replied, which is short for Teion. "Oh," I said rather startled. "Then, you must be Torey," I said smiling down at the littlest one. "No," he shook his red head with a grin, so enchanting it would charm the devil. "okay, Cline, Faux pax number two in less than two seconds — this is gonna go well," I said to myself in a "titch" of self-chatter. "This is trouble — but we call him 'Nek,' which is short for Nikko," replied the young mother. "T-O-R-E-Y!!! Someone is here to see you." "okay, Mom," came a reply from upstairs. The two legwraps disengaged themselves and bounded to the top of the stairs to retrieve Torey.

Charity McKnight invited me into their new home where she and her mother, Gayla Knight, a nurse, are combining efforts to raise three boys. They recently moved to Georgia believing this is where Torey would receive the best medical care. Thankfully he is in remission today, though not out of the woods yet as he still has another year of chemo. He raced down the steps after his mother's third call. A little speechless he said "Hi" and plopped down on the couch at his mother's side.

"I am so tickled to meet you," I said. I detected a shy smile. "I hear you like baseball a lot." I received a slight smile (great… second base.) "Maybe you'll like this then," and I handed him a gift bag with colorful clowns on it containing an Atlanta Braves hat and a limited edition signed baseball. YES! We had a full-blown smile — we had made it to third base! I was speaking his language. Though he already had a Braves hat, he assured me that one more was not a problem. Apparently, even at this early age, it's a man thing that you can never have too many hats. As I listened for the next two and a half hours to the brave story of Torey McKnight and his beautiful family, I realized it is appropriate that he loves the Braves. For that is what this leukemia fighting family is — brave. This little boy has a shunt in his arm and leg where he receives cancer treatments once a week. Every third

Wednesday, the medication makes him so sick, it takes him until the next Tuesday to recover. He "coded" once in his mother's arms where, thank God, they were in the hospital. She stood by helplessly as they miraculously revived her son. I said to Ms. McKnight, "I know you've heard the saying 'We're not given more than we can handle.' But, girl… you've got a ton heaped up on your plate!"

"I know that saying, but I don't know about the handling it part," she replied. "I know that we would not be surviving this thing were it not for the help we have received from Egleston Children's Hospital and the wonderful programs such as the Leukemia Team in Training. We need people like you who are willing to give of themselves, their time, and money."

What a humbling experience to meet such a challenged and dedicated family. And what an honor and inspiration to know Torey. It will take all of us to help Torey and the 30,000 like him to get out of a pothole that at times seems bigger than life. He's a fighter. "Every challenge is an opportunity to become more than you currently are." Torey is already there.

## Most Planning Doesn't Include Potholes

I am often reminded of Torey's determination by the green hospital band I wear daily in his honor to help me prepare for race day. It reminds me that I, too, am a fighter. It's been two weeks since I fell into that pothole in the road at Chastain Park. Today, I did my first two miles back toward the Marathon. I have been gentle with myself, trying not to beat myself up emotionally over stepping into that dumb hole. And I have taken care of myself physically by not pushing the healing process so I don't injure myself further. I am learning to listen to my body. I hope you will do the same for yourself whenever healing of any type is required. My ankle does *pop* more than it did. With a little practice, I will be able to pop out Beethoven's Fifth Symphony. I'll have a new *ankle act*. Who knew? Success is all about how we look at things and then what actions we choose to take. I am confident that I will be 100% ready for the Honolulu Marathon in December. One of my favorite quotes is "If you want to make God laugh…tell him your plans." That is my plan… "God willing and the creek don't rise!" to quote an old Southern saying. I do think planning is highly overrated. It does not allow for the pothole factor. Of course, I do plan. In fact, several years ago, I wrote a poem about it…

### The Plan

Foxy forties...
Nifty fifties...
Sexy sixties...
Skiing seventies...
Elegant eighties...
Naughty nineties...
Happy hundred...
Reassess the plan!

I wrote this when forty seemed old and a long way off. What's interesting is that back then the thought of being around after one hundred years to "reassess the plan" was meant to be funny. But now sitting in the middle of forty, it sounds like a pretty darn good plan! For my generation, the reality is that we may very well live to be one hundred plus years old. "If I had known I would live this long, I would have taken better care of myself." There is a ton of wisdom in that old quote.

Today, we had better know what our success looks like and how to take care of our health, wealth, and happiness. My life management theme song is "Roll With It, Baby!" sung by Steve Winwood. Of course, I hate that I had to take that line literally and actually roll down the street. We do have to roll with whatever life throws at us. I did not see that pothole, and I'll bet there are other potholes out there. I believe it's a good thing we can't see them. Just think of the roads that we might be tempted to miss for fear of the potholes. Do plan... just plan to be flexible! I would have missed some wonderful opportunities, friendships, and experiences had I been stuck strictly to *the plan*. A prime example of that would be the very pages you are reading now.

**How to Avoid Rose-Colored Potholes**
Know when to say "no." This is the hardest success strategy for me. There are so many colors on my pallet, and I want them all. I sometimes can't choose one even to get started. Canadian Country Singer Michelle Wright has my favorite line in one of her songs: "I know I can't taste it all — there are just too many flavors." But, man, do I want to try! And, in order to be successful, we must be selective. It sounds so cold and calculated...and yet we must be

selective of friends, time, energy, money, projects, and opportunities. Are you too busy to be successful? What are you busy about? Are all of your activities congruent with who you are, with what you want to be and with where you want to go? This week I have had the opportunity to join three different and wonderful organizations, which would not only be exciting, informative, and fun... but could also help my speaking and training career. And with my current schedule, I cannot be a responsible, contributing member to each of these organizations. As difficult as it is, I will have to choose. I will do that by matching my values, goals, and dreams and, yes — plans to these organizations to determine which will be the best fit for my investment of time, money, and energy. Of course, I want to do it all. A dear friend and former colleague, Charmaine Elegante from Price, Utah, once taped this saying to my phone: "Thank you, for asking. However, I cannot say yes to all that my heart responds to. Thank you, again, for asking." Whew! That response has saved my bacon on many an occasion. Memorize it and use it to simplify your life. Then do a friend a favor by taping it to her phone and forehead — so that you can continue to see it! Speaking of friendship — you will lose some and gain some along the road of success. Some of the most painful and loving lessons I have learned have been from the coming and going of relationships. After a very painful experience with a friend, I called a handful of my dearest ones to ask them, "Am I a good friend to you? Am I meeting your expectations as a friend?" Nobody was home. (!) The information and love that I gained from those eventual conversations is priceless. One of them, whom I choose to keep nameless — her ego doesn't need it and she knows who she is — sent me a card that read: "Silences make the real conversations between friends. Not the saying but the never needing to say is what counts — Margaret Lee Runbeck." I believe that true friendship can't go away... if it does, it wasn't anyway. That's all I have to say about friendship.

I don't know what your current challenges are. I do not pretend to know or to have the answer to "What is true success?" My truth is only my experience in what has and has not worked for me. I have come to understand that lying to myself is the quickest way for me to lose energy, power, and self-esteem. And I find it to be gut wrenchingly tough to be totally honest with myself. Often, I look for the deeper meaning of events, like falling into potholes. I ask myself questions like: Was this a sign to tell me to slow down? Do I have a fear of moving forward? Am I heading in the wrong direction? Did my angel take a break? Can I sue the idiot that didn't fix the pothole? That's when the-light-of-my-life-the-flame-of-my-eternal-being in all his electrical engineering internal pragmatic wisdom says to me, "June, sometimes a pothole is just a pothole." An outside perspective can be very eye opening when we are too close to the situation.

That too has been a major part of my success — knowing when to ask for input and guidance. I've had some of the best teachers and mentors on the planet. It has taken years off of my learning curve. Do invest in yourself by buying the expertise and coaching that you need to become outstanding in your business. Equally important is to know when not to ask for input. To quote Carol Burnett's grandmother, sometimes it's better to "let it lie where Jesus flung it." Listen to your gut and your angels to know when to and when not to seek council outside of yourself. Last, but never least, is to remember to have fun! Get very clear on what fun is to you and to those you love. Then spend more time doing it. "Laugh often and much for that is the truest measure of success." The quicker you can laugh at yourself, the quicker you can let it go — whatever it is. Do you know people who seem to have lost their sense of humor somewhere between "Snellville and Texas"? How else are we going to keep the crazies in perspective except with laughter?

I was *CRAZY* from trying to meet the deadline on this book. Deadline day, I ran by the dry cleaners to get a new fall skirt hemmed. The owner that I have done business with for years was kneeling at my feet to adjust the hem. She looked up into my eyes and very sincerely said in broken English, "You too besy?" I said, "yes, I am busy." She repeated with more emphasis and concern, "You too busy. Two dif-far-ant shoes." Sure enough, there they were, two very different shoes on my feet. It had been that way all day. I hadn't even noticed. I began to show my two shoes proudly as other customers came into her business. We all laughed hysterically. It really lightened up their day — and mine. Always take the initiative to instigate laughter. It will bring you recognition, respect, reward, and a darn good time.

**In Summary of Potholes**

I wish you such joy, luck, love, and laughter as you continue to reach for the stars. There is no better way to serve than to honor who you are. To be successful and to pass it on is the greatest gift to give back to the Universe. Get involved with big ideas, even if it is in a small way. Allow your challenges to help you become more than you currently are. And know that what and who you are currently is enough. Understand that sometimes, a pothole is just a pothole. I am *tickled to life* to have had the opportunity to share my thoughts and ideas with you. Take what you need and leave the rest. Thank you for being a part of my success. Enjoy your journey to health, wealth, and happiness… whatever that looks like for you. Watch your step and remember to have fun — even with the part that you cannot see coming. I'm sending you Angels… *to help you enjoy the trip*!

**June Cline**


Poised, polished and pfun, she was awarded, by her peers, as the "1995 Showcase Speaker of The Year" by the Georgia Speakers Association. June is a nationally known speaker, trainer and humorist. June has been interviewed on radio and TV talk shows addressing the power and value of incorporating humor into our personal and professional lives. Thousands of people have enjoyed her warm, heartfelt fun as she helps them find a higher quality of life. Her fun philosophy is reflected by her company name, The Court Jesters Club, which she started in 1990.

Though she grew up in Alabama, June says she graduated "magna cum la-la" from Westminster College in Salt Lake City, Utah, with a B.S. in Social Science. She spent sixteen years in the profession of student financial aid. Five years as a Senior Business Development Officer for Signet Bank, taught her invaluable communication, marketing and sales techniques. June honed her training abilities at American College Testing (ACT.) Her experience as Director of Financial Aid, at the College of Eastern Utah provided her with both counseling and leadership skills (and, enough student blooper material to create a new career and write a book!).

You can reach June at the Court Jesters Club, 935-A Cobb Place Blvd., Kennesaw, GA 30144 Phone (770) 423-7278, Fax (770) 423-7279, or E-mail: junejester@aol.com.

# A Fish Out of Water: Defining Values for Success

by **Jean Houston Shore**

> *Where wisdom is called for, force is of little use.*
> HERODOTUS

Imagine for a moment that you have been asked to put together a new weeknight show for one of the television networks. Since you are on a tight deadline, you decide to combine elements from hits of the past. After months of planning, you present your finished concept: June Cleaver, Fonzie, Lucy Ricardo, Captain Kangaroo, Columbo and two of the girls from *Baywatch* all living on the same street. Each episode will feature a problem that arises when the values systems of your chosen characters clash with one another. Can you imagine June Cleaver meeting the *Baywatch* girls or Columbo greeting Lucy Ricardo? You call your show *A Fish Out of Water*.

All of us can relate to occasionally feeling like fishes out of water, struggling desperately to get back into our comfort zones. When we recognize that in leadership all eyes are on us, assessing our every move, the discomfort increases. Even though most of us will not feel the same fickle scrutiny as America's top executives do, we do find ourselves "on stage," playing to an audience of constituents who judge our leadership abilities by determining whether we consistently practice what they believe we preach. Even without the challenges of a leadership role, employees frequently say they feel vaguely dissatisfied with their work situations, for reasons they cannot explain. To solve these fish-out-of-water problems, we must look deeper into the issue of defining our personal values.

Many of our business and personal choices today are tinted in shades of gray. A personal set of values can be like a giant magnifying glass, allowing us to distinguish between those confusing shades. We look to our system of values to determine how to proceed in situations that require action. It's like our personal rule book, helping us determine the distinction between good, better, and best in any situation.

Practically speaking, there are two areas we must constantly monitor with regard to value systems and daily life. First, our personal value system must mesh with an acceptable value system for our employer. Fish-out-of-water feelings easily spring from unacceptable values matches. Second, our day-to-day behaviors should be consistent with the personal value system we say we embrace.

## Employer Values in the Workplace

Once we have defined our own value system, we will become aware of differences in the value systems of those around us. As our culture continues to change, many companies are finding it helpful to publish for their employees a list of acceptable values. Charles Brewer, Founder and CEO of MindSpring Enterprises, Inc., a national Internet Access Provider, believes that "the key to creating a remarkable organization, internally and externally, is through an intense focus on values that guide its employees' actions." MindSpring publishes its list of Core Values and Beliefs on its Web site and in product training manuals, inviting customers to let them know if company employees do not seem to be living up to them.

Here are some things you can consider to determine what value system is acceptable at your workplace:

- Does your company publish a list of company values? If so, conduct an informal reality check on the effectiveness of your company's values list.

- Do people really live by the company values or is the list just a meaningless piece of paper?

- Do the behaviors of people at your place of work imply other values that should be added to the list?

- Do departments of the same company appear to be living by different values? Create a values list for the department you work in.

Once you have a values list you think truly represents the behaviors of your organization, examine it to see if the company values are aligned with your personal value system. (More information about how to define your personal value system is given later in this chapter.) Remember: great stress is created when you are forced to behave in ways contrary to your personal system of values. If the behaviors expected of you at work run counter to your closely held personal beliefs, you may be well advised to make a change in your work situation.

**Attaining Values System Consistency**

The second area to monitor relates to consistency. Are your day-to-day behaviors consistent with your personal value system? Internal fish-out-of-water feelings arise when we know that we are compromising our beliefs. Other people respect us if we stand firm on our values. It may be even more important, however, for us to earn that level of respect from ourselves. Knowing that the choices we make allow us to uphold the values we say we hold dear gives us a sense of peace. Building a track record of personal integrity gives us the strength to fight our most difficult battles.

**Stages of Values Development**

Being able to manage values in the workplace, and attain personal values system consistently, requires us to clearly and deeply know our personal system of values. Unfortunately, many adults do not enjoy the benefits of a well-defined system of personal values. For most people, at least some components of the value system are clear. For example, most people adopt at least some part of our country's legal do's and don'ts into their personal value system, agreeing readily that murder, stealing, and rape are *wrong*. We reject other parts of the legal system, at least in practice, as people regularly choose to litter the streets with trash, cheat on their taxes, exceed the posted speed limits, or jaywalk across the street.

The most common reason we do not consciously use our values system is because we never take time to thoughtfully consider what we believe. When we are children, parents and other influential adults in our lives help us begin the values development process. They impress upon us daily the importance of virtues such as honesty, sharing, and respect for the property of others. This first stage, which begins shortly after birth and lasts well into the school years, is commonly called *values inculcation*. Many of our most strongly held beliefs can be traced back to that early values teaching we received in our homes. Fish-out-of-water feelings can arise when we act in ways that go against this early teaching.

The second stage of values development begins, generally, when a child enters school and lasts throughout high school, college, and even into early work experiences. This stage is called *informal role modeling* and starts with the child/adult recognizing a person or group of persons he or she would like to emulate. The child/adult observes this person's behaviors and unconsciously infers that, to attain what that person has attained, the child/adult should behave like the role model. The behaviors of these strongly influential role models then become a part of the child/adult's value system, whether or not the behaviors truly lead to the outcome the child/adult hopes to attain. If a young girl sees an older girl and judges that girl to be attractive, she might assume that the older girl's behaviors of wearing suggestive clothing and being promiscuous will lead to attractiveness. So the younger girl develops a value system that will allow for suggestive dress and promiscuity so that she may attain attractiveness. Role Modeling continues as young parents determine how to raise their children, young workers define how to treat customers, and young managers determine what management style is appropriate. Fish-out-of-water feelings can arise here whenever our role models somehow let us down.

The final stage of values development is what is often missed in adult development today — the stage of *values clarification*. Values clarification is the structured consideration of the many components of a value system, along with a study of what values in the system should stay and what values should go. The study also includes an examination of how to prioritize the values you choose to keep. As an example, a value system may include both honesty (which would preclude stealing) and care for family. Which value would be subjugated if the family was starving for food? Would the subject become dishonest in order to care for family? Or would care for family be subservient to the need to be honest at all costs? Neither answer is wrong — they are simply alternative priorities of personal systems of values. Values clarification is a time-consuming and deep-reaching process, a process that should begin early and continue throughout adult life.

Since the development of a well-defined system of values through values clarification is time consuming, why should you go to the trouble? There are some benefits that accrue to you simply because you have gone through the process of values clarification. You will realize other benefits as you use your value system in everyday situations. Still more benefits come to you as you interact with other people in accordance with your value system.

**Benefits from the Process of Values Clarification**
When you embark on a values clarification adventure, you examine each of the values you hold by using a structured and objective method. (Some questions to use in clarifying your values are presented later in this Chapter.) When clarifying your values, you think critically, carefully considering your preferences, habits and beliefs. During this process you ask why you identify with those preferences, hold onto those habits, and maintain those beliefs. What results is a set of personal definitions that expresses how you feel life should be lived. Your set of personal definitions can be expressed in words, symbols, and colors or a combination of all three.

One of the chief benefits of going through the process is that, once it is created, your well-defined value system will function as a moral compass to guide you and give you direction. Understanding your value system helps you find and embrace the purpose in your life. As you fit together the raw materials of your closely held beliefs, the patterns of your behaviors (both effective and ineffective) begin to emerge. This suggests ways you could become even more successful than you are now.

In addition, actively identifying the components of your value system helps you stretch your limits. By examining (possibly for the first time) areas where you may be biased in your approach or where you may lack the inner drive to turn your beliefs into appropriate actions, you gain valuable insight. In both cases, as you bring about changes to become less biased or to enhance your inner drive, you become a stronger, more self-aware, more effective individual.

Examining your value system can help you realize that you may be prioritizing daily tasks incorrectly or at least executing them differently than your value system would suggest. This enlightening experience again puts you in control and gives you the freedom to realign your priorities as you refine your value system.

Going through the process of values clarification also allows you to see your value system dimensionally. This means that you clarify how you see one value (e.g., a desire to help those less fortunate than you are) in relation to the other values you hold (e.g., wanting to be financially secure or environmentally responsible.)

### Benefits from Everyday Situations

Our business and personal lives require us to make values choices every day. Having a well-defined personal value system will help you make these values choices more effectively and less painfully. A well-defined value system gives you the basis for making decisions by identifying the critical components of those decisions at the outset. Let's say that your value system placed a high importance on developing your subordinates' interpersonal skills and a lesser importance on developing their technical skills. In this case, the choice between spending your budget dollars on technical training versus spending it to send your group to a team-building intervention would be simple.

Another way that a well-defined value system helps you in everyday situations is that it lets you judge your progress toward business goals. Business goals are composed of more than just dates and dollars; they incorporate values choices, too. You can motivate your team to perform better by emphasizing the values element of the business goals the team is pursuing. For example, a push to reduce scrap and rework at a plant producing child safety seats could be clearly linked to employees' personal values of integrity, the worth of a hard day's work, and the importance of child rearing.

A well-defined value system can help simplify your life by removing the emotion and confusion from difficult choices. With a well-understood personal system, the biggest decision becomes "Where does this issue fall within my value system?" not "How do I feel about this issue?" In this way, decisions that were formerly made in the heat of the moment can be reviewed logically and measured against thoughtfully established personal standards.

All of us lose focus on our ultimate life goals from time to time. If you have not taken time to define your personal value system, you may not even recognize when you may be losing focus. Having a well-defined value system gives you a yardstick against which to measure each of your actions, ensuring that your highest priority life values remain sharply in focus.

Finally, having in place a well-defined value system can result in inner peace and reduced stress. There is sense of accomplishment when you succeed in living your life by your own value system. A well-defined value system helps you feel safe in changing times, since you have a secure mental foundation that will remain fairly constant no matter what situations change around you. A well-defined value system allows you to plan your future with confidence. When you know clearly what is most important in your life and what your value priorities are, you have painted a vision of what you want your life to be. Making plans to move your life from where it is to where you want it to be becomes simply an administrative exercise.

## Benefits when Interacting With Others

Understanding your own value system is valuable in and of itself. But the real power is found in what knowing your own value system can tell you about interacting with others. Our society's understanding of the diversity among us is steadily increasing. Even so, we must work hard to remember that, though they maybe similar, our personal value systems are not identical.

When a group of people has similar value systems, a common bond and understanding are created. Many corporations have established company "Values Statements" that define the hierarchy of values that supposedly govern the behaviors of company employees. If your personal value system closely resembles your company "code," you will feel comfortable and confident in exhibiting the behaviors your company requires. Conversely, if your personal value code differs greatly from the code your company expects you to follow, you have two choices. You can either choose to compromise your values or find employment with a company whose values more closely reflect yours.

Another advantage that having a well-defined value system affords is that of enhancing your ability to select compatible relationships in your life. We do not always have the chance to pick and choose the relationships in our lives; however, for those choices we do have, having defined our own values system gives us a basis for making wiser relationship matches.

Some business situations are uncomfortable for us for reasons that up until now we could not explain. Let's say you are on a team where one person believes the company should win a contract at any cost, including compromising on quality specifications. You may be reluctant to go along, thinking that customer satisfaction is at risk. Another person might also be reluctant because he or she believes that the company reputation would be tainted. The team could not move forward without someone making a values system compromise. Understanding more about the pivotal roles our personal value systems play in our behavior choices helps us see why these problem situations arise. A well-defined value system helps you recognize situations when others are trying to impose their value systems on you. In my opinion, we should always listen as others explain their choices to us. However, the specific components of your value system are up to you.

Similarly, a well-defined value system helps you recognize situations when others are trying to force you into polarized values choices. You have a dimensional value system with many components. Yet, sometimes others want you to believe that your actions must be all or nothing. You can define your values choices (and your responses to those who would polarize you) but remember that there are many shades of meaning within even a simple values choice.

## Well-defined Values and Success

If having a well-defined system of values offers all these benefits, can we draw a clear connection between values and success? To answer that question we must define what being "successful" really is. Some people would define being successful as having plenty of money. Others say success is being able to spend your time the way you want to spend it. Still others might say that having success means enjoying the respect of your family and community. Since a person's definition of success reflects his or her value system, there are as many interpretations of success as there are variations in values. For example, some people choose to become financially "successful" by buying and reselling illegal drugs. Most adult value systems do not allow for that definition of success. For now, most of society withholds its admiration from *successful* people who break the law to succeed. It is disturbing to note that many of our young people are building their value systems using these very individuals as role models. For our purposes, let us define success as having two components. First, a successful person is at least law-abiding. Second, a successful person lives a meaningful life that others would admire. Within these two facets, most any slant on success would fit.

A quick review of any periodical reveals that values go in and out of style. As society changes its definitions of success, your value system may become more widely popular or unpopular. This does not mean you should change your value system. But it does mean that some parts of your success (money, respect, admiration from peers) may become easier or harder to attain as society changes its views.

Does this mean you should change your value system with the winds of social change, just to make *success* easier to achieve? In a word, no. You could become wishy-washy in your values system, but in the long run you will be the loser. People do not look up to hypocrites. A weak value system is the enemy of long-term success.

Living your life according to a strong set of values gives you a better opportunity to be successful. You have an advantage in the playing field if you know what you stand for. A strong system of values results in consistent, predictable behaviors, and people will look up to you if you seem to be a person of integrity. You can be successful if your actions tell others that you are a regular person just like them. Your actions should be consistent with your stated value system. When your actions are perceived as being inconsistent, people become confused about who you are. Your public actions tell others what your value system is. When your actions are telling people one thing and you say you believe another, people cannot feel comfortable trusting you and supporting you. Unless your actions and values mesh, your long-term success will be limited. You earn respect and admiration when others see you demonstrate consistent behaviors.

### Defining Your Personal Values

There are Seven Life Questions to be answered when you begin to define your personal value system. They are presented here in a given sequence; however, you may address the questions in any order you like.

**What do I believe about my Heritage and History?:** Who are my PEOPLE? What is most important to me about those who were my literal or figurative forefathers? Is my heritage primarily a physical one, a spiritual one, a set of cultural norms? How much influence does this heritage have on me now?

**What do I believe about my Gifts and Talents?:** What thing(s) do I seem born to do? Are there activities that particularly "click" with my feelings about whom I was meant to be? In what pursuits do I feel most grounded?

**What do I believe about Significant Relationships?:** In what way(s) is my life here on earth connected to other lives? What are the relationships that are clearly most important in my existence? How would I describe the significance and character of these relationship(s)? What are the priorities in these relationships?

**What do I believe about Purpose or Calling?:** Why do I think I am here on the earth? Is there a contribution I want to make before I leave here? What do I hope people will remember me for most?

**What do I believe about Faith?:** What do I think about faith and/or spirituality? Do I have faith in a Supreme Being? If so, how real is that faith in my life? How much do my beliefs about faith affect the other parts of my life? What are the tenets of the faith I hold?

**What do I believe about Giving to Others?:** What are my beliefs about giving or not giving to those outside the realm of my significant relationships? Do I feel any responsibility for those less fortunate than I am? How does this belief relate to my other beliefs?

**What do I believe about Life's Cycles?:** What is my overall view about the journey of life? Do I feel that all people are on a path to an uncertain end? Do I think good things only happen to some people or do I believe everyone has an equal chance at happiness? Is there such a thing as "bad luck?" Is my overall view of life an optimistic one or a pessimistic one? How do I believe we should deal with life's ups and downs?

## A Process for Uncovering Values

As you can imagine, discovering and sharing your answers to these seven questions is an enlightening experience of self-discovery. Here is a process other discoverers have used for working through the questions:

1) Find a quiet place with no distractions. Sit quietly for a few moments and clear your mind of the day's current issues. Silently commit yourself to using this time for discovery that will make your life even better than it is today.

2) Choose one of the Seven Life Questions. Take a sheet of unlined paper and write in the center of the page the keywords from the Life Question you chose (above). Then consider the Life Question keywords in your mind and begin to write on the piece of paper other descriptive words to express your beliefs about this question. If you like, draw pictures to represent the ideas. Write in different sections of the paper, write sideways or even upside-down. Take as much time as you need; try to fill the entire paper. This technique is frequently called "mind-mapping."

3) On another sheet of blank paper, begin writing your answers to that Life Question in paragraph form. Begin at least two of your sentences with the words "I believe." As you write, refer frequently to your mind-mapping sheet for key words and phrases.

4) Once you have finished your paragraphs, put the papers away at least over night. After a short amount of time has passed, retrieve your answers and review your work. Add or change your answers as necessary.

5) Once you have uncovered or clarified a particular value, you should publicly claim it. Choose a couple of people you trust and respect and set up a time to share your work with them. Tell them that you are not trying to convince them that they should embrace your value system, but that you wish to move forward in your personal development by publicly affirming what you believe. Ask your confidants to support you in clarifying what is most important in your life by asking about anything they do not understand. Allow this time to be a special sharing time for all of you.

6) Repeat this process for each of the Life Questions.

7) When you have completed the process with all Seven Life Questions, review your answers as they relate to one another. Note any areas of conflict. Prioritize the values you have uncovered.

8) Make a list detailing what you have learned about yourself having completed the first round of values clarification. Continue the clarification process throughout your life.

No matter what our ages, job titles, or career aspirations, we benefit from having a well-defined value system. Understanding more about our beliefs allows us to be aware of the role those values play in shaping our everyday interactions. By making an active effort to live according to well-defined personal values systems, we will not flop around helplessly like fish out of water.

## Jean Houston Shore

Jean Houston Shore is a professional speaker and seminar leader who helps executives, managers and employees improve their lives by improving themselves. She owns the Business Resource Group, a seminar company assisting both businesses and associations. Jean is best know for her educational and inspirational presentations including *Change and Your Career*, *Leadership with Vision*, and *The Banner*. Jean's programs help her audiences align vision and values, producing practical results. Jean's consulting clients repeatedly say that she possess an uncanny ability to uncover core business issues and ask the tough questions needed to get them back on track.

Before founding the Business Resource Group, Jean traveled to Canada, the United Kingdom, and throughout the United States, teaching the principles and application of Total Quality Management. She began her career as a Certified Public Accountant, having passed the CPA exam in her first sitting. She is a trained facilitator, frustrated singer and songwriter, and a terrible cook.

You can reach Jean at Business Resource Group, 408 Vivian Way, Woodstock, GA 30188 Phone (770) 924-4436, Fax (770) 924-1128, or E-mail: shorebrg@mindspring.com.

# ★ 4 ★
# Lead By Example

by **D.J. Harrington**

Several of my good friends are writing chapters in this book.
I know them as professional speakers. I wish you could have the
personal privilege of meeting Austin McGonigle… what a great man!
Dr. Shirley Garrett, or Meg Croot, whoa, together watch out!

Let me see if I can add by giving one or two examples of my
thoughts on success. To me success is not a destination; it's a journey.
First things first. Have fun on your journey. Let me begin where I think
success starts, when we are young.

So often during seminars across the country, I have a chance to tell
humorous things that happened. One night while on the road I called
home. My wife Sheila told me about a package that I received in the
mail. I told her to go ahead and open it. As she did she said, "Oh, my!
There's a can and it looks like it has eyes all over it. Who would have
sent you such a thing?" I answered, "Oh, honey, that is an Eye Can."
She wasn't as concerned about receiving a prototype of an eye can than
she was that I had been telling my audiences about the incident. "You
haven't been telling people about the eye can have you?" she said
accusatively. More for my defense, "Yes," I responded proudly because
I had been telling audiences for the last couple years about what
happened to us. Now let me tell my readers.

I came home late one Friday evening to find a note that read, "Mr.
DJ Harrington." As I opened it, I realized it was from my daughter's
first grade teacher. My six-year-old daughter, Erin was attending
Boston Elementary School. The teacher was asking me to call her
during the weekend to set up an appointment to meet with her the next

week. Well, because I was leaving Sunday night to go back on the road there wasn't any way I could accommodate her.

I called the teacher Saturday, explained that I was Erin Harrington's dad and asked her if there was any possible way to discuss this problem over the telephone. "Oh, no,... we have to meet," she said, her comment signaled a major infraction. Later that day, I asked Erin if there was anything that she might have done in school during the week which would generate a call from the teacher. Her come back was something like, "Dad, she wrote the letter to you ... maybe you did something wrong!" It's like they say, "The fruit doesn't fall far from the tree." When I asked my wife why she hadn't read the letter, she politely told me that it was addressed to DJ Harrington, and, "Dear, that's you."

On Saturday, I connected again with the teacher by phone, but she insisted on an appointment Sunday afternoon at the school. After church, my wife and I went to the school where we saw the principal's car was in the parking lot, alongside an unfamiliar automobile.

The principal kindly unlocked the door for us, and we meandered down to Erin's classroom while making small talk. We took our seats on small chairs indigenous to classrooms for six year olds; I call them midget chairs. Then we started to discuss what happened that Tuesday while I was traveling. My daughter was involved in a notorious spelling bee — a classical test of boys against the girls! The teacher described the background detailing that the girls stood up, and my daughter proceeded to the line. The teacher stopped her story and asked me if I have ever been in a spelling bee. I looked at the lady and said, "Mam, get to the chase... what did my daughter do?" She said, "In a spelling bee, Mr. Harrington, you have to say the word, spell the word, and then say the word again. If you are correct, then you proceed back to the end of the line."

"Okay, Mrs. Warren, I've been in a spelling bee before." With knitted eyebrows, I questioned her, "What happened?"

She replied, "Your daughter was next in line, and her word to be spelled was *can't*. I asked Erin to please spell the word CAN'T. Your daughter looked at me with sternness, and said, 'That word is not in my vocabulary. I'm not allowed to say that word.'" The teacher told me her mouth dropped open, and she asked Erin, "What? Who told you that?" "My daddy," Erin said, "Can I write it on the board?" So, Erin went to the front of the classroom and did just that. The teacher then instructed Erin to go to the end of the line as usual when the answer was correct. As Erin was walking to the back of the line, the teacher asked what her daddy does for a living. Erin told her that her daddy makes people feel good even if they feel bad.

Oh, brother! I guess she imagined that I sell drugs or something. I don't really think little children know what their parents actually do for a living. Much of my time is spent in airports, and if I had a little person at home now, he would probably think that I work at the airport.

Well, as she was going to the end of the line, Mrs. Warren said, "Erin has your father ever done anything else weird?" A helpful little girl offered, "Erin, tell the teacher about your dad!" In Kindergarten, I sat Erin down in the living room and gave her a pair of plastic scissors and Elmer's glue, and located and removed pictures of eyeballs from magazines and newspapers. We cut out Ronald Reagan's eyeballs, Margaret Thatcher's eyeballs, and bloodshot eyeballs of Willie Nelson. Every pair of eyeballs we found, we glued onto the side of a tin can.

The tin can was a large Campbell's soup can perfect for eyeballs. I meticulously removed the soup label, and we glued the eyeballs to the side of the can until every inch of the can was filled with eyeballs. She brought the "eye can" in for Show N' Tell and displayed it for everybody at the school. Erin was asked to go around and show to every grade from kindergarten to 6th.

Today my daughter is a sophomore in high school and excels in tennis. One day a person asked her why she wears a pin and where did she get it. The pin reads, "Attitude is Everything." She responds proudly, "I got it from my dad. My dad gave me the 'eye can' attitude."

"What does your dad do for a living?" Today, at age fifteen, she told the interviewer that her father helps people develop from within, so they don't go without.

My wife was off to the side listening to this interview, and on the way home, she questioned Erin about her answer. "What do you mean, your dad helps people develop from within so they don't go without?" Erin interrupted her impatiently with, "Mom... I listened to one of his talks."

I'm going to tell you if you have little people in your family, you need to avoid, as much as possible, saying the word can't. A young person or a middle-aged teenager may need to occasionally use can't. If there are little people in your family sit down, take out the plastic scissors, cut out eyeballs, and glue them to the side of the can.

Train them that as Americans they should always have an "I can" attitude. America wouldn't be where it is today if our forefathers had developed an 'I can't' attitude. Let me ask you, is there an 'I can' in your life?

One weekend, I asked my daughter Erin to help sell videos in the back of the auditorium after one of my speeches. She watched inquisitive people attending my classes ask questions about my unusual props. When they walk into the auditorium, take a swift sight inventory of my prop table, they see many things. One prop is actually a prospector's hat. Crowned with a big red light on the metal helmet, it is capable of illuminating a large portion of the auditorium as well as a cave just as it was intended.

They recognize others such as the headgear of a train conductor and a fireman. One or two of the bravest attendees walk over and boldly ask, "Why all of these hats?" My answer… "Well, a lot of times we have to don a fire chief hat, because as managers, we usually extinguish fires." If we don't have a fire to put out, what do we normally do? That's right… we create one!

Through my travels and sales training studies across the United States, Australia, Canada, and in the UK, I find there are many sizes and shapes of managers, and generally the only hat they know how to wear with expertise is the fire chief hat.

There is a book called <u>ZAPP</u> written in which William Byham talks about this. What hat are you wearing? There is a train conductor's hat and a train whistle which I purchased from a major toy company. When I blow the whistle, the whole room comes to attention as if I have just told the entire group "all aboard the train to success is leaving." That's when I relive my entire trip between Germany and France. The episode went like this.

It was four o'clock in the morning when the conductor came to get my ticket. As I rubbed the sleep from my eyes, I looked at this seasoned gentleman and located my American passport and rail pass and handed both to him as he had requested. Expressionless, he glanced at me and then at my credentials, and in broken English smothered with a French accent, he said, "Where are you going; where have you bEEn; and how are you going to get there?" My instincts told me that it really wasn't his business to know mine especially at four o'clock in the morning.

I could still hear his words ring in my ears for miles down the track. Later, I would know how important his question was to be to me.

Wouldn't that be a good message for me to carry back to the United States while donning a conductor's hat and blowing a whistle? When speaking to audiences, I could ask where have we been... where are we going, and how are we going to get there. Are we on the right track? Are we going in the right direction? Have we taken too much baggage?

There are times when a person who goes through divorce or alienation carries unnecessary baggage forever. This baggage could be from physical, emotional, or professional problems; regardless, he goes through life forever carrying past hurts on every trip. Every time I return from a trip, the first thing I do is unpack, or depending on how quickly I leave again, I weed out certain items I don't need for the next trip.

Am I going in the right direction? Do I have the proper ticket for the right trip? Sometimes I like to look down at the ticket I have purchased and see if the destination and the amount that I paid to board the train or plane was really worth it. I want to ask the same of you. How much are you willing to pay to reach your final destination? Are you willing to take time out to learn, to read, and listen?

Further down my prop table, I spot my priest hat. It was a cool day in spring spent running errands with my wife. Since it had to be an original priest hat, Sheila and I searched unwaveringly for a church supply store that had one in stock. Under the disapproving eye of the sales clerk, I bought the complete ensemble. I reassured the clerk that I was appearing as Father Carforu on the Automobile Satellite Training Network and needed the outfit for credibility. Without that explanation, I doubt she'd have sold it to us.

My bishop was known as Bishop Uselli. The segment was well-received, and I kept the hat. Father Carforu told managers that they should pray for the salespeople in their department because they all laugh and joke around. That was said in fun to teach, but truthfully, I believe that we should have prayer, providence, and perseverance. Prayer changes; providence provides; and perseverance accomplishes.

Next to the priest hat is another hat that looks like a Russian-Soviet, winter hat. It is made of fur with flaps that can be untied to cover the ears. Generally, it is worn by a person who brightens up the whole department by leaving the room. Reminiscent of uncompassionate faces of Russian soldiers, I call it my stinking thinking, and doom and gloom hat. It's a depressing hat. Some people easily identify with the hat, because they, too, were weaned on a dill pickle and hated their mothers since age three. Those people are really out there.

Another one that I recognize is the Chevrolet hat or Caterpillar hat, one of the hats from Mohawk Carpet, or Cal Pro, and I wonder whether people realize it's not the cap or the garment that we cover ourselves with but what's inside that counts. It doesn't matter if we're wearing a hat with a logo that says, "Tommy Hilfiger," "Genuine GM Parts," or "Federal Express." The final truth is what's inside. Expecting an overweight individual to be a pole vaulter seems an impossible feat. If I was a coach, my advice would be, "Just throw your heart over the pole, and the rest of your body will go with it."

The prospector's hat which I told you about earlier is the last one on the prop table. Primarily the prospector's hat is used for mining caves. When I put that hat on I hear gasps of, "Oh, my! Where is he going with this?" Then I have an opportunity to tell them that it's similar to when I spoke to the disaster recovery group that responded to the Oklahoma City bombing several years ago. I don't change my delivery or material to groups such as Caterpillar, IBM, or the disaster recovery group.

Recently I had an opportunity to wear that hat again and share this story once more. We were in the middle of the ocean on a dark, rainy night and all of a sudden through the fog, there was a light. We immediately contacted the captain and said, "There is a light in our sea lane." The captain said, "Signal to it, and tell them to move." So we did just that, we signaled, "MOVE FROM OUR SEA LANE." Surprisingly the signal came back, "MOVE YOURSELF." The odd response was given to the captain who again answered disdainfully, "MOVE YOURSELF!" This time the captain also instructed us to tell them, "We are the great Missouri, the largest ship in the fleet, move from our sea lane." So, we signaled that message... WE ARE THE MISSOURI, THE LARGEST SHIP IN THE FLEET, MOVE FROM OUR SEA LANE." The retaliatory message came swiftly… "WE ARE THE LIGHTHOUSE!"

I want to turn the light on many times and tell audiences that we are the lighthouse in the community. Where people live and go to bed with integrity and honesty, they will talk about you and your place of business. When they talk about a great place to work, are they, without a doubt, referring to you and your fellow employees? When they talk about someone who is giving back to the community, are they talking about you? I'll add, put a light on in customer service; and we as a company or individual need to be customer-focused.

So, my different hats project different things. In the last couple of years I have thoroughly enjoyed my Secret Recipes hat because we have so many successes. All of us are a part of a secret recipe of success. You were kind enough to purchase this book and are reading it one-on-one as if I am sitting next to you. Before going on to the next chapter, I want you to answer this question honestly.

What hat are you wearing? Are you wearing the fire chief hat putting out recurring fires, or are you wearing the priest hat… always praying for the situation. I heard one man tell me he kneels down to pray knowing it depends on God, and then works relentlessly like it all depends on him. That's when you'll be truly blessed.

Don't be like the person who gets motivated, runs around his house, sings in the shower, does all the affirmations, and then goes back to bed. What hat are you wearing in life?

## GARDEN FOR SUCCESS
### BY D.J. HARRINGTON

**FIRST PLANT 7 ROWS OF PEAS**
Presence
Promptness
Preparation
Patience
Perseverance
Positive Action
Prayer

**THEN PLANT 8 ROWS OF SQUASH**
Squash Gossip
Squash Indifference
Squash Indecision
Squash Negativity
Squash Worry
Squash Envy
Squash Greed
Squash Fear

**THEN PLANT 9 ROWS OF TURNIPS**
Turn-up For Training
Turn-up On Time
Turn-up With a Smile
Turn-up With Good Thoughts
Turn-up With New Goals
Turn-up With New Prospects
Turn-up With Excitement
Turn-up With a Positive Attitude
Turn-up With Determination to Make Everything Count
for Good and Worthwhile

**NO GARDEN IS COMPLETE WITHOUT LETTUCE**
Let Us Be Faithful to Our Duty
Let Us Be Honest With Ourselves
Let Us Be Unselfish and Loyal
Let Us Be True to Our Obligations
Let Us Have Fun and Enjoyment
Let Us Obey the Rules and Regulations
Let Us Love and Help One Another

**AND LAST BUT NOT LEAST,
LET'S ASK FOR GOD'S HELP**

# D.J. Harrington

D.J. Harrington is President of Phone Logic, Inc., an international telemarketing and training company based in Atlanta, GA. He serves as a consultant to over 600 businesses throughout the U.S. D.J. appears every week on ASTN, the national cable training network. Programs focus on "Prospecting" to "In-coming Calls." As a syndicated columnist for 33 newspapers, D.J. writes monthly articles that appear from Atlanta to Los Angeles.

His years as sales trainer and motivator for a variety of companies have provided D.J. with a diverse back ground which he combines with energy and his dynamic personality to provide memorable presentations for companies such as: UniRoyal, General Motors, American Bank Systems, Bloomingdale's, IBM, American Express, and Mohawk Carpet.

You can reach D.J. at Phone Logic, Inc., 2820 Andover Way, Woodstock, GA, 30189 Phone (770) 924-4400 or (800) 352-5252, Fax (770) 516-7797.

# ★ 5 ★

# Develop Your Ethical Edge!

by **Arthur (Mano) Manoharan, M.D.**

An individual or an organization that has the reputation of being ethical has a distinct advantage over others. This increases the level of trust or confidence in the ethical person or the ethical organization. People are happier to enter into business contracts and deals with such a person or organization. On the other hand, if individuals or institutions are known for unethical activities, they have lost their ethical edge which can lead to disastrous consequences. Recently there was some publicity about "Toys R Us"; the company was alleged to have been involved in promotional activities that were considered to be unethical. This can have a reaction that may have a serious negative impact on the company!

Ethics is the very basis of human interaction; and, if there is no ethics, everything can break down. In many trades and businesses a person's word is his bond. This cannot be so without trust and confidence between business people. In the United States a great deal of business advertising and promotional activities are unsavory. Barbara Walters, the well-known TV personality, said that most of the advertisements on the TV screen are not true. If something is advertised on TV, she would not buy it!

What will happen to the world if we all behave ethically towards each other? The world would be a much better place. There will be no cheating or deceiving. People will speak the truth to each other. Organizations and businesses will not indulge in false advertising or promoting half truths and lies. People will trust each other and help each other to behave more ethically. Will this ever happen? I think it will, if a <u>critical mass</u> in the community believes and acts according to its beliefs. Many people pray every day "Thy Kingdom come!" It cannot come unless we change the way we behave towards each other. I believe that behaving in a more ethical way could be the first step. If we accomplish this, the rest will follow.

What is ethics? What is involved in behaving more ethically towards each other? Ethics is an area in moral philosophy dealing with what is right and what is wrong. Although there are universal norms in ethics, but culture, religion, and politics play major roles in determining what is right. One of the first principles is "Do no harm." When the Dalai Lama addressed the United Nations General Assembly, he said, "We are here to help each other. If we cannot help, please do not hurt anyone!" Our dealing with each other should not result in mental or physical hurt. Mahatma Gandhi would call this "Ahimsa," or non violence. In the 20th Century we have a new responsibility of protecting the environment. In other words, we will not destroy the environment that surrounds us. No industry should be encouraged to pollute the land, water, or air.

The most serious health problem facing the world is environmental pollution. There is but one ocean, one land mass, and one atmosphere for all the peoples of the world. Whenever the water, the earth or the air is polluted, it is a disservice to the whole human community. The destruction of the rain forests, the production of carbon dioxide leading to global warming, or the uncontrolled fishing of the oceans are all dangerous activities leading to disastrous consequences. Industries and governments that promote these activators have to realize that this is a form of violence against future generations. What has happened in the past cannot be permitted to continue. There have to be educational activities teaching individuals and communities about the serious consequences of global pollution. It is considered that 80% of cancers are caused by environmental toxins. One of the major priorities of all governments of the world is to fight pollution to promote the health and well-being of all peoples of this planet.

There are two main principles involved in deciding what is right and what is wrong. One is called <u>deontological</u> ethics, or studying the nature of an act to decide whether it is right or wrong. For example, truth telling would be right compared to lying. Being kind and generous would be right compared to being rude and selfish.

The second principle is called <u>utilitarian</u> ethics. This deals with the examination of the outcome and is used to decide whether an act is ethical. For example, surgery by itself cannot be justified unless it is done to cure or correct a condition. If one gives money to an individual or an organization, it cannot be justified until we know how the money was utilized. Giving has to be done in a responsible manner. Education, construction, and a host of other activities are justified by their results or outcomes. Most of the state and federal laws are considered ethical because of their usefulness or utility.

Justice or fairness is another important principle in ethics. However, what is just or fair depends on political ideology and culture. When it comes to distributive justice, <u>most people do not wish to deal with it.</u> For example, in the United States, we have extremes of wealth and poverty. This issue is so sensitive that most people do not wish to deal with this problem. We believe that we are all created equal, but we are not ready to work towards economic and social justice!

There is another aspect of ethics dealing with structural issues. The way our institutions and laws are structured, they are expected to be fair to everyone. For example, the State of Hawaii had a law that stated that police officers should have a minimum height of 5 feet 10 inches. On the face of it, it looked good because a member of the police force should be big and strong to apprehend a criminal. However, this excluded many men of Japanese ancestry, and a number of women from applying for the job of a police officer! This law was changed to make it fair for everyone. Similarly, there are organizations and firms that make it difficult for women and minorities to reach certain positions. These have to be changed if the organization desires to become an ethical organization.

Another important principle in ethics is respect for the human being. Human beings should be treated with utmost respect and consideration. They should not be considered as objects to be manipulated or utilized towards reaching a goal. Human beings are not objects. This is often forgotten; and instead, people love their possessions like cars or houses. They end up using the people in their lives. The objects are meant to be used and people are meant to be loved and respected. When people act with <u>love and respect</u> towards each other, it is likely that they will follow the other ethical codes.

What is it that prevents us from being ethical? Why are we finding it difficult to make ethical decisions? The main reason is that we do not reason or think when we make decisions. We make decisions from our previous experience or, in other words, we make a conditioned response. A Russian physiologist called Pavlov did an experiment with dogs. He rang a bell and fed the dogs. Every time he rang the bell, the dogs salivated and then he fed them. He did this regularly so that the dogs salivated every time he rang the bell, even when there was not food. This was considered to be a conditioned response. The dogs associated the ringing of the bell to the serving of food. They salivated even when there was no food.

We have been conditioned from childhood by various experiences. My mother, when she fed me with spicy food, conditioned me into liking spicy food for the rest of my life! Similarly, we learn what to like, whom to dislike, and what choices to make. Even ideas on patriotism and religious beliefs are accepted by children without critical thinking. When they "group up," they react or give a conditioned response to many situations without thinking. The unfortunate aspect of this is many individuals, or most individuals, are not aware of the fact that they are behaving like Pavlov's dogs. Words like "black," "communist," "undocumented alien," "Baptist," or "Catholic" produce different kinds of responses in different people depending on their conditioning. Sometimes society as a whole responds with a conditioned response. For example, the outpouring of patriotism during the Gulf War was nothing but a condition response. The media and politicians are skilled in utilizing these public sentiments in creating mass hysteria or mass support!

Since people respond to situations by conditioned response, some philosophers have concluded that the notion of free will is not true. People do not think or use their free will. Are such people morally responsible? If individuals have been programmed like machines and give a programmed response to situations, they cannot be held morally responsible. When Jesus was crucified, he said "Father forgive them, for they know not what they do." The soldiers were just following orders. We have all been conditioned in such a way that our brains have these programmed responses for most situations and we respond in a conditioned status, thinking that we are responding adequately and correctly!

Imagine a world full of people, not using their free will, but responding as conditioned beings! No wonder we are in such a mess!

What is the way out of this situation? How can human beings regain their free will and break away from these conditioned responses? The first step is to become aware that one's response is indeed a conditioned response. Whenever the response is immediate, or quick, it is invariably a conditioned response. The education of children and adults should include this principle of human behavior and how it can be overcome.

The next step is to become a more contemplative person. Never respond to any situation with an immediate response. If one gets excited, with a rapid pulse and a quick sweat, that response is bound to be a conditioned response. A contemplative person learns to put himself in other people's positions. To do this, one must learn about other cultures and belief systems. Knowing more than one religion helps people to look at religious questions in a different way.

During the end of the 20th Century, one has to think of the world as one community and not as countries with different interests. Industry has to be conscious of global issues like global warming, acid rain, destruction of the rain forests, population growth, and environmental degradation. This will give some perspective and understanding in looking at local problems as they relate to global problems.

Every individual who wants to use his or her free will has to become aware of his conditioned behavior. It will be a great liberating experience to step out of one's conditioned universe. Introspection or self examination is an important step in understanding one's conditioning. "Man know thyself" is an old saying but it is very true. Once people understand how they have been conditioned, they can begin to use their free will.

When people do not use their free will, they are likely to repeat their mistakes over and over again. This happens to be true in most people's lives. They operated from their conditioned states, and so there is no learning when they make mistakes. For example, there is a great deal of regional loyalty in the United States. It is because both the southerners and the northerners condition their children to develop these prejudices. Such prejudices are strengthened by the community. Parents have an obligation not to create prejudice in their children. Why do countries repeatedly go to war? We cannot have peace in the world or promote goodwill between people if we do not let go of past prejudices.

**Conclusion**

In a world where science and technology seem to rule, the ethicist may seem irrelevant. But, unless society develops a moral basis for living, science and technology can lead people into chaos.

As business interests dominate social decision-making, profit-making at any expense may appear to be the driving force. The United States is a classic example of a society where the very wealthy and the very poor live side by side, with the poor often looked upon as being responsible for all the social problems!

Specialization of knowledge has led to the neglect of studying what is right and what is wrong. When people have no sense of moral values, their decision making is not influenced by ethical considerations. Many of the social problems like violence, use of drugs and the break up of families are the consequences of the "business as usual" philosophy.

If moral values are not infused into our society, we are in danger of developing a more violent, chaotic, and undisciplined society. But if people are aware of their moral obligations, there is the opportunity to reorganize society where the care and nurturing of all human beings will be the top priority. Children should be taught what is right and wrong. They should be given an opportunity to watch the moral decision-making of their elders in society, these elders can influence the children by setting standards for ethical decision-making.

Industrial organization must develop a code to improve their ethical priorities. Employees and employers have to learn their rights and obligations. The use of mass media in promoting sales requires a great deal of attention. Industrial and trade organizations have to set standards and ensure that false advertising and misleading publicity are excluded. Business has to be conducted within moral standards. If the Chambers of Commerce and business people learn to impose restriction on themselves and follow ethical values, they can create a change in society. In the advent of the 21st Century, the protection of the environment is a top priority. Industries and governments have to work together to eliminate the pollution of land, water, and air. The reduction of waste and the cleaning up of pollutants have to become major priorities. This will include the need to protect animals and plants that are being threatened to extinction. Moral standards must become the normal practice of business. Respect and love for all human beings has to be the most important moral principle.

The failure to observe ethical principles can lead to disastrous consequences. More poverty, more violence, and more social disorder will be the result if individuals pursue their own profit-making paths without concern for society at large. Humans are smart enough to recognize when they are heading for disaster. The neglect and exclusion of moral priorities is the downhill path to more chaos and confusion. If we are smart enough, we can change our course and follow a more ethical pathway. If people develop their ethical edge, they cannot only benefit themselves, but all of society!

## Arthur (Mano) Manoharan, M.D.

Arthur (Mano) Manoharan, M.D. is a citizen of the world. He was born in India where he attended medical school. He specialized in public health, initially at the University of London and later at Columbia University in New York. He has worked for many of the special agencies of the United Nations including the World Health Organization. He speaks on ethics, believing that the world will be a better place when we behave more ethically toward each other.

You can contact Mano at 2006 Azalea Circle, Decatur, GA, 30033 Phone (404) 352-0592.

## ★ 6 ★
# The What, Why, and How of Self Esteem
## What is it? Why is it important? How do we develop it?

by **Myra McElhaney**

*Self esteem comes from a developed and considered sense of what we will put up with and what we will not and our abiding knowledge that these parameters are essential and absolutely unbreachable.*

UNKNOWN

Many years ago I read this quote in a newspaper. It seemed so powerful to me that I cut it out and carried it in my wallet for several years. I reread it many times over the years.

I had always thought self-esteem was a "thing." Something you had or could get. I read this quote for the first time. Then I read it again. I rolled the words around on my tongue, and I thought about each one asking myself, "What exactly does this quote mean?"

For the first time I realized that self-esteem is more than whether or not we like ourselves. Our self-esteem is the value we place on the core of who we are. Self-esteem isn't just there. It isn't given or found. Self-esteem grows from beliefs we "consider" and "develop." To have "parameters" which are "essential and unbreachable" takes a lot of thought and deliberation.

As a teenager I was shy, quiet, and very self-conscious. I both admired and envied the girls and guys who seemed to be totally confident, comfortable with themselves, able to speak up and voice their opinions without hesitation. I thought they had self-esteem. And I wanted it.

In my personal quest to have self-esteem, I've learned and am continuing to learn a lot. I found that I had some misconceptions and illusions regarding self-esteem. Most importantly, I've learned that we are constantly in the process of developing self-esteem. It fluctuates like the stock market. Some days it's up; some days it's down — maybe just a point or two, maybe a crash. Self-esteem is more about what we are than what we do or achieve.

We all have self-esteem. Sometimes it's just low! Our self-esteem ebbs and flows as we go through life. Our experiences, beliefs, and knowledge can effect it. Other people can also affect our self-esteem, both by the way they treat us and by our perception of what others think.

Let's look at what self-esteem is. Why it is important to our success and how do we develop it?

## WHAT IS SELF-ESTEEM?

Doesn't everyone already know what self-esteem is? Not really. Self-esteem is a word that is often used, abused, and confused. It is often confused with self-confidence, conceit, and even arrogance.

Self-confidence is based on our belief in our abilities. This is usually based on past history. For example, if we enjoy computers and have had experiences working successfully with them in the past we are likely to feel self-confident in our abilities to learn a new program or software package. This has nothing to do with feelings about how worthy we are as persons. Self-confidence is based on something we believe we can do, not what we believe we are.

Arrogance, self-centeredness, and conceit are based on excessive or exaggerated ideas of one's own importance. These characteristics imply a feeling or impression of superiority and this can result in overbearing or cruel behavior.

Put simply, self-confidence is about what we believe we can do. Self-esteem is about what we believe we are. It has nothing to do with what we think of other people. Genuine self-esteem isn't a competition or a comparison. Arrogance, self-centeredness, conceit, and all the various negative traits we were warned about as children operate from a basis of building ourselves up by putting others down.

Let's take a closer look at the meaning of self-esteem.

According to our trusty old friend, Webster, "self" means "the entire person of an individual. The union of elements as body, emotions, thoughts, and sensations that constitute the individuality and identity of a person."

"Esteem" means "respect, the worth or estimation in which something is held. It implies greater warmth of feeling accompanying a high valuation."

But "esteem" is also a verb — an action word. "To esteem means to take into consideration or account, to appraise, to recognize the worth of."

Self-esteem is not simply something we have; it is something we do.

Then self-esteem is much more than confidence and satisfaction with ourselves. It is a constant evaluation of who we are, what we believe, and what we value. Self-esteem is our appraisal of our entire being — our core person.

This appraisal or "value" can fluctuate from time to time just as the value of gold, the dollar, or a stock certificate fluctuates. Just like a market analyst constantly analyzes a stock, we must constantly "esteem" or evaluate who and what we are. Our "self" or our core can remain stable while our "esteem" or the "value" we place on ourselves fluctuates.

What are the beliefs and values at your core?

Have they been "developed" and "considered?" Have you simply accepted the beliefs and values you were taught as a child or have you questioned, challenged and explored them?

Where are your parameters or boundaries? Are they "absolute" and "unbreachable?" Do you have a sense of what you will and will not put up with? Without a sense of our boundaries, we are more likely to allow ourselves to be taken advantage of or treated badly.

Once we are clear on what our personal values, principles, and standards are, we are better able to make decisions that build rather than deplete our self-esteem.

For example, Tom and Mike are both Account Executives for a large well-known advertising agency. A big client is coming into town and the boss strongly suggests that they take this client out to a strip club for entertainment. Will agreeing to go along with this effect the self-esteem of either Account Executive?

For Tom, who is single and known as a playboy who likes to party, probably not. However, for Mike who is a family man, active in his church, and leader of the local scout troop, it could.

It is not the behavior that affects our self-esteem as much as it is how well the behavior fits in with our personal values, principles, and standards.

**WHY IS SELF-ESTEEM AN IMPORTANT ELEMENT OF SUCCESS?**

*Of all the judgements that we pass in life, none is as important as the one we pass on ourselves, for that judgement touches the very center of our existence.*
<u>Honoring The Self</u> by NATHANIEL BRANDEN

You may be asking:

"So what does the value I place on myself as a person have to do with success?"

"Once I'm rich and famous won't I have all the self-esteem I need?"

The value we place on ourselves, as persons will affect the decisions we make, the people we choose to associate with, and the habits we form. Those things certainly affect our success!

Wealth, fame, or even love will not make us value ourselves highly if we are not living our lives in tune with our values and with the "self" we see as our core being.

Princess Diana was one of the most beautiful, most wealthy, most loved people in the world. Yet in an interview near the time of her divorce, she discussed her personal bouts with low self-esteem.

There are many ways self-esteem is important in achieving success or reaching for the stars. Self-esteem is the value we place on ourselves, based on our beliefs about ourselves, our values, principles, and standards. With this in mind, it seems that self-esteem not only effects whether we become successful but it also affects our definition of success — the goals we set, our ability to believe we can achieve them, and our belief that we deserve to achieve our goals. The more we value ourselves; the more we are true to ourselves.

The self-esteem we project is important to our employers, associates, and customers. Research has found a definite connection between the degree of a person's self-esteem and the degree of his or her overall mental well-being. There is also a connection between self-esteem and our behavior in our professional and personal relationships. Our self-esteem will influence our expectations and judgements.

People with healthy self-esteem expect to do well. Our self-esteem affects how we relate to ourselves as well as how we relate to others. People with healthy self-esteem are more accepting of others and of differing beliefs and opinions.

People with high self-esteem seek the stimulation of demanding goals. People with low self-esteem tend to prefer the safety of the familiar and undemanding.

People who feel they deserve respect are more likely to treat others with respect. Feeling that we deserve respect is not the stern authoritarian ogre we picture with a pointed finger demanding, "You will treat me with respect!" That demand usually comes from a basis of low self-esteem. True respect is earned not demanded. People who truly feel they deserve respect earn it by their treatment of themselves and others.

People who project high or healthy self-esteem tend to be more flexible, more willing to take responsibility, think independently, and feel confident in expressing their ideas. Don't we all want to work with someone like that?

Now that we've examined what self-esteem is and why it is important in our journey of growth and success, how do we get it?

## HOW DO WE DEVELOP HIGH SELF-ESTEEM?

In an ideal world we would all be born with unconditional high self-esteem and have that esteem or value recognized and acknowledged throughout our lives. Unfortunately, that isn't the case.

Where do we get our self-esteem? We form our self-perceptions as we grow up. We base our value of ourselves as we are treated by others and by the judgements and expectations they place upon us. As we grow up, these self-perceptions are affirmed, strengthened, modified, or rejected.

Most of us grew up at a time and in a world where selflessness and humility are commonly regarded as synonymous with virtue. Many families and religions, with the best of intentions, set out to make sure we weren't arrogant, conceited, vain, haughty, insolent, or any other of that whole passel of "bad" things. Humility is exalted as a virtue. "Humility," by the way, actually means "submissive." As a verb, "to humble" means "to destroy the power, independence, or prestige of."

We were supposed to learn that we were not better than other people were. Most of us internalized that as "not as good as." Somewhere in there we got the message that we had little or no value as persons, thus, low self-esteem. So here we are, confused about our value as persons.

The good news is that like the value of a stock or commodity, the value we place upon ourselves can change. We can revise our self-image through new experiences, beliefs, and knowledge.

The first step in increasing our self-esteem or value is to *question*.

To value ourselves, we need to truly get to know ourselves. In seminars when we are discussing self-esteem and self-confidence, I find that many adults have never stopped to consider what they believe.

We read the mission statements, guiding principles, and value statements of companies and organizations. How often do we think about our personal mission, principles, and values? What are our standards of performance?

What are your personal values? What are the things in life that are most important to you? If you had to rank them, could you?

Are your values, principles, and standards of performance based on something you've "developed" and "considered"?

What parameters do you hold to be "essential and absolutely unbreachable?" Where are your boundaries?

When we know ourselves well, we think and act in a manner that is consistent with our true selves. We have personal integrity when our behaviors integrate our values, principles, and beliefs. To have a clear sense of our identity allows us to behave in a more consistent manner.

Without a clear sense of our identity, we can be more easily persuaded to behave in a way that doesn't align with our beliefs and principles. When we were children, our parents set rules and guidelines to help us make good decisions. As we mature or really "grow up," we begin to set our own boundaries.

Several years ago I was working for a company that was a vendor to retail stores. There was constant pressure to produce sales and keep "our" stores fully stocked and looking great. In preparation for an important visit from the National Sales Director the Regional Manager directed us to fill the cases with empty boxes where stock was low to give the appearance that the stores were fully stocked with merchandise.

I did as I was directed. Although it didn't seem right, it wasn't illegal or immoral and refusing to do it would certainly get me in hot water. At that time I had not given a lot of thought to my personal values, principles, and standards. However, I knew I felt uncomfortable about misrepresenting the situation.

That was just a small thing. The key is that it is not the behavior, but how the behavior aligns with our core values that affects our self-esteem. When we are consistently put in situations where we act in ways that "go against our grain," our self-esteem suffers.

The second step in developing self-esteem is to *accept*.

Accept ourselves as we are. Our core persons have worth. Unconditionally. How do we know we are valuable? Our creator thought so!

Does this mean that now that we've given ourselves permission we will magically begin to value ourselves more? No. It's not that easy — still more accepting to do.

According to Psychology of Adjustment by Eastwood Atwater, our self-concept is made up of several selves. We express different aspects of ourselves at different times.

The ideal self is the self I would like to be.
The subjective self is the self as I see me.
The social self is the self I think others see.

The ideal self reflects our aspirations, expectations, and values. It reflects who we want to be. At various times in our lives it may be necessary to take a look at our ideal selves and reevaluate them. The ideal self we created years ago is likely to be different from the ideal self we hold today.

The subjective self is based on experience, limitations, decisions, habits, needs, interest, traits, etc. We can increase our "value" of this self by developing competence in one area or another. Our associations with other people and our experiences of success and failure will affect the way we see ourselves.

The social self is based on our perception of how others see us. This will be influenced by the way we are treated by others. Some people are more aware of and influenced by the social image than others. How we are affected by this is related to our tendency to either look to situations and people to guide our actions or looking inward to our own standards.

If our subjective self (the way we see ourselves) is vastly different from our ideal self (the way we want to be) or from our social self (the way we think others see us), our self-esteem will suffer.

Accepting ourselves doesn't mean that we do not want to grow and change. It simply means we accept reality. We meet our selves where we are now. We look at the facts about ourselves; whether or not we like them, we accept them.

Once we accept ourselves where we are, we can then evaluate where we would like to be and develop a plan to grow in that direction. We can improve and evolve through embracing new experiences, increasing our knowledge, developing new skills, changing our thought patterns, and learning to persist through adversity.

We are always in the process of self-creation. Through experiences, knowledge, and relationships we can constantly redefine ourselves. Every moment of the day, we get to decide who we will be.

The third step in increasing our self-esteem is to *acknowledge*.

Look at the values, principles and beliefs we have developed and acknowledge them as valuable and worthy. Striving to live by our own personal code will help us to live true to ourselves. Some days we may be closer than others. It's the working toward it that makes us better.

Acknowledge that we decide what our ideal, subjective, and social self is. We decide on our behaviors, experiences, habits, etc. We are adults now; it is up to us to take the responsibility for our self-esteem.

The fourth step in developing self-esteem is to *adjust*.

In our journeys toward the stars, we must constantly reevaluate and adjust to make sure we are on target. Our journey toward success is also a journey of personal growth. The self that we value or esteem is constantly changing and growing.

We may need to adjust our ideal self. Our ideal self must be realistic. Our ideal self is the yardstick we use to measure our subjective self. If our ideal self is unrealistic and far beyond our reach, we are likely to devalue our selves. Result: lower self-esteem. It is up to us to determine what is realistic and what is attainable.

We may need to adjust our subjective self. This is where we could develop a plan to get us to where we want to be.

Example: Debbie is self-conscious about her looks. Since appearance ranks highly among her values, she is always berating herself by saying that she is too fat; she looks old, etc. Her ideal self is definitely different from her subjective self. What could she do to raise her self esteem?

That depends. Is Debbie ten pounds overweight with an ideal self that is model thin? Or is Debbie obese and behaving in ways that are unhealthy?

We can look more closely at our ideal self and decide if it is realistic. If not, we have the power to adjust our ideal self. If we find that our ideal self is reasonable, we may want to develop a plan to get our subjective self more in line with our ideal self.

Look again at your values, principles, and standards. Now look at your ideal self. Is your ideal self in line with your values, principles and standards? Is it realistic?

Now let's look at the subjective self. How does it line up with our values, principles, and standards? How does it line up with our ideal self? There are many steps we can take to adjust our subjective selves so that we behave in ways that are true to our ideal selves.

We can improve our image or value of our subjective self by increasing our knowledge and skills. Reading, taking a class, having a new experience can help us to feel better about ourselves.

Another way we can build self-esteem is to improve our thought patterns. Do you frequently beat yourself up for your perceived shortcomings? Do you hear the voice of your mother/father/teacher/boss/etc. when something goes wrong?

"How could you be so stupid?"

"You'll never amount to anything."

"It's good you were born with brains because your looks sure won't help."

Most of us have *old tapes* that haunt us. It takes time and practice, but we can change these *old tapes*. We can develop new *self talk* to encourage ourselves, affirm our abilities, and validate our value. Each time we hear one of those old voices we can consciously argue with it. Replace the comment with a positive affirmation.

Here are a few simple steps we can take to improve the way we feel about ourselves.

Accept compliments. The next time someone gives you a compliment, just say, "Thank you!" Too often we reject or diminish a compliment with a qualification or explanation.

Relinquish responsibility for things beyond our control. Too often we allow people and things outside our area of control to make us feel bad about ourselves.

Keep a success file. Keep special thank-you notes, certificates of appreciation, a copy of a report or project that we did well. Any documentation that we contributed value will do. Looking through these items on a day when your self-esteem is slipping can perk you right up.

Visualize yourself succeeding. This exercise is most effective if you take the time to close your eyes and imagine in great detail the look, feel and smell of your idea of success. Visualize your small successes that you experience along the way.

In my own journey of personal growth and success, I find self-esteem very important. For me, maintaining a healthy level of self-esteem is a daily process — constant redefining and reevaluating. High self-esteem or placing high value on myself comes through knowing myself well and behaving in ways that are true to my core. Remember: *It is up to us to decide who we become and what our value is.*

# Myra McElhaney

Myra McElhaney has fifteen years experience in sales, customer service and training. Her broad industry experience includes fashion, retail, advertising, and real estate.

Myra has conducted training programs and keynote speeches professionally for six years. She has worked with several Fortune 500 companies as well as small and mid-size companies. She is a member of National Speakers Association and serves on the board of directors for the Georgia Speakers Association.

You can reach Myra at McElhaney & Associates, 8531 Birch Hollow Drive, Roswell, GA 30076 Phone (770) 664-4553, Fax (770) 752-0817, or E-mail: pmcelhaney@aol.com.

## ★ 7 ★

# It's a Juggle Out There

by **Shirley Garrett, Ed.D.**

*I can sometimes resist temptation, but never mischief!*
JOYCE REBETA-BURDITT

Every time someone reads that title, they want to edit it to read "It's A *Jungle* Out There." And I chuckle to myself as the reader begins to recognize that the world is not made up of lions, tigers, and bears — but is made of phone calls, E-mails, faxes, children, partners, demands, misunderstandings, meetings, deadlines, meals, social events, and on and on and on. And unlike the jungle, where the fight-or-flight response enables us to either confront or run away as fast as we can, the *juggle* involves relationships, work patterns, self worth, and virtually all everyday experiences that can keep us earth bound — or help us reach for the stars.

Dan Thurman, a very accomplished and wise juggler (and speaker), once told me that when juggling, the important thing is not what you catch, but what you are willing to let go of. And I think in life the same can hold true. In order to make sense out of the chaos that we seem to create, we must be willing to let go. You are invited to let go of some old assumptions, let go of some traditional beliefs and let your mind play with some of the ideas presented in this chapter. In doing so, you may find yourself moving off your point of view onto a new view point.

In The Magic of Conflict, Tom Crum challenges us to get off our point of view (something we need to defend) and move to a new viewing point — a place of increased perspective and greater possibilities. As Tom explains, "rising up to a viewing point does not mean totally forsaking your point of view. It puts your point of view in perspective, in relation to the whole." Imagine an eye looking out, focused in one direction — to a point in the distance. That is a point of view. One point. One idea. One place. Now, imagine an eye on top of a viewing point (like a mountain top). What is possible for the eye to see? Many points. Many ideas. Many places.

It wasn't very long ago that I thought I had become *enlightened* and knowledgeable about what is good and right and thus equally clear about what is bad and wrong. Life has a funny way of putting us in our place and before long, I realized that I had literally become a point of view, complete with limiting possibilities and potential. It was easy for me to jump in immediately and offer "good, sound advice" to anyone who was having trouble at work, with relationships, or in finding peacefulness, joy, or balance in life.

During my journey, there are lessons that have worked for me and will perhaps awaken a thought for you. In reading of my own discoveries, perhaps you will be reminded of some of your own. I invite you to sit back, relax, think, pause, and connect with the words I share. Listen to the internal voice that might suggest that this or that thought has potential value in your life… and dismiss those ideas that don't seem to fit for you.

### It Is a Juggle Out There!

In another era, we might resemble "whirling dervishes" appearing to spin, as if in a trance. Whirling and spinning, and turning with no apparent goal — simply letting the trance-like nature of the dance carry us from one moment to another. Or perhaps we more closely resemble the "plate spinner" on the Ed Sullivan show. Spinning one plate, rapidly followed by another, and another, and another, and then rushing back to re-spin the first one, keeping an eye on the others, ready to catch a plate just before it falls to set it into motion again, and WHEW!

It's time to stop the spinning, the whirling, the juggling!

The truth is that many of us are moving so rapidly from one activity, project, job, family/social event or personal quest to another that we rarely take time to stop — and celebrate the world and people around us. We have put so many objects into our juggling pattern that we barely touch one aspect of our lives before another appears — demanding immediate attention. Before we have a chance to catch our breaths, or determine if what we are doing is adding to our lives or simply depleting us of energy, we move to another event or crisis.

We've all read books, listened to tapes, and attended seminars about achieving balance, harmony, or peace within our work and personal life. Why then is it so hard to put into practice? I believe that for the most part, we look at quick fixes — things to make us feel better in the moment. Instant solutions, instant fixes. However, when the going gets tough or we don't take the time to de-stress, we are suddenly confronted with the same old issues we have always faced.

In the remainder of this chapter, I encourage you to look at the systems in your life that adversely impact you. We will discuss the work and social world and the world of your personal well-being. Additionally, I will invite you to look inward for some of the answers. In doing so, I'll share tips from my own journey — as well as some shared with me by family, friends, and audiences. My intention is to help you analyze your current state of affairs and share with you tips for making the changes that will bring you peace and joy.

## The World of Work

♬ ♪Hi! Ho ♪!, Hi! Ho♬ ♪!, It's off to work we go!♬ ♪ Recently I listened to a "futurist" explain that after years of preparing to be a nurse, he was startled to realize at the orientation for his first job, nothing was as he expected. Unlike the majority of the Seven Dwarfs, he did not feel the excitement and anticipation of the work in the day ahead. Many of us arrive daily at our work or our careers to find that nothing is quite what we expected… and perhaps we feel futile in our attempts to make it different. Sometimes the rapid changes in the work world leave us confused, feeling used-up, and burned-out. Other times, we feel challenged by the job ahead and then discover to our dismay that the direction we were going is not the same as everyone else's. Or maybe, we feel isolated and determined to just get through by doing the job and expecting little support or encouragement from any one else.

The following concepts became clear to me as I taught school for several years, owned my own business, and was fired from a splendid career (that's another story for another day!)

## Determine What the Right Job Is

In any given career position, you probably have at least 10 different responsibilities. In fact, it is suggested that you to take a minute and list everything you are responsible for on your job. Now, look at your list and determine the order of importance each responsibility has (in your opinion). Here's the tough part. What importance would other people (boss, co-workers, clients, customers, vendors, stock holders, etc.) assign to the tasks. There are so many people who have opinions about the importance of each of those tasks. The opinions are based on each individual's own agenda and beliefs. For example, a teacher may see her most important job as helping students get their behavior under control enough to learn the lesson. Parents may think that teaching reading is the most important function of the teacher. The principal may think that classroom discipline is a priority. The school board might believe that raising the test scores is most critical. The curriculum director my take the position that teaching critical thinking skills takes precedence over everything else. And the students may think that creating a place to have fun and feel good is the absolute most important thing a teacher can do.

No wonder we might feel confused. As professionals, we feel that we know what is important. However, if we want to stop the whirlwind in our jobs, we must find out from all the stakeholders, "What is the most important task at hand?" This may mean real dialogue with the many people who influence your work day. It may mean being able to defend your position, yet honor the position of the other person. It may mean that your organization might have to be involved in some strategic planning. The more you can get everyone on the same page (with the same agenda), the less work-related stress will occur; the more successful the work will feel; and stronger team work and cooperation will emerge.

### Whose Problem Is It?

It has been my experience that people often become confused about whose problem or responsibility something is in the workplace. Perhaps you have become well known for how you handle one aspect of the job — so, when there is a fruit-basket turnover in administration or leadership, or you become promoted, you are no longer responsible for the same tasks or issues as before. However, instead of letting go, many of us often hold on to our old responsibilities, refusing to relinquish control of the task, although it may be in our best interest to do so. In doing so, we might find ourselves constantly trying to *fix* someone else's problems.

Several years ago, I married Randy and was anxious to please him and do the things that I thought a *successful* wife should do (which in the South was strongly influenced by a clean house.) We live in a small house that Randy built at a time when he thought he would only need a *bachelor pad*. In no need of large nonessential areas, Randy built a closet for the washer/dryer along one wall of the kitchen, diagonal to the front door, and behind louvered doors that have never been closed.

When we first married, I thought it was important to keep a clean, sparkling home at all times. I did pride myself on keeping a relatively neat home: keeping the clothes put away, vacuuming occasionally, putting dirty dishes in the dish washer, and keeping the kitchen floor swept.

Randy is a cattle farmer and after working in the hay fields all day, he would come home from work, remove his shoes at the front door, roll his socks off his feet, and shoot them like basketballs into the washer. He was good at this, being All County on his high school basketball team. I would then wash the socks, and as I removed them from the washer to the dryer, I would unroll them. Needless to say, hay would fall all over the floor, leaving me another job of sweeping.

At this point, it is probably important to admit that I am not a happy housekeeper. In fact, unless all is right in the world, I find housekeeping to be my least favorite job — right up there with pulling weeds from the flower beds. Once I get the house work done, I expect a lot of help keeping it done. Great expectations! Little results.

However, I wanted *this* marriage to last, so I would say very little about the mess that these socks were creating. I would grudgingly get out the broom and dust pan and get the hay off the floor, muttering under my breath all the time. This attitude lasted a couple of weeks. Next, I tried the *talk with your husband about your needs* approach. Somehow, Randy could not see the magnitude of the problem. I continued to sweep hay, muttering a little less under my breath as time went on. One day it occurred to me that I may be approaching the *nagging* stage about those darn socks! If there's one thing I hate worse than housework, it's nagging.

Suddenly I had an idea. I would no longer own the problem. I would give the problem back to Randy! I continued to wash the socks. Then, I would casually remove them from the washer, set myself up and *shoot* them into the dryer. Two points! I, too, could be Michael Jordan! (For those of you not familiar with Drying 101, you can dry a sock ball for 24 hours and it will never completely dry!) So, after the usual drying cycle, I would remove the socks from the dryer and put them into

Randy's drawer. And when he opened the sock balls — suddenly, Randy had a whole new assessment of the sock problem!

Think about your work world — on the job, at home, or the work you do in the community. Are there times that you add to the juggling routine by owning responsibility for someone else's work? Someone else will pick up the slack if he sees the need to. But as long as you keep on doing what you've always done…

### Be Willing to Say, "I Blew It"

We all make mistakes — we all blow it! However, many of us struggle with being able to own up to our mistakes. Abbott-Jeffer, Inc. (A speaking, training, consulting company) created small cards with the words "I blew it… I made a mistake and would like to own up to it without being criticized or judged." On the reverse side of the card are tips for when you blow it. What wonderful wisdom they share. They suggest three steps for when you blow it. First, lighten up on yourself. Everyone makes mistakes. It is simply a part of being human.

Second, be accountable. Because we all make mistakes, the notion of *hiding* our mistakes can be interpreted by others that mistakes are not allowed here! I'm reminded of a couple of children I know. In one of their households, mistakes are accepted as learning experiences so the child immediately lets an adult know if he has had an "oopsy daisy!" (His words for spilled milk, a broken toy, or other major catastrophe). He takes responsibility for his role in the accident, helps find a solution, and is able to discuss any lessons that might be learned. Another child may grow up in a home where mistakes are seen as "bad," "childish," "mean," or other terms indicating unacceptable and inappropriate behavior. When he has an "oopsy daisy," he is quick to hide it, hoping he will be long gone before it is discovered. He has learned to hide or deny any mistakes that he might have made. Two very different approaches, two very real situations. Think about the lessons we are teaching others around us when we are unwilling to be accountable for our mistakes.

Third, Abbott and Jeffers suggest that you take action immediately. I, for one, have never found a mistake to decrease in magnitude because I put off owning up to it. It is important to try to find solutions to problems and help determine the next course of action. However, prolonging acknowledgment of a mistake sends out a message that you are hiding. Think about it.

## Relationships

We all live in relationship to each other. How our relationship works and how much value the relationship adds to our lives could be dependent upon its authenticity. By authenticity, I mean that each person is willing to bring honesty to the relationship — that each person is willing to listen for understanding and willing to speak honestly enough to be understood. This is not unlike in <u>Seven Habits of Highly Effective People,</u> Stephen Covey's habit number five which suggests that "we seek first to understand, then be understood."

## Authentic Communication

So often I find myself anxious to be understood, then I'm outa here! The more I try to live by this principle of reciprocal understanding, the more I find my relationships becoming more whole, less stressful, and more abundantly fulfilling. And this is a tall order! Like many professional speakers, I suffer from the desire to talk a lot and, if I listen at all, to hear just enough to be assured that you have heard me.

It has also come to my attention that if I take the time and commit the energy to really listen with the intent of understanding, every relationship in my life can be catapulted to a new high! This skill seems so simple, yet takes so much energy. This is truly one of those cases where we have "to let go of our ego" and give credence to what the other person is saying.

Being able to express ourselves is a powerful gift of preservation. If there is an issue that is of great concern to us, it behooves us to talk it out enough to be able to "name" the problem. As Joel Goodman says, "Name It, Tame It" or paraphrased, if you can talk enough to give name to your problems or concerns, you will be able to find resolution. Robert Johnson, author of <u>Owning Your Own Shadow</u> discusses the importance of "talking." According to Johnson, "You can give another person a precious gift if you will allow him to talk without contaminating his speech with your own material." Once again, the emphasis is on listening for understanding — as opposed to listening for the speaker to take a breath so you can jump right in!

Another example of what has been termed pseudo-listening is discounting the speaker. For example, when a child falls down and whimpers, "It hurts SOOO bad!" it is easy to deflect her sentiments as being attention-seeking. What would happen if we acknowledged that,

"Yes, it must really hurt to have a cut on your leg"? How much more validated would the child feel? Or what about employees who might express their concern about corporate down-sizing? Assuring them that they have nothing to worry about might prevent them from talking with you about their dream to receive training in another area or try for another position within the company. Sometimes I try to be really conscious of the number of times I invalidate someone within a day. It is incredible. Instead of really listening, I often find myself discounting the other person's concerns or wanting to give my tried and true solutions. The only problem is, the solutions are only tried (and not always true) by me!

It is true that the greatest need that each of us has is the need to belong. And often, the need to belong is in direct opposition to speaking our truth. Somehow we have been conditioned to believe that if we speak our truth, no one will like us. What I have discovered is that we can avoid speaking our truths and everyone will still not like us. And perhaps the most valuable lesson of all is knowing: "It really doesn't matter if *everyone* doesn't like me!"

Being able to speak our truth is a tremendous undertaking. To this day, I do not find it always easy to say what is on my mind. Or to be able to state a position without sounding defensive or "tunnel visioned." Owning what is truth for me is a challenge. Daily I am confronted with people whose lack of tolerance appalls me. Racial, gender, and sexual preference jokes abound. How do I speak up and say, "This makes me uncomfortable"? How do we speak our truths without sounding prophetic or self-righteous? This is one area that remains a struggle for me. However, I have found that the more I become connected with other people — really trying to say hello to their soul as well as the empty space between us, the more I am able to externalize the message of being connected.

## Looking In Our Faces

When my grandsons were very small, for whatever reason, I realized that saying "please," "thank you," or "I'm sorry" seemed to be flippant after-thoughts to wanting something, receiving a gift, or trying to make amends (usually after some adult's prompting). One day it occurred to me that the "polite words" were being spoken without conviction, and I sensed the importance of changing the dynamics. So we started a habit that eventually became known as "looking in his/her face." Very simply, when the occasion called for "polite words," I insisted that the children look into each others' faces and watch for the response, Without understanding the concept, they began to "feel" the power of their words. After several years of this practice, it amazes me when one of them will come tattling, "Gran-Gran, he did not look me in the face when he said he was sorry!"

It is amazing how challenging it can be to look into someone's face. When I am centered and focused and in the moment, I try the following. When I drive up to a takeout food restaurant, or I pay for gasoline in a quickie market, or I cash out at the grocery store or bank, I try to look directly into the eyes of the attendant. It is amazing how often they are surprised, and genuinely delighted, to receive a connecting smile and comment. Give it a try. Let me know how it works for you!

## Forgiveness

In every relationship, there will be moments when someone needs to be forgiven. For some people, it is easy to forgive any pain or problem that other people have created. For others, forgiveness seldom, if ever happens. Holding on to anger and past hurts takes a lot of energy. It also sends the message you are living in the past, not the present. Forgiveness is a way of letting a person know that you accept them in the present. You accept them for who they are today — not who they were yesterday.

Not long ago, my friend Kitty's son was getting married. Through mixed communication, I arrived for the wedding weekend several hours later than Kitty expected me. I could tell that she was upset. At the time, I did not recognize the depth of her disappointment and hurt. A few days later, Kitty invited me over to talk. As we sat on her deck, quietly talking, she expressed to me how hurt she had been the week before. My response was typical. I felt flustered and defensive. I felt embarrassed and like a failure. I wanted to restate my reasons for the mix-up. I wanted to figure out how to fix the situation. I wanted to perform a penance. In the matter of a few seconds, my feelings about myself had plummeted. I did not know how I could right the wrong.

As I told Kitty that I was sorry and began what I considered the long journey to repair the damage, she immediately hushed me with these words, "I forgive you." She said them with such power and such conviction that I never doubted they were true. I was startled. In those profound moments, I looked into Kitty's eyes and knew that I was forgiven. I knew that the event was forgotten. I knew that she loved me and that no penance was expected or even desired.

In the course of the next few days, I thought often of the feelings that were a result of our encounter. It became clear to me that very seldom in life do I experience true forgiveness. In fact, more often than not, I feel that I am on probation and just as soon as I make a mistake there will be someone anxious to remind me of my lack in value. As I pondered this insight, I wondered how many other people have the same experience. Through discussion with friends and family, I realized that this feeling of probation is not unusual. Other people felt the same way. They felt that their acceptance was only conditional, based on the condition that they met every one else's expectations and needs — and did not "drop the ball" in the process.

The experience with Kitty held three valuable lessons for me. One, forgiveness is a gift we give to each other. All my life I heard of God's grace, His ability to grant us forgiveness regardless of what sins we might have committed. Until that afternoon on Kitty's deck, I don't believe I understood the power of that grace. Somewhere, unconsciously, I had doubted that grace, or forgiveness, could be so easily given. It was emotionally and spiritually inspiring to have had such a profound experience with forgiveness.

Second, it came to me that asking for forgiveness is not an easy task. For some reason, it has always seemed easier to try to justify a mistake (stay committed to my point of view) or begin to scramble to pay penance for a mistake. Asking for and being able to accept forgiveness is a powerfully enriching experience in a relationship.

And, third, I feel the importance of letting someone know when I forgive him. That I don't easily repeat the words, "Oh, it's okay." But that I truly affirm his self worth by giving the gift of forgiveness. That I really let them know that their past is indeed in the past and that I accept them in the moment.

As you read this, you might have images of people whom you need to forgive. You may want to take a few minutes and think about their worth as human beings. You might want to look for ways to affirm their goodness and be willing to accept them as they are today, not yesterday. You might want to give them the gift of forgiveness.

And as you think along these lines, you might want to think of people who feel hurt or anger toward you. Simply asking for forgiveness can be freeing. And a word of caution. Although you ask for forgiveness, you may not immediately receive it. That's okay. Asking is the first step in healing. Marcus Aurelius said that "The art of living is more like wrestling than dancing." I disagree. When we really connect with each other — at a soul level, the art of living is a beautiful dance.

## Personal Well-Being

The third aspect of our lives that we juggle is our personal well-being. There seems to be a wake-up call sounding throughout our country. People are achieving financial and career gains beyond their dreams. They are living in beautiful homes, driving new cars, wearing this year's fashions, and traveling more than any other society in history. And yet, there seems to be a profound sense of emptiness — a lack of wholeness.

When we spend our lives juggling so much "stuff," it is almost impossible to take good care of ourselves — our physical, intellectual, spiritual and psychological needs. In the preceding paragraphs, I have challenged you to look at where your energy goes. You have been asked to do a little reflection. At this time, I encourage you to review the self that is sitting, reading this book — and reaching for the stars.

Take a few minutes and think about those stars in terms of yourself. Define what a physical star would look like for you — not for someone else. It is out of your physical well-being that you have the energy to do every day what you need to do, what you want to do, and then have enough energy left over to take care of an emergence. What activity brought you joy as a child? Rediscover bike riding, dancing, walking, swimming. Just remember to go just a bit slower — and wear a helmet!

What would need to be accomplished for your intellectual star to shine? For it is out of our intelligence that we develop knowledge, and out of knowledge we find wisdom, and out of our wisdom we develop a sense of understanding... understanding of ourselves and understanding of each other. Are you like many of us who shut down at times in our learning processes because of an unkind remark by a teacher or another adult? If so, move beyond those words and challenge yourself to read more, learn more, experience more.

Reaching for the spiritual star seems to be permeating our culture. Look in any bookstore and you will find volumes written about spirituality and spiritual awakening. I'm not talking about religion, but of spirituality. Scott Peck says that spirituality is when your knowledge about God is replaced with an experience with God. Respecting your own definition of what *spirit* is to you, I would like to encourage you to look toward a spiritual path if you are not already on one. For it is out of our spirituality that we find hope. And out of hope we can find internal and eternal peace.

And finally, you are who you are. Your psychological self, the very core of who you are is your precious gift. As you peel back the layers of behaviors that you have learned are "acceptable" and rediscover parts of yourself that brought you joy, then you will find bits and pieces of yourself that are unique and powerful. Celebrate and value who you are.

## 3 Wishes

Unlike the dust that a magic wand sprinkles, the words that you are reading will not magically transform your life into one that is balanced, meaningful, and abundant but instead, perhaps they can serve as a catalyst for thought that will inspire you to take the necessary actions to discover the aspects of life that bring you joy — to do more joyful things and fewer of those that bring you turbulence.

My first wish for you is for the peace of incubation. When you think of an incubator, are you reminded of a safe, self-nurturing place? Webster defines incubate as "to keep under conditions favorable for development," and an incubator as an apparatus for providing those suitable conditions.

What conditions do you need for development? For so many of us, we simply need some quiet time in which to think and focus within. I have found that if I will create a space within my day to sit, breathe deeply, empty my thoughts and head of my "to do" list, that I stumble upon answers to previous confusion, solutions to major problems, and release from old blocks. Amazingly enough, creativity begins to flourish, not only in work production, but also in addressing conflict. It seems that the more time I spend quietly *emptying* my head of thought, the more clear my thoughts become.

## Some Ideas for Incubation

1. Find a quiet place — one that automatically instills a sense of joy — simply relax, breathing in through your nose and out through your mouth. As you inhale, imagine your breath as flowing throughout your body, into the trunk, arms and legs, fingers and toes. As you exhale,

imagine the breath swirling out and into a continuous path back into your nose. Visualize your breath. Straighten and open the chest on the inhale, bend forward at the waist during the exhale — pushing all the air out of your body. Breathe slowly, deliberately. Let your mind become blank. Do not try to solve your anxieties — let go of them.

2. Turn on some music that relaxes you; sit quietly as the music causes your mind to drift to other places and pleasant memories. Remember comforting moments, comforting people, comforting places. Visit them in your mind. Don't worry if you fall asleep — your body needs the rest. Be aware, though, that you might need more rest in your life.

3. Pull out old photographs, mementos, and souvenirs. Remember the joys surrounding the moments. Hear the laughter of old friends. Remember the celebrations of family. Honor the emotions that arise. Understanding that all emotions won't be joyous; some will be sad, some will be hurtful. Try to visualize yourself in your memories — celebrate the moments of joy and growth. Acknowledge the pain. It is out of both joy and pain that we find balance in life.

4. Write. Julia Cameron in The Artist's Way suggests writing three pages first thing every morning... before the news, before the paper, before the rush of the busy day. Don't plan what you write. Write randomly, with abandonment. Write whatever comes to your mind. Don't edit and don't read your work for a long time. Simply write your thoughts, let them flow.

5. Find a centering activity. A centering activity is an activity that brings you into the moment. Sewing, arts and crafts, fishing, digging in the dirt, watching animals feed or leaves falling, or rocking in a chair, or painting, drawing, or dancing. Feel yourself really present in the moment. Notice the physical appearance of objects around you. The billowing clouds against a blue sky; the path that a stream makes as it tumbles over rocks and stumps; the way a squirrel eats an acorn; the colors of the flame as logs burn. Hear the rustling of dry leaves blown across the ground, the chirping of animals as they search for food and for mates; the sound that silence makes; the noise of traffic. Smell the air — the aromas of the season. Experience the textures of touch — fresh vegetables, soft wools, sensuous silken, comforting cotton.

6. Move. Walk, jog, ride a bike or a boat. Dance, stroll, strut, and skip. Stretch, reach, turn, and jump. Create large free movements. Expand yourself; draw yourself in. With music — without music. Move. Let your body experience your mind. Let your emotions find expression

in your movements. Breathe, laugh, shout, and sing.

My second wish for you is for the joy of laughter. Laughter is such a precious commodity. Like precious silver or gold in the ore, when laughter is mined out of the spirit, the value is great.

It has been said that the average child laughs 200 times a day. The average adult laughs 15 (I know some people who are way below average — don't you!). What happens between childhood and adulthood? I remember hearing things like: "Settle down, Shirley Ann!"; "What are you laughing at?"; "What's so funny?"; "Quit being so silly!" In fact, it wasn't that long ago that someone said to me, "You're going to magic school? That's the silliest thing I have ever heard. A 40-something-year-old going to magic school."

Now I celebrate and delight in my silliness. After years of worrying about my spontaneous mischief and laughter, I appreciate the part of my spirit that refused to be squelched. It also helps to know that the word *silly* evolved from the English word *saelig* and German word "seely." Loosely translated, the word means blessed, happy, prosperous, and wise. And indeed, when I evoke just a bit of silliness into my day, I do feel blessed, happy, prosperous, and wise.

So where do you go for a dose of laughter? I begin each day by reading the comics. When children are around, I try to pay close attention to their play, their questions, and their delight with the world. Even the Internet provides me with humor. For example, go to the following Web page and discover a chuckle traveling through out-of-space and into your life: jcooper@mindspring.com.

My third wish for you is for the wisdom of Aikido. Aikido is a martial art, and like all martial arts is based on a philosophy. Literally translated Aikido means "the way of blending energy."

In order to visualize this concept, imagine a bull fighter. Do you know what happens when a bull begins to run toward the bull fighter? The bull fighter steps out of the path of the bull (at least the smart ones do). The bull with all it's power and energy can neither stop nor turn quickly enough to redirect its energy. The bull fighter is positioned to use the bull's energy for his gain. Let me emphasize that I am not an advocate of bull fighting. Additionally, there are other nuances that separate bull fighting from the martial art of Aikido. But, isn't it easy for you to know where the bulls in your life are coming from? Sometimes they are heading straight at you. While at other times, they are sneaking around the corner. Occasionally, you might even find the "bull within." But, how often, when confronted with the bull, do you immediately respond by attacking "head on"? What would happen if you stepped to the side? Let the bull pass by? Develop new strategies for dealing with old problems? With old bulls?

When we begin to think in Aikido terms, wisdom is forthcoming. We move off our position of trying to "win" at conflict, and instead honor and acknowledge the place from where the attack is coming. When this happens, all sort of new and peaceful possibilities arise.

I'm reminded of a funny story once told that can show how disarming Aikido can be. An older woman found herself sleeping alone in her house for the first time in her life. Her husband had to leave town for an emergency and she was unable to go. She was assured that she could take care of herself. Wouldn't you know that in the middle of the night the phone rang? At the other end of the line was a very deep masculine voice asking, "Can I take off your panties?" Without missing a beat, she asked, "What are you doing with them on?"

As funny as this story is, it is a great example of deflecting a possibly negative and attacking situation into one that neutralizes the tension… even adding humor in the retelling!

It can be a juggle out there. You are busy doing so much. But you alone have the control over what can be done to change the dynamics. We have looked at what you "do." I've shared some suggestions for *doing* things in a little different way. Additionally, you are busy "being" who you are. Sometimes the "being" gets lost in the juggle of the "doing." As you reflect on what is truly important, reach for the stars. Oh, you'll have to keep juggling, but reach for the stars. Be willing to let go of some "things" so you will have the freedom to reach. And reach for the stars with your name on them. Capture a few called peace, joy, and wisdom.

> *The growth of understanding follows an ascending*
> *spiral rather than a straight line.*
>
> JOANNA FIELD

# Shirley Garrett, Ed.D.

Shirley Garrett, EdD, is a speaker who helps audiences refocus on what is truly important in life — balance, self-esteem, and relationships. Her delivery style is humorous, yet sincere, as she weaves personal anecdotes, humor and a touch of magic into her programs. Shirley's talent for blending the needs of the audience into powerful presentations makes her a sought after keynoter, workshop leader, and retreat facilitator.

Orphaned at age three, Shirley's life has included challenges and adventures that have included being honored as a Georgia Business Woman of Achievement and elected to the board of directors of a national organization. And throughout the journey, Shirley has remained full of life, spirit, and mischief!

You can reach Shirley at Shirley D. Garrett, PO Box 1195, Carrollton, GA 30117  Phone (770)836-1926, Fax (770) 834-9969 or E-mail: drshirl@mindspring.com

*Note: If you have stories to share of how you have discovered the art of juggling in your own life, or if you are challenged by an overwhelming attempt at finding balance, Shirley would love to hear from you. Be a part of her next book,* It's A Juggle Out There. *Simply write, phone, or fax Shirley to share your experience.*

BIBLIOGRAPHY

*Shirley recommends the following books as resources for self-discovery.*

GOING DEEP: EXPLORING SPIRITUALITY IN LIFE AND LEADERSHIP, Ian Percy. If you continue to struggle with meaning — whether it is in a difficult business environment, personal circumstances, or a desire to understand the meaning in ourselves, this book is a must read. Ian takes the reader through six stations of the Inner Journey as a method for understanding your potential for accomplishment in life.

SIMPLE ABUNDANCE: A DAYBOOK OF COMFORT AND JOY, Sarah Ban Breathnach. Although written for women, this book of daily meditations and thoughts is designed to help the reader experience how daily life can be an expression of the authentic self.

THE ALADDIN FACTOR, Jack Canfield and Mark Victor Hansen. From the "Chicken Soup" authors, this book is a wonderful lesson on learning how to ask for what you want in life.

THE ART OF THE FRESH START: HOW TO MAKE AND KEEP YOUR NEW YEAR'S RESOLUTIONS FOR A LIFETIME, Glenna Salsbury. When you reflect on your life, do you ever feel that you are not really accomplishing what you would like? Use Glenna's tools to uncover the values that guide you, and lead you to discover what you want to achieve and how to get there through internal motivation.

THE ARTIST'S WAY: A SPIRITUAL PATH TO HIGHER CREATIVITY, Julie Cameron. Not just a book for the aspiring visual artist. This book will take every reader on a journey toward spiritual awareness and creative living. The twelve week program can have lifetime influence. A must for anyone who wants to live their passion.

JOURNEY TO CENTER: TURNING A LIFE OF WORK INTO A WORK OF ART, Tom Crum. Using anecdotes from his own journeys and from the extraordinary people he's met around the world, Thomas Crum introduces the principle of centering — a skill for unifying the body, mind, and spirit. Learn to break out of the pattern of constant conflicts in life. Learn how to change a conflict from a contest to an opportunity to connect and grow. Phone Aiki Works at (970)925-4532 or (716)924-2799 for information about the book and other materials available.

# ★ 8 ★

# Return to Success

by **Marcia Steele**

We are living through a fast moving era of rapidly accelerating change, where the business world often feels like Disney World and life is like a ride on the latest gravity-defying roller coaster. But the truth is 'we ain't seen nothing yet.' Ahead of us lies the scariest, most exhilarating ride of them all – the 21st century. It's time to sharpen your skills and fasten your seat belts because despite the g-force twists and turns the business world will be taking in the next millenium; corporations and organizations of all kinds will still be looking for people to become change agents in creating success.

The German philosopher Nietzche wrote, "Our destiny rules over us even when we are not aware of it. It is the future that makes laws for our day." That may be true but when the future becomes difficult to predict because of the crazy rate of change, how can we know what laws the future is making for us for today? Paradoxically, the answer lies in the past. Why? Because one characteristic of change is that it often moves us full circle. An English playwright Arthur Wing Pinero said it best when he wrote, "I believe the future is only the past again, entering through another gate." So, one way to get a preview of what lies ahead is to look back and take account of two things: our own experiences and those of the people who went before us. By doing this, we can learn to return to success.

Our ancestors sought two key things: the opportunity to be free, and a way to take care of themselves and their families. They found that the answer lay in working for themselves and at the start of this century, over ninety percent of people were self-employed, with less than 10 %

of the labor force working for other people or the government. At that time, we Americans were a self-sufficient people, but gradually we changed. We began to work for big companies, believing they would provide security for us. We began joining big unions that promised to take care of us and elected officials who would sponsor legislation to protect us. We changed from an independent, self-reliant society within which we took responsibility for ourselves, to one that depended on other people or the government for its livelihood.

By the early 1980's, a complete reversal had taken place. We had changed to a society where less than ten percent of the working population were self-employed. Then suddenly, a major upheaval occurred and our security blankets were torn from us. In one turbulent decade, from 1980 to 1990, the corporate business climate changed dramatically, and two hundred and thirty companies disappeared, a whopping 46% of the Fortune 500. Some went due to acquisitions and mergers; some succumbed to competition; some died because of their inability to change. And today, the trend continues. Many people who thought they would have job security for life are finding themselves standing in unemployment lines, as companies continue to realign, downsize, merge, and outsource.

Like our ancestors, the challenge we face is twofold: to survive these scary times, and to re-position ourselves to prosper in the future. Years ago I heard someone say, "One of the greatest tragedies in life is to have the experience and miss its meaning." So I started to reflect on my own experiences and discovered one common link between all my successes: D.B.A. This does not stand for "Doing Business As," but for "Dreams, Beliefs, and Actions." I realized that whenever I had been successful, it was because I had dreams and beliefs, and took action on them. I now believe that D.B.A. can bring success in every aspect of life.

Let me give you an example of the power of DBA: The story of my coming to America from my home in Jamaica. Like many people from small countries or towns, I wanted the bright lights and glamour of the big city. So I left my island in the sun and headed for New York City. I arrived on a chilly Saturday in March. I spent the next day pouring over the New York Times, circling every help-wanted ad for any position on Wall Street that had anything to do with computers. To me, Wall Street was exciting and magical, the Disneyland of the business world, complete with the scary rides, highs and lows, and crashes! The thrill of money made and the despair of money lost fascinated me. So, the next Monday morning, as I sat on the F train heading to Wall Street, I was overflowing with excitement.

A few minutes into my first interview with a man seated behind a big shiny desk, I was told something I had not remotely considered: "Sorry, you're too young." Although I was disappointed, I went on to my second interview. There I heard more chilling words from behind a big impressive desk, "Sorry hon., we have no females in the computer room." My first day on Wall Street was not going the way I had planned. After all, this was America, the land where dreams come true. I was beginning to suspect that the folks back home in Jamaica were right. Maybe I was crazy to think I could get a computer job on Wall Street. Then I remembered something my mom told me when I was little: "Never quit. Never!" She also taught me a Jamaican expression that serves me well to this day: "If you want success your nose got to run." In other words, on your way to success you might have difficulties that bring you to your knees and bring you to tears — your nose got to run.

Remembering this helped me muster the courage I needed to move on to my third interview, which was with a big bank. The name Franklin National Bank was carved in gold on one of those impressive buildings fronted by huge marble columns, and at least a hundred steps. My heart pounding, I ran up the steps, entered this "temple," and asked for the personnel department. Once again I learned that there were few, if any, small desks on Wall Street. This time, the man seated behind yards of polished mahogany looked up from my resume and said: "You have no U.S. experience." I thought, "No, this can't be happening again." I had brought my dream of making it big in the computer industry to the land where dreams come true, and it was crumbling by the minute!

Even today, Jamaica is not exactly on the cutting edge of technology (our version of E-mail was, "stop the mailman — E got the mail.)" I really wanted that job. I knew that in baseball you are out after three strikes, and I didn't plan on striking out. So, I gathered my thoughts, looked him straight in the eyes and said, "Excuse me, sir, but how would a computer know I wasn't from around here?" There was an unnerving silence before his smile finally broke the suspense, and his eyes were sparkling when he said, "okay, I'll try you out for 90 days." Yes! I had done it. My dream had come true. I had a computer job at 130 Pearl Street, smack dab in the middle of Wall Street. I had been told it would take weeks, even months, to get a computer job in New York, much less on Wall Street, but thankfully I hadn't listened to the prophets of doom. Now I had attained my dream before lunch on day one. How? Through the power of D.B.A. — dreams, beliefs, and actions.

The first key to D.B.A. is, not surprisingly, to know how to dream. As I go around the country giving talks and conducting workshops, I often ask people "What is your dream?" Sadly, most shrug their shoulders and say, "I don't know." Many have forgotten how to dream. We are fortunate to live in a country of endless possibilities, but before you can have a dream come true, you've got to have a dream!

So let me take you on a journey. Pretend you are a kid again. Imagine you are off to see the Wizard of OZ with Dorothy and Toto. And the wizard is going to grant you anything you want. What would you ask for? If you could have anything in the world, what would it be? Let your imagination go, and dare to dream like a child. Children have prolific imaginations and are excited by their dreams. Ask a child if he wants a swimming pool, and he'll say, "Oh yeah, let's get a great big one with a diving board. And a slide… and so on." Ask an adult and the chances are you will hear this: "Well, it would be nice, but it's too much work. It's not practical. And can you imagine the cost of heating it?" We adults sometimes forget how to have fun, just as we forget how to dream. To learn to dream again, we must search for the child inside, and unleash our creativity. What do you want? What is *your* burning desire? What do you want to be famous for? What excites you? If the laws for today are made in the future, then make your future big. Dream BIG.

The second key principle in returning to success is belief in yourself and your dreams. Why do so many talented people fail to achieve much in life? Why do so many dream of making a difference but never actually do? One reason is because they don't believe they can. The great Roman poet and philosopher Virgil said; "They can because they think they can." Another reason is that instead of propelling them to excellence, their dreams and goals do exactly the opposite. Having limited beliefs and aspirations will forever condemn us to a life of mediocrity. This is unnecessary, especially since we live in a country where anything is possible. I have met many talented people who have shortchanged themselves with limiting beliefs. They succumb to negative talk and give up. They fail to pursue their dreams and settle for what comes along, rather than going after what they want.

Others refuse to take responsibility for themselves. They cast themselves as victims by blaming their lack of success on everything from their parents and friends, to their companies and the government. Low self-esteem is at the root of this self-defeating behavior. It is difficult to soar like an eagle when you are surrounded by expectations that limit you. It is true that your attitude determines your altitude.

The slide into negative thinking can be subtle — buying into self-defeating commercialism like <u>PC's for Dummies</u> and entertainment like <u>Beavis and Butthead</u>, or <u>Dumb and Dumber</u>; heeding expressions like, "You are not good enough" and "I told you so," or taking a victim's stance as a result of real life tragedies. If your career and your business future has been crushed by downsizing, realignment, or outsourcing, it is easy to fall victim to disempowering beliefs.

So, how can you "pick yourself up, dust yourself off and start all over again"? First of all, realize that needing help does not mean you have failed in some way. If you have been laid off, transferred, or somehow displaced, realize that it is normal to have feelings of insecurity and depression. You are not alone. You might need professional help in working through the healing process, but sooner or later you have to get back in the saddle. You need to face the challenges and the fears, and get your life back on track. Here are some things that could help:

First, realize that fear is the number one thing that stops us from moving forward.

Second, understand that most fears are self-imposed.

Third, recognize that fear is usually what gets in the way of our believing in ourselves.

My friend Mike Donahure, of the Colorado Mountain School, helped me climb to new heights by showing me how my beliefs were keeping me down. He helped me to understand that there are many different kinds of fear, and seven different levels:

Level 1: Paralysis. This is sometimes called the deer syndrome. Like a deer staring into the lights of an oncoming vehicle, we are frozen in position. In this fast-paced, ever-changing world some people get shell-shocked into in-activity. Changes come at us so fast that we often don't know what to do. So we do nothing. We stand frozen in the headlights of change and become a casualty.

Level 2: Inefficiency. This is also called "Beginner's Dilemma." We realize we must do something, but we are afraid, either of doing the wrong thing or doing the right thing badly. Either way, we would see ourselves as ineffective and inefficient.

Level 3: Catastrophe. What if I make things worse? I think I'll leave things alone. It's safer to do nothing.

Level 4: Holding On. This is also known as "turf protection." We are afraid of losing what we have so we hold on tight. We forget that in order to get to the other side of the swimming pool we have to let go of the ladder. We fool ourselves that we are making progress by doing more of the same thing. We even work twice as hard at it, fearing that doing something different would be a mistake, and turning "business" into "busyness."

Level 5: Self-Doubt. This is the fear that we won't be able to do it. We fear being laughed at or being ridiculed and criticized. Again, we do nothing.

Level 6: Rejection. The fear of not being accepted. What if they don't like me? What if I don't make the cut? What if they reject my ideas, my proposal, and my product because I'm not good enough?

Level 7: Disbelief. I don't know the size of the problem, the competition, and the answers. I don't know what to do. I don't believe I can. I simply don't believe. This is the worst kind of fear because, if you don't believe you can succeed, you won't even try. That is why most athletes are taught to visualize themselves crossing the finishing line. They must see it "in their mind's eye," and believe that winning is possible, before it can become a reality.

Don't let fear rob you of your dreams of success, which usually lies just beyond level seven, in the form of belief. If you truly believe you can succeed, you'll never quit. If you never quit, you cannot fail because success is inevitable. Here are two suggestions to help increase your belief systems:

Build a support system. Surround yourself with people who believe in you and can help you believe in yourself.

Expose yourself to everything that will help you reflect, rediscover, and reaffirm your strengths.

This book is an excellent start. Listen to inspiring, motivational talks on tape as you drive in your car. It is time for introspection and action. Take time to sharpen old skills and develop new ones. But take it one step at a time. Try doing at least one thing each day that will move you closer to your dreams of success. To quote Chris Evert, "Whatever your goal in life, be proud of every day that you are able to work in that direction."

We can learn from our ancestors. Whether they came over on the Mayflower, by plane or refugee boat, whether they begged, borrowed, or stole the money to get here, they believed that their dreams would come true once they were in this land of opportunity. The faith that brought most of our forefathers here was pure belief, and the same belief still brings hundreds of immigrants here today from all over the world. They believe that their dreams will come true in this land of opportunity, no matter what those dreams are. Belief is power, because when you truly believe, you create a passion that burns so deeply that it propels you to action. And action is the third key to unlocking the doors to success.

Action is essential. If your dreams are big or noble, strong and heartfelt, then action is sure to follow. But you must be the one to take the action. This nation achieved greatness because it was blessed with hard workers. Theodore Roosevelt said, "I am only an average man but, by George, I work harder at it than the average man." Many of our unsung heroes were simple immigrants who came here with nothing but a dream and a belief. But once they got here, they took action. They worked one, two, and three jobs at a time to make their dreams come true. Few of them turned to other people or the government to take care of them. Usually they were willing to do just about anything in order to show their appreciation for the opportunity of a better life. Sociology studies confirm that an immigrant is seven times more likely to become a millionaire than someone born in America. Undoubtedly, this is because of their appreciation for freedom and the opportunity to pursue their dreams.

There are many examples of immigrants living the American dream, but no modern day corporate leader better exemplifies this than the late Roberto Goizueta CEO of the Coca-Cola Company. He left Cuba in 1961 with his family, a suitcase, and 100 shares of Coca-Cola stock, to pursue his dreams. He believed that in the U.S. all things are possible. This was a man of vision, courage, and action who believed in his company and his abilities. Roberto Goizueta made a difference everywhere he went, and when he became CEO in 1981, he displayed vision, courage and leadership by introducing diet Coke, and extending the company's trademark to products other than Coca-Cola. In his 16 years at the helm, Coke's market value grew from $4 billion to $150 billion. Roberto Goizueta had an appreciation for freedom and other things of real value. He would often remind people: "Don't get too tied to material things. Somebody can take them away from you." As a leader with great compassion, he helped thousands of others to realize their dreams, showing extraordinary courage along the way. As he said, "Once you lose everything, what's the worst that can happen to you?"

If you could make anything happen, what would it be? What changes would you make? What difference could you make? We are given opportunities every single day to make a difference and to steal success, but we seldom take them. We must dream, believe, and take action. If you take action on your dreams, and never quit, you are bound to be successful. Ask Olympic champions what part dreams and beliefs played in their success, and they will tell you that dreams and beliefs had everything to do with it. They will also tell you that dreams and beliefs by themselves wouldn't have been enough. They had to practice, practice, practice. When they were tired, they practiced. When they were injured and hurt, they still practiced. Nothing stood in the way of practice, because they knew that without that daily discipline and determination, they would achieve nothing.

Today we are being asked to work harder and work smarter. We are encouraged to learn to do more with less. To excel at work and still spend quality time with our families. Every day we are called upon to reach higher and higher, to do the seemingly impossible. It is easy to get overwhelmed by it all or get over-worked, stressed out, and dejected. Don't. Here is how I learned to cope and still be successful.

As a child in Jamaica, I would often lie on my bed and look out the window at inchworms as they crawled along the outside windowsill. These centipede-like creatures with their many tiny legs fascinated me. I imagined that traveling any distance must have been a daunting task to such a small insect. Maybe that is why they were constantly on the move, I thought. They kept moving, one itsy-bitsy step at a time. Those little creatures taught me a valuable lesson. We don't have to do everything at once. If we take life one step at a time, we will eventually get there, providing we never quit.

What is one small challenge you could set for yourself? What is one small thing you could do to move towards your goals? Suppose each month you decided to improve just one little thing by 2%? What if you did that every month? At the end of the year you wouldn't be 2% better, you'd be 2% plus compounding every single month. Even in this competitive fast-paced world, with the help of the inchworm principle, you can move to the next level and achieve your dreams of success.

We can also prepare for a successful future by looking at trends, and seeing what actions we need to be taking. Current trends indicate that success in the future will be delivered in "care packages." Take a look at the actions and trends being set by two highly successful companies: Southwest Airlines and Starbucks Coffee.

The secret to Southwest Airlines success is outlined in its book NUTS! Colleen Barrett, Vice President of Administration, is fond of saying, "We are not an airline with great customer service, we are a great customer service organization that happens to be in the airline business." This kind of thinking permeates the company. They are a caring company. One of my favorite quotes from the book is this: "The tragedy of our time is that we have it backwards. We've learned to love techniques and use people." Southwest's Chairman, Herb Kelleher, is a pioneer and a leader of the future. He believes in, "treating employees with care and concern, if that is the way you want them to treat each other and the customers," he says. "To know what really makes the Southwest Spirit, you have to look beyond the machines and things because running a fun, productive airline defies science. It is an art that comes from working hard, with feeling." Working hard with feeling is action delivered with care. Is it any wonder that Robert Levering and Milton Morkowitz list Southwest Airlines in the top ten of The 100 Best Companies to Work for in America. One of the reasons that Southwest is the only airline to earn a profit every single year since 1973 is because the company consistently deliver "care packages."

Starbucks is another company which believes that success comes in "care packages." CEO Howard Schultz joined Starbucks in 1982. At that time, the company was a small Seattle coffee retailer. His dream was to offer the romance of Italian espresso across the country. When he bought the company in 1987, it consisted of six stores with less than 100 employees. Today, Starbucks is worldwide, with more than 1,300 stores and some 25,000 employees in North America, Singapore, Japan, and Hong Kong. In his book Pour Your Heart Into It, Schultz explains that one of the keys to the company's success is respect for employees and others. He says, " I want to work with people who don't leave their values at home, but bring them to work. I want to work with people whose principles match my own."

To be truly successful, we must wrap our actions in "care packages," as Schultz and Kelleher demonstrate so effectively. If you don't care about the job you do, the people you serve, or the attitude you bring to work, we don't just rob your employer of success, you rob yourself. When you "work hard with feeling," you feel successful. Ignore people and they will ignore you. So, learn to care about the job and about the people with whom you interact. This is the springboard to higher levels of success, as well as the feelings of success that can become a self-fulfilling prophecy.

Happily, a new spirit is emerging today. A re-birth of that self-reliant, cooperative, pioneering spirit that existed at the start of the century. People are once again taking personal responsibility for themselves and their families, acting as free agents and raising their own standards of excellence. They are becoming forward-thinking entrepreneurs who take responsibility for their decisions, actions and results. People recognize that they can achieve unparalleled success if they are dedicated and determined. They are moving full circle, stepping into the future through the revolving doors of the past. Returning to success.

The early pioneers were willing to do what it took to achieve their dreams. It took belief and courageous actions to make the journey to discover the West. In covered wagons they faced danger from man and beast. They braved storms, crawled over mountains and sweated through deserts, sometimes going for months without seeing another living thing, even without water for baths. But they pressed on until they reached their destination. Are you prepared to make sacrifices and do what ever it takes?

Stop looking to others to validate your decisions and actions. Shift back to self-reliance. Rediscover that pioneer spirit, that entrepreneurial zest, and set your own path. Remember, you can create your future by learning from the past. We live in an unprecedented time in history. The innovations of today present enormous opportunities for anyone willing to unleash imagination and envision the kind of future that was once inconceivable. The time to decide what the next decade and the next century will bring is now! Our destiny and our future depend on how we respond to the laws and pressures of today. Don't be robbed of your future. You can have it all!

If we apply the formula of Dreams, Beliefs, and Actions like many before us, we too will achieve success. Start to dream again, believe in your dreams, and take action. The wonderful thing about these three keys is that they have been making dreams come true ever since mankind started dreaming. And they will continue to make dreams come true into the next century and beyond.

We each have a unique perception of what constitutes success. Dreams are very personal, as are beliefs and actions. But if you apply the DBA formula, you will get what you want, and want what you get. This is the time to dream, to believe, and to take action in a country where anything is possible. But never forget that on your way to success, your nose got to run. So never quit! Begin today by saying, "I will chart a new course. I will dream, believe, and take action. I will return to success."

## Marcia A. Steele

Marcia Steele is an international, world-class business speaker and president of Steele Success, an organization wholly dedicated to bringing out the best in others.

She say's from an early age she knew selling coconuts to tourists was not in her future. So she immigrated from the West Indies and headed straight for the big city and Wall Street. That's where she learned the keys to achieving success no matter how great the odds or how many the rejections.

Her programs reflect her global experience having worked in eight countries with industry leaders like 3M, Coca-Cola, Chrysler, General Electric, Procter & Gamble, Texaco and Xerox. As a management consultant she works with industries from manufacturing, distribution and consumer goods, to universities, associations and foundations.

As a professional speaker, Marcia is known as the *international high content motivator*. She offers a unique mix of business acumen, creativity, and leadership, all blended with motivation to inspire all to Steele Success[SM].

You can reach Marcia at Steele Success, Inc., 11250 Quailbrook Chase, Duluth, GA 30155 Phone (770) 813-9767, Fax (770) 813-9864, or E-mail: success@discom.net.

# Coach and Praise with the E.R.A.S.E.R. Method for Courageous Conversation

by **Patti Wood, CSP**

Are you mad at your boss; irritated with a co-worker; upset at your teenager? Are you frustrated because you'd like to tell them how you feel, but are not sure what to say or how it will be taken? The E.R.A.S.E.R. Method is a step-by-step process to script out your message requesting that a behavior stop or change. It helps you word it in such a way as to lessen conflict and defensiveness in the other person. Ideally, it will *erase* the offending behavior.

Would you like to motivate your employees? Have a more positive work and home environment? Would you like to be a better leader and/ or parent? Do you want to ensure that good work and good deeds are rewarded but you're not sure how to begin? The E.R.A.S.E.R. Method can also offer a step-by-step way to script out praise so you can catch people doing something right!

It's not easy to talk to someone about something negative and there's often an awkwardness in telling someone he's done something well, but a courageous conversation script makes it easy. We aren't used to clearly stating what we want from people especially if it involves a criticism. We may avoid it or we may yell in frustration, but clear communication isn't the norm. Because it's not easy to sit face-to-face with someone and say you don't like something he's doing, we take what we perceive is the easier route. We complain to someone else, "You won't believe what Frank did." We stuff it and grumble to ourselves and it comes out in other ways. Or we wait so long that we finally explode all over the person. The E.R.A.S.E.R. Method is actually the easiest way to deal with criticism and praise.

It's direct; it's honest; and it produces positive results. In the acronym E.R.A.S.E.R each letter stands for a step suggested for a courageous conversation. **E** for EXACT, **R** for RESULT, **A** for AWARE, **S** for SWITCH, **E** for EVIDENCE, and **R** for REWARD.

First, we'll detail how to use the E.R.A.S.E.R. Method to give effective criticism, then we'll give examples how to use it to praise someone. Though we'll go through all the steps of the script in a particular order you may not need to use all the steps every time or use the same order every time; pick and choose what's right for your situation.

## Before You Begin the Conversation

### Timing

The timing of a courageous conversation is important. You want to say something as soon as the behavior occurs or as soon as you see a pattern of behavior. Waiting a week to tell someone he's left the toilet seat down last Tuesday or forgot to turn in a project due a week ago has little positive effect. The closer the conversation is to the behavior the more likely it is to change.

Using the time wise E.R.A.S.E.R. Method eliminates surprises on your employee's performance review and the "why didn't you say so" conversations in your relationships. If you're talking to someone about a behavior she does over and over, simply tell her as soon as you notice the behavior becoming a pattern.

### One Behavior

Only use this script to ask for a change in one offending behavior. If you wait and serve up a laundry list of complaints, the person is certain to become defensive. "You're ugly and your mother dresses you funny and you've got bad breath" is not the best opener of a courageous conversation and could get you a lovely black and blue eye. Choose one behavior at a time so you don't overwhelm the receiver.

### Whose Problem?

Next, you must take an honest look and decide whether this behavior is her problem or yours. If a co-worker gives you detailed directions on how to do your portion of the project and you think she's bossy, is that an accurate assessment or could you be overly sensitive and your co-worker merely helpful?

If your teenager doesn't clean his/her room, and it bothers you because you are embarrassed by what your house guests might think, it may be your issue and not your teenager's. In other words, would it be okay if he just kept the door shut and kept the mold and fruit flies away. We often think if the other person changed, our lives would be great; but sometimes we need to change. Once, with an older co-worker who was always asking about my personal life, always giving me unsolicited advice, and criticizing how I chose to do things, I felt patronized. Before I formed the E.R.A.S.E.R. Method, I did some research and discovered this woman was the oldest of 11 children and essentially raised her brothers and sisters. "Wow," I thought. "She's just mothering me!" She didn't need to change! My perception of her behavior needed to change. And when it did, I discovered she mothered because she liked me and we became friends. Examine whether the other person is the problem or whether you need to change the way you look at the situation. In most cases it's a little of both, so try not to approach the situation assuming the other person is wrong. Make the conversation a collaborative effort to create a better situation.

**Something Good**

If you decide that the behavior warrants a courageous conversation, you start your script with something positive. The most awkward part of a courageous conversation is the beginning — so make it easier, start with something positive.

Say something positive and sincere. Something good about the person or your relationship with her. You can talk about your project or, when all avenues are negative, say something nice about the weather.

"I know you are a hard worker who really put in a lot of overtime."

"I really value you as a teammate."

"I know you really want this project to be successful."

**State Your Intent**

Let them know the intent of the courageous conversation, be clear and specific and ask if they can talk. Don't make them stress out or guess at your intentions. Tell them your objective for the conversation; ask them if they're got time.

"I've got something on my mind about our meetings. I'd like to talk to you, do you have a minute?"

"There's something I've noticed lately concerning our report and I'd like to discuss it with you. Is this a good time?"

Be careful. Don't use the dreaded phase "we need to talk." That creates a sinking feeling in the receiver. It's obtuse and the projector in the receiver's head begins playing a horror movie.

## Exact

In the first step you examine the person's behavior. Is there a pattern to it? Look at it as a journalist would a news story. Stand away, look at it objectively, and ask yourself the journalists' questions: "What is the behavior?" "When does the behavior occur?" "Where does the behavior occur?" And "How often does the behavior occur?"

Express your concerns in *exact* terms. Don't use generalizations like, "every time you..." or " you never..." or "you always..." If you say to someone "You're always late," she's likely to reply defensively with "No, I'm not!" "There was that time last week..." Don't use words that have inexact meaning such as, "difficult," "bad," "initiative," or "conscientious." Don't guess or express an opinion as to why they do what they do. For example, "If you weren't so busy with..., you would _____." Also, be careful about asking someone why he did what he did. It's almost certain to create defensiveness. Instead, state the specific time, action, and frequency of the behavior to create a clear understanding in the receiver. Separate your opinions and perceptions from the behavior, state only the facts.

Below are some examples of constructive ways to word your concerns:

"Five times in the past three weeks, you have been at least 15 minutes late for work."

"I've noticed that the last four times you've taken a message for me, the full name of the caller and the phone number were not written down."

"When I called and e-mailed you twice from the sales meeting asking for the figures, I didn't hear back from you at all."

After you state the *exact* behavior, ask for a response, such as, "Is that accurate?" or "Is my perception correct?" Create a real conversation, don't just steamroller them. This information may surprise them and even though you see it as just stating facts, they may see it as a strong message. Create a dialogue that allows them to express their perception not the situation. Don't assume you're right.

Step E     Be *exact*; describe the offensive behavior. Answer the journalists' questions noted above regarding the behavior.

## Result

After you've described the behavior, the person may still not understand why he should change his behavior. You may need to give him a *result*,.i.e., tell him what happens as a result of the behavior. "When you _____. This is what happens _____."

"When you are not at your desk at 9:00 a.m., Ann or Mike must take your calls and cannot make their own sales calls."

"Because you didn't fill out the message pad, I did not have a last name or phone number and could not return the call and we lost an $8,000 booking."

"When you didn't call me back with the figures, I had to go into the client meeting unprepared and we didn't look good to the client."

Remember when you were little and your mom asked you to do something? Didn't you almost always ask yourself, "Why do I have to do it this way?" "What makes this important?" When we grow up, we still want to know. The result step lets them know their actions have an effect. It lets them know why it's important for them to change their behavior and that may motivate them to change.

Step R     State the *result*. Answer the question, "What is the concrete result of the offending behavior?"

## Aware

Make them *aware* of how you feel. There are times when it's obvious from the steam escaping from your ears that the person's behavior is upsetting to you.

Sometimes it is not so obvious, especially to the offending persons, so clue them in. Notice what emotion their behavior arouses in you and communicate it.

"When you are late, I feel anxious that the work won't be done."

"I was frustrated when I did not have a way of returning the call."

"I was upset that I was unprepared for the client."

Notice these statements are worded carefully. Absent are statements like, "You made me angry." By using an "I" statement, you avoid arguments. No one can argue with an "I" statement. When you say, "I feel...," it's pretty difficult for someone to disagree and tell you that you don't feel something; your feelings are your feelings.

There are times when this step is very significant. Some people just don't know how their behavior effects others.

For example, I once told two friends that I got upset when they teased me about my posture. They individually apologized and said they would stop. They didn't know it was bothering me. So, for them, knowing it bothered me was sufficient motivation for them to stop the behavior.

Granted, there are people who only need to know what really aggravates you to be motivated to continue the behavior! Fortunately, those people are rare. You might just as well skip this step with them. Why throw gasoline on the fire? You may need to have other forms of conversation with an individual who fits this mold. Also realize that you don't always need to put emotions into the conversations. Some issues require "just the facts."

Step A        Create *awareness*. When appropriate, state how you feel in response to their behavior.

### Switch

Create a *switch*. Ask them what they might do instead of their current behavior. Suggest a different behavior. If you've ever tried to stop a habit, you know how difficult it can be. Something to make it easier is to replace the old, negative habit with a new, positive habit. This technique makes a return to the old habit less likely. So, why not help the offending person out by suggesting a new, less offensive behavior to adapt. Suggest an alternative behavior that would work for you and for her! Remember the gentler approach is to ask her for a switch.

"I would like to see you sitting at your desk at 9:00 for the next three weeks."

"Could you please put the full name and phone number down on the pink slip?"

"What do you think would work instead?"

"How can we stay in touch when I'm on the road?"

Step S        *Switch* behavior or ask them what could be tried instead of the current behavior. Suggest the behavior you would like to see.

## Evidence

If you're concerned that the person may backslide into an old behavior, or it is critical that he do something a certain way, you may wish to add an *evidence* step to your script. This eliminates the need to repeat a request over and over. Outline what will happen or stop happening as a result of the behavior modification. Support it with an expressed agreement as to what the change will look like. Perhaps you can give a time frame when you will be observing the behavior, or a specific number of times you would like to see the behavior. This step is appropriate for speaking with subordinates or children. In most cases, it's too directive for co-workers and friends.

"I would like to see you sitting at your desk at 9:00 a.m. for the next three weeks."

"Please try to completely fill out the pink slips for the next two days. See how people respond to your asking them to give their full name and telephone number."

"So, if we talk every day this week at 8:00 and 4:30, we will stay in touch."

"The next time we make dinner plans, could you get home from work one-half hour earlier than usual?"

Remember, you may want to open up some dialogue here and ask what the evidence would look like. "So, what do you think better communication would look like?"

Step E     *Evidence* — establish and agree on the behavior change.

## Reward

Some people are motivated by *rewards,* some are persuaded through the prospect of punishment. Think about what motivates the person you are talking to. Would it be helpful to give a specific reward if he erases the old behavior and switches to a new one? What could you do to support them in their new behavior? What punishment could you present as a possibility if he doesn't? Caution —make sure it's something you absolutely, positively will do. If you won't carry through on this step, it's powerless. They must know you mean business. Again, this step is not appropriate in all situations, sometimes you can just leave it out. The best option is to make the change a collaborative effort. You can also adapt it by trading rewards: "If you do this, I'll do this," or by offering your help, ("What can I do to help you make this change?").

*Reward*    Give a small specific reward [that you'll do or that will happen] if they continue good behavior.

"If you are 10 minutes early for three weeks, you can leave at 4:00 p.m. the third Friday."

"If you take complete messages and it results in a booking this week, we'll go out to lunch on me."

"On this next proposal, I'll make my request to you before noon and you try to get figures back from engineering before the end of the day." Then we'll get the contract... and our bonuses.

"If you keep your room clean this month, I'll help you paint it the color purple you like."

Step R        *Reward* good behavior.

After you've finished your script, look it over and make sure all the necessary steps are included. E for *Exact*, R for *Result*, A for *Aware*, S for *Switch*, E for *Evidence*, and R for *Reward*. Not all conversations require all the steps. Edit out any generalizations or ambiguous terms like "good" or "bad." Fill in the Quick Reference sheet at the end of this chapter. If it is difficult for you to give criticism, practice the E.R.A.S.E.R script with a friend. Have him respond as the offending person might, and ask for suggestions. Make sure your body language and voice are calm and sincere. If you're still nervous, it may help to preamble your conversation by stating you are practicing a new method of communicating and solving problems. Then, do the most important part, deliver the communication! No communication—No result. Go for it and good luck!

If you want to use the E.R.A.S.E.R. script to give a piece of praise, follow these guidelines.

Step E       Express your praise in exact terms. Don't use generalization. What exactly have they done when, where, and who was involved?

|  |  |
|---|---|
| **RESULT** | What was the wonderful concrete result of their behavior? |
| **AWARE** | How did you feel when they did it? |
| **SWITCH** | Ask that they continue this behavior, perhaps suggesting other behaviors they can also act upon and switch. |

| | |
|---|---|
| **EXACT** | "Last week at the team meeting you contributed three ideas that we can really use to solve our budget problem." |
| **RESULT** | "Because you took the time to prepare for the meeting and think through how these ideas could be implemented, we were able to vote on them and implement them immediately." |
| **AWARE** | "I'm really pleased with your initiative. It makes me feel great." |
| **SWITCH** | "I'd like to see you contribute like that again at our next meeting." |

The world needs more great behavior, so use the E.R.A.S.E.R. Script for praise often. You'll be amazed at the results.

### THE E.R.A.S.E.R. Method
### Quick Reference
### by Patti A. Wood

Write out the script as if you were saying it out loud to the person.

**Exact** Using exact terms state the person's behavior as it exists now. Answer the following questions in your statement. Don't use generalizations such as, always, never, ever, time, and don't guess at why they do what they do. What is the behavior? When the behavior occurs? Where did the behavior occur? How often did the behavior occur?

Example: "Seven times in the past three weeks, you have been at least 15 minutes late for work."
Write your **Exact** step:_____

**Result** What is the concrete result of that behavior? What happens because they do or don't do something?
Example: "When you are not at your desk at 9:00 a.m., Ann or Mike must take your calls and they cannot make their sales calls."
Write your **RESULT** step:_____

**Aware** Make the person aware of the emotion(s) the behavior arouses in you. How do you feel in response to their current behavior?
Example: "When you are late, I feel frustrated and anxious that the work won't be done."

Write your **AWARE** step:_____

Switch Ask for or give a behavior to switch to. What would you like them to do instead of their current behavior. Make sure it's one small concrete replacement behavior.

    Example:      "I'd like to see you sitting at your desk at least three minutes to 9:00.

Write your **SWITCH** step:_____

**Evidence**     What will be the evidence that the behavior has changed? How will both of you know? Give a specific time frame when you will observe the behavior or a specific number of times you would like to see the new behavior.

    Example:      "I would like to see you sitting at your desk at 9:00 for the next three weeks."

Write your **EVIDENCE** step:_____

**Reward**     What specific reward will you give if they erase the old behavior and switch to the new one? Or, what punishment will you give if they don't switch behaviors? Make sure it's something you will absolutely, positively do.

    Example:      "If you are 10 minutes early for three weeks, you can leave at 4:00 the third Friday."

Write your **REWARD** step:_____

# Patti Wood, MA, CSP

Patti Wood has been a professional keynote speaker and trainer for fifteen years. Her hundred's of clients include: AT&T, BellSouth, Colgate-Palmolive, Hewlett-Packard, McGraw-Hill, Merck Pharmaceuticals. She is cited as an expert on Body Language in publications such as Time Magazine and Entrepreneur Magazine. Patti Wood was a university instructor in interpersonal communication for eleven years. She has written five books including, <u>Success Signals, First Impressions and Body Language</u>, and <u>I Have to Give a Speech Tomorrow</u>. Clients love her humorous, high energy, interactive style that leaves participants talking in the halls about what they've learned.

You can reach Patti at Communication Dynamics, 2343 Hunting Valley Drive, Decatur, Georgia 30033 Phone (404) 371-8228 or 1(888) 4 PattiW.

# ★ 10 ★
# Choosing Your Success Path and Finding Fulfillment in Your Work

by **Vicki McManus**

*Dream big, plan well, work hard, smile always
and good things will happen.*
Sally Huss, artist-La Jolla, CA

*I can't imagine a person becoming a success
who doesn't give this game of life everything he's got.*
Walter Cronkite

On average we will spend two thousand hours per year engaged in our chosen profession. I say chosen, the reality is, most people never consciously choose the work they do. They "fall into it" or take the job because it was the only one offered or available in their area.

When I am traveling, I often make conversation with strangers and find out what they are passionate about in their lives. I love watching the expressions on their faces as they tell me about themselves. They usually speak about art, music, reading, or a particular craft that they enjoy. They share their cycling, racing, or sports passion. Often, people will tell me about their volunteer projects, environmental efforts, or other ways that they are contributing to their communities. I learn a great deal about their children, grandchildren, and pets. The excitement and passion are apparent. Their whole being changes as they begin to share things they love doing.

The second question I ask is what they do for a living. I am amazed at the stark contrast in their physical appearances when I ask this question. They usually respond with comments like, "That's not what I really want to be doing" or "I can't wait to retire." When I ask what they really want to do, they reply "I couldn't make a living doing what I want to do." I say hogwash (a traditional southern term.)

Why would you spend more than 2,000 hours a year doing something that makes you unhappy? We have this illusion of separation of work and personal interests. Unfortunately, that is not how life works. To create true happiness and success, you must create a harmonious balance between career and personal life. Some of the most successful people I know never 'go to work.' They certainly put in a lot of long hours at what we would call a job, but for them their purpose in life is supported by the contribution they make in their chosen fields.

How do you turn interests into interesting careers? Find something that you have a talent for, nurture this gift, and take steps on a daily basis to lead you toward your goal. This is exactly what Erma Bombeck did. Since I was a little girl and read my first 'Erma' The Grass is Always Greener Over the Septic Tank, I was a fan for life. This lady was an ordinary housewife who had the extraordinary gift of turning the mundane into magnificence.

When Erma passed away, she had contributed over 4,500 columns and twelve bestselling books that deeply touched millions of fans. She was a member of the original team on ABC's *Good Morning America* and appeared on the program twice weekly from 1975 to 1986. Not bad for a mom and aspiring writer whose first piece of fiction writing (in her words) was the weather forecast in the Dayton Herald. Surely if she could do this with dust, dogs and kids, you can turn your talents into a career.

When I began looking at career options in high school, I took stock of my interests. Here are some of the things I knew about myself: I was a leader; I enjoyed having control over my work environment; and I loved working with my hands. I had a way of making people feel comfortable around me and I enjoyed a wide variety of friends. So how did this help me in choosing a college major? Take a look at the following job description.

*Dental Hygienist: Paraprofessional who works in conjunction with a dentist in the identification and treatment of dental disease. Job description includes gathering medical / dental history, exposure of x-rays for diagnostic purposes, patient education, removal of deposits and stains from teeth, application of topical medicaments to prevent dental disease.*

This may not sound like a glamour job to you; but for fifteen years, I absolutely enjoyed being a dental hygienist. (Just for the record we don't like to be referred to as mouth maids, tooth pickers, or gum gardeners.) Here's the way I interpret the field: loving individual needed to support others; opportunity to educate people in ways to improve their health and prevent dental disease; personal skill set must include humor, flexibility, interpersonal communication and strategic thinking; must have outstanding hand-eye coordination and the ability to organize your day; tremendous opportunity for personal growth and development.

Perhaps you read the description and thought — dental hygienists work with people dealing with fear and anxiety. Most clients will profess their disdain or outright hate for you, and you must be able to tolerate bad breath, blood, and tooth decay. Your work environment is extremely structured with very little time for breaks from the stress of the day. The pay is good, but opportunities for advancement are limited. Weak at heart need not apply.

My point is to share with you that each of us is suited for different roles. While I found clinical dentistry exciting, challenging, and fulfilling, others may not. As I was growing up, I always knew that I had the ability to influence others. I also enjoyed listening to people and helping them relax. After school, my mom taught me how to work with ceramics and to crochet. I was always using my hands. Becoming a hygienist was a natural choice. As a result of following my unique talents, I have always been one of the highest paid individuals in the field.

As I matured in the field, a desire to support my community on a broader scale emerged. I listened to that inner voice and discovered a new career path built upon the first. I have now transitioned from clinical dentistry into consulting, where I assist dentists, and their staffs in creating their own success strategies.

A friend once shared his secret to decision making. Whenever he was faced with a decision about his career, he would imagine that everyone he knew no longer existed. After he freed himself of the expectations of others, he would consider the proposal. If he decided that it was something he could be passionate about and committed to, he would begin to bring others back in. If there was anyone who would have an objection with his decision, he could readily isolate and anticipate the situation. This enabled him to see the impact of his choice clearly through other people's eyes. By completing this process many times throughout his life and career, he has been able to stand steadfastly by the decisions that he makes.

You must discover your own unique talents and the way that you can contribute. As you read this chapter, I am going to ask you to work through several processes. Space has been provided at the end for you to begin designing your ideal career path. I encourage you to record your feelings while you are in the moment. Do not let a busy life-style rob you of the opportunity to journal your thoughts.

Right now, turn to your journal pages at the end of this chapter; take a moment to jot down things that you are passionate about. What really piques your interest? Without regard for others in your life, if you could create a career out of your hobbies, interests, and passions, what would it be? Identify the occupations that align with these interests.

All high achievers began where you are today, contemplating their future. Here are five success strategies for leveraging your unique talents.

1. Believe in yourself. Only you know what your true desires are.
2. Model others. There are many successful people doing what you are dreaming about.
3. Gain skills and resources that will lead you into the future.
4. Build a network of support.
5. Know when to make a move.

The first step is to believe in yourself. Give yourself permission to dream big dreams. Did you realize that 50% of all the jobs that will be available in 10 years have not been created yet? If you think this is a bold statement, look back just a few years. Where are the keypunch operators, and the secretaries that took shorthand? Service industries have taken over manufacturing's position as the leading employer. Computers and robots are now performing many routine, mundane tasks, once requiring vast numbers of man-hours to perform. Find your passion and look at the marketplace and see where you can make an impact on the future.

Does the name Fred Smith ring a bell for you? It should. He is the founder of a little delivery company called Federal Express. Fred came from a fairly influential family and was able to attend Yale Business school. Now I know you're thinking "No wonder he's a success; he was born with a silver spoon." But wait, there's more to the story. Fred maintained a 'C' average in school. He was not considered acceptable material for the business school. In fact, his most coveted paper received an 'F.' That paper outlined the business plan for a company to deliver overnight packages. The professor laughed at him and said, "Why would anyone pay that amount of money to send a package overnight? Especially since we have the U.S. Postal service."

Fred left Yale and took all the money he had and recruited others into joining his effort. On his first day of business, they were scheduled to deliver nine packages – seven were lost and the other two were delivered to the wrong address! How's that for great beginnings? His family did not support him. He had lost everything chasing his dream. Everything, except the belief in himself and his dream. He managed to keep the company together long enough for the concept to gain acceptance, and the kinks to be worked out of the systems. Today, he's doing Okay. Wouldn't you say?

Go back to your list of interests, passions, and dreams; add to this list as you continue to explore this chapter.

Next, you must model others. If anyone has ever achieved a result, then it is possible for others to achieve that same result by doing the same thing. You need to make keen observations to analyze exactly what that person did. More importantly, you must understand his beliefs about what he is doing.

My advice to you is to take a rich person to lunch. By this I mean, find someone who has already achieved the results you are looking for and find out how he/she did it. You can do this in several ways. Yes, you can take someone to lunch; be sure to pick up the tab. You can also listen to audiocassettes or read books written by people whom you admire. Most authors are distilling 15 – 20 years of accumulated knowledge when they publish their works. Take advantage of this time compression and learn from their experience. You could also watch cable learning channels, biography and history channels. Use the Internet as a research tool. Keep copies of current magazines with you at all times. I find that I usually have five to 10 minute segments of unexpected time each day. Having resource material with me keeps me in a mode of constant learning. These all offer low-cost ways to discover the strategies of achievers.

We have all heard the story of how Thomas Edison invented the incandescent light bulb. He conducted more than 10,000 separate experiments prior to the invention. My first thought when I heard this was to focus on his failure. How can a person continue to follow a path that has created failure 9,999 times? What I didn't understand was his commitment to his vision and his beliefs about experimentation. His vision wasn't to invent a light bulb; it was to light cities.

He also had a belief that he could learn something from every experiment that would take him one step closer to his dream. He never considered the first 9,999 attempts at creating the light bulb as failures. He only saw the value that they produced. How can you apply this to your search for success?

First, you must gain clarity about your personal vision of success. For Fred Smith it was to revolutionize communications and delivery of parcel packages. For Thomas Edison it was to light cities. In each case, these men saw a need or a way to improve the lives of those around them. They did not know how they would accomplish their dreams, and that is the key. A vision is something that you know is possible, but have no tangible proof of this possibility. A vision is a journey, fulfilling it will come through time, trial and error.

In order to sustain your vision, you must adopt beliefs that support it. Put these in writing, so that when life gets tough you can reconnect with them. Phrase your beliefs into empowering statements, such as: Change equals opportunity; I am uniquely qualified to become successful; I must live boldly in my conviction; by letting my light shine, I unconsciously give others permission to do the same; by helping others, I help myself.

Reinforce your beliefs with your goals. Goals, like Edison's goal of creating the light bulb, support your vision. Set lifetime goals in the areas of career, family, finance, service and contribution. Then back up to 10-year goals, 5-year goals, and 1-year goals that will create a path to your ultimate lifetime goals. This process could take up to 30 days to complete. It is vital that you begin the process now, and be as complete as possible in this moment. Review this daily for the next 30 days and continue to add your thoughts. By carefully planning now, you can create a positive impact on your future. You are now ready to move to the next step.

We have briefly modeled two highly successful achievers. You have discovered their visions, some of their action steps, and the beliefs that supported them through tough times. Think about your heroes. Whom would you choose as your role models?

Now that you have a list of your talents and interests, and role models, add the element of vision. Take a moment to explore your inner voice and driving force. What do you envision for your life? Rest in a quiet place, and get fully connected to the vision of your life. Imagine what people will be saying about you when you are 92 years old. How will you be remembered?

Vision quickly fades without supporting beliefs. What empowering beliefs must you have in order to sustain your commitment to your vision? Strengthen your beliefs by outlining your goals and action steps for achievement. Turn to your journal and begin recording your role models and some of their beliefs. Then explore the vision and beliefs that you will need to support this vision.

Gaining skills and resources leads you into the future. You are never too old to learn. Surround yourself with people who know more than you do. They are your best resources for learning new skills. Increasing your skills may also include formalized higher education, professional continuing education, and independent study.

When I discovered my desire to become a dental hygienist, I knew that I would need training. I needed to complete the academic requirements for entry into the field. In my case this was one year of prerequisite work with a two-year associate of science degree in dental hygiene. After college, I continued my education. Taking night classes at the University of Georgia and going back full time to study business and liberal arts after seven years of clinical practice.

Each year I would take at least 40 hours of professional continuing education. My employer paid only a portion of this. I considered continuing education as an investment in my future and was happy to pay for the portion that my employer did not cover. As I made the transition from clinical dentistry to consulting, my level of education and training rose once again. I needed new skill sets to be competent. I began to prepare about eight years prior to making the transition by taking courses in marketing, finance, business law, and psychology. I continue today by reading current journals, taking courses, and being in touch with the trends in dentistry and the general corporate environment. I typically spend over 200 hours per year in professional continuing education. The learning never ends.

Adopt this belief, and for the rest of your life you will be successful: Learning is a lifetime process. It is my responsibility to get the training and education I need to create success in my life.

"Get yourself ready for a bigger job and the job will be ready for you," once said Napoleon Hill, author of Think and Grow Rich. What do you need to do right now to prepare for the next phase of your career development? Remember 50% of all the jobs available in 10 years have not yet been invented. Will you still be in the job market 10 years from now? If so, then you should continue to grow and develop new skills.

Get involved in corporate training programs. Take advantage of every course offered through your company. Attend, even if you are not being paid for the day, and participate fully. If you are not learning while you are earning, you are cheating yourself out of the best part of your compensation. Turn to the journal page and list opportunities for gaining new skills. What classes do you need to take? What organizations should you join? What publications should you subscribe to?

Build a network of support. From the time we are born, most of us have a network of people that supports us. Hillary Rodham Clinton wrote about this in her book It Takes a Village. She speaks about the responsibility of our communities to support their children. This type of support has been a key element in my success strategy. Building a network of people who believe in you, constantly challenges you to grow and excel. Remember that in networking, it's not always who you know, but rather, who knows you that counts. There are also distinctions in networking. Your social network is not your business network, which is not your medical network. However, the principles are networking are the same.

First, you must give before you expect to receive. One way to accomplish this is to get involved in your community and professional organizations. Volunteer for projects that you would enjoy participating in regardless of the contacts you make. Give without expectation of receiving and I guarantee that you will reap the benefit. Begin to take a genuine interest in everyone you meet. One great way to show interest is to memorize the color of people's eyes the first time you meet them. This allows you to maintain eye-contact for a brief period of time and shows other people that you are truly interested in what they are saying. Valuable contacts can be made in unlikely places and must be followed up and maintained. It is your responsibility to nurture them.

If you haven't read Harvey Mackay's Dig Your Well Before You are Thirsty, *the only networking book you'll ever need,* put this at the top of your reading list. If you have read it once, read it again. This time with a highlighter in hand. In his book he shares that there are several key people that everyone MUST include in their network, among them: Doctor, Lawyer, Banker, Real Estate Agent, Travel Agent, Headhunter, Local Elected Official, Celebrity, Auto Mechanic, Best Friend; I would add Dentist. These are individuals whom you should seek out long before there is a need. Have you ever heard the phrase "Bankers only lend money to those that don't need it?" Life's important decisions should not be made out of scarcity or desperation. You want to have time to research physicians, attorneys, and financial backers. Building these relationships well before the need arises will give you added advantage in time of crisis.

When creating your business network, include such people as mentors, contacts in competing organizations, and sources for hard-to-get tickets. As you review your list of people whom you admire and would like to model, consider asking one of them to become your mentor. Have scheduled times to meet and discuss your career. Many top-level managers and successful business owners are more than happy to share their strategies with young achievers finding their paths.

Staying in touch with competing companies, or similar industries, increases your capacity to serve in your current position. It may also serve you well when making a lateral move into another company that would offer more opportunities for advancement. By knowing someone inside the organization, you get a feel for their corporate culture and will be one of the first to know of openings within the company.

Every budding entrepreneur or advancing manager needs to know how to appear to perform the impossible. Few things would impress a boss or prospective client more than to be able to provide tickets to their favorite sporting event, play, or concert. If you can do this even when the event is sold out, then you've created magic and a reputation to go with it.

Networking is more than being seen at the right places with the right people. It is cataloguing facts about the people whom you meet. Be curious about your friends' and co-workers' interests, likes and dislikes. Surprise them whenever you can with your creativity. Not only will this support your career, but it will support your relationships as well.

By knowing details about other people's interests and remembering special occasions in their lives, you show that you care and are interested in them. Developing these types of relationships will assist you as you make transitions in your career. Once again, turn to the end of this chapter and quickly jot down the names of business and personal contacts that you need to add to your network.

Know when to make your move. There will never be a perfect moment to make a change. My husband I often laugh that life pushed us off the career high dive. Within three months of our wedding, we both made changes in our careers. He started his own company in freelance art sales and photography while I started a temporary placement service. Just like any other business, we had our high and low cycles. We were faced with start up costs, a new marriage, and a new home. We questioned our sanity at times but always remained true to our convictions. Within a short period of time, we were each thriving in our new careers; however, the transition was not without anxiety. Sometimes you just have to take a leap of faith into your future.

Here are several things you can do to prepare for the transition. Use the time you have now to prepare for your desired position or career. Take night classes, attend seminars, and begin subscribing to the industry journals and newsletters. By attending local professional meetings, you gain powerful contacts; you may even meet your next employer or business partner. Volunteer for committees that will put you in touch with key people within the industry. Put yourself in a mind set of already being successful in the field. Nothing attracts success like the appearance of success.

Next, you must become financially prepared. This is especially true if you plan to start your own business. Prior to our marriage, Kevin and I made the decision to base our life-style on one income. This meant that, when we bought our house, we applied for the mortgage based on one salary. We could have stretched our budget and reported both incomes, but why put that added pressure on our lives? We knew that each of us had strong entrepreneurial spirits and that at any given moment we could change careers. We also knew that we wanted to have a family someday and that would take me out of the work force for a period of time. There have been some tough times through the years, yet we have each had the freedom to choose our career paths. This freedom to be happy in the work that we do is without a doubt the number one contributing factor to our success.

Remember the questions that I ask strangers during my travel? What do you enjoy doing? How do you make your living? Anytime your level of enthusiasm is noticeably different when answering these two questions, it is time to consider making a change. This could include changing the environment of your current position by restructuring your work, making a move within the company, or creating an exit strategy.

In his autobiography, John Paul Getty states that in order to become rich you must change jobs 12 times between the ages of 21 and 35. My friend, Gayle Oliver, took this to heart. She held eight jobs between the ages of 18 and 26. These positions included employment with Fortune 500 and entrepreneurial-based companies in the areas of sales, marketing, and business administration. In fact, she tells me that she became so good at interviewing that she decided to start her own business — "Buckhead's Best Resumes." Since its inception seven years ago, she has created a sterling reputation within the Atlanta business community. Her passion for writing, communication, presentation, and client relations has turned into a prosperous business. Her success has been so great that she is now establishing a franchised company — America's Best Resumes, Inc.

While switching jobs may work for some, others have found ways to stay at the same job for 20 years and make the work different each day. Bill Haber, special advisor to the president and cofounder of Creative Artists Agency, found this to be true. He never allowed himself to become stale. One of the ways that he accomplished this was to keep a list of 100 life objectives — things he wants to do before he dies — in front of him at all times. Things like: fly an F-18, spend a night on a nuclear submarine, have tea at Buckingham Palace. Keeping this list encourages him to reach out to people and experiences that he otherwise would not have known about. What would be on your list of 100? Write these in your journal.

There are other ways to bring creativity into your work place. Simply drive to work a different way or if possible alter your hours. Make time to visit museums, parks, or other places of interest during lunch. Take walking breaks or workout. Order something different for lunch, something you have never considered eating before. Keep meeting new people. In other words, get out of your rut. If you are bored, chances are you are in a boring routine. Shake it up and see what happens.

Take a moment right now and mastermind ways that you could make your present position more enjoyable. How could you create more value for yourself and the company you serve? How can you shake up your routine and simultaneously become more productive?

Now make a list of ways that you could make your life in general more enjoyable, more successful, more fulfilling. Do you see a common theme emerging between ways you could make your work more fulfilling and ways to make your life more enjoyable? Can you realistically create an atmosphere of growth in the position you are currently in? If the answer is yes, celebrate. If the answer is no, then it is time to move on.

In making any transition, you want to remember to stay in relationship with your current employer if at all possible. Don't burn your bridges. Some of the most successful people I know have left their jobs, worked for competitors, and returned to the original company at two to three times the salary they previously earned. Why? Because they maintained the relationship, were recognized for their contribution, and were welcomed back as an asset. Take Steve Jobs, founder of Apple, for example. Here's a man who revolutionized an entire industry, was dismissed from his own company, and now years later is being asked to come back on board. He is recognized for his creativity and ability to get others to align with his vision. He possessed the talents that this ailing company needs.

What unique qualities do you possess? If you left your present position, why would they hire you again? By focusing on your unique talents, you can build a career that may span a variety of industries and positions. The thread that ties it together is you.

Creating success in your career is simple. You have to believe in yourself and your desire to contribute. Find others who are successful and model their beliefs and principles. Prepare yourself with the skill sets and financial resources that you need. Most importantly, create a network of people that will support you. Continuously grow and learn. By keeping your eye on your dreams, you will know when the time is right for you to make your move.

## Career Success Journal

What am I truly passionate about? _____
_____
_____

What are my interests and hobbies? _____
_____
_____

Which occupations align with these interests, hobbies, and passions? __
_____
_____

Identify role models: _____
_____

What are some of their beliefs? _____
_____

Vision: In my lifetime, I want to create _____
_____

Beliefs that will support my vision: _____
_____

Goals:
**Lifetime**
    Career _____

Family_____
    Finance _____
    Community service _____
**Ten Years**
    Career _____
    Family _____
    Finance _____
    Community service _____

**Five Years**
    Career   _____
    Family   _____
    Finance   _____
    Community service _____
**One Year**
    Career   _____
    Family   _____
    Finance   _____
    Community Service _____
    Skills I need to acquire: _____

Courses I need to take: _____

Degree Completion? What level _____
Join the following professional organizations: _____

Subscribe to the following publications: _____

Developing a network:
Business: make contact with: _____

Personal: _____
How can I make my current work situation more interesting, productive? _____

How can I make my personal life more interesting, fulfilling? ____

Begin list of 100 things to see and do _____

# Vicki McManus

Vicki McManus is a management consultant and coach for dentists and their staff. She creates success strategies that impact both their personal and professional lives. Her latest book, <u>FUNdamentals of Outstanding Teams</u>, gives dental practices the tools they need to develop peak performance teams.

Vicki is the co-founder of Creative Excellence, Inc. and is the director of Fortune Practice Management of Connecticut. She is a member of the Institute of Management Consultants, National Speakers Association, Georgia Speakers Association, Candidate member — Institute of Certified Financial Planners, and the American Dental Hygienists' Association. She speaks throughout the United States and Canada.

You can reach Vicki at Fortune Practice Management, 5579-B Chamblee Dunwoody Road, Suite 207, Atlanta, GA 30338  Phone (770) 512-0341 or  (888) 347-4785 or Fax (770) 512-0341.

# ★ 11 ★

# Increasing Your Sales with Emotional Intelligence

by **Dr. David Ryback**

The secret is out: Underlying the strategy for successful selling is the need to be emotionally sensitive. But before emotional intelligence became an acceptable concept in the workplace, there was no working language to describe it well. Now it can be done.

The notion of emotional intelligence has been known to social scientists for decades. But only in the last few years, since Daniel Goleman's best seller on the topic, has it found acceptance in the business community, particularly among salespeople.

Is this important? Only if you want to increase your sales by having your customers think of you as their partner.

The basics of emotional intelligence include greater self-awareness and management of inner emotions, as well as self-motivation through such awareness.

Self-awareness is the first step to experiencing others' emotions. Without the personal experience upon which to base it, how can you possibly know another's feelings? Successful sales involves being finely tuned to your customers' emotions. If you don't know how they're feeling, you're not going to be able to reach them. If you can't reach them, selling them will not be easy.

The superior salesperson acts as a guided missile, following the customer through the twists and turns of interest, resistance, indecision, hesitation, excitement, intent, back to resistance and more twists and turns, until the deal takes place. The missile is not heat-seeking but rather heart-seeking, always pulled to the emotion that is predominant at any given moment. If the heart-seeking is true, i.e., accurate, then the communication channel remains open and the possibility of a sale is maximized.

The importance of managing your own emotions comes into play when your intent is to maintain rapport with your customer. This involves not only knowing the other's feelings but being able to respond in kind as well. If your customer's feeling afraid, any intense tactics might well be counterproductive. Much better would be a sympathetic response. If the customer's ready to sign and needs encouragement to sell the deal to a committee, then more intensity on your part at this point might be quite appropriate. So both steps are important — sensitivity to others' feelings as well as management of your own emotions.

The self-motivational component of emotional intelligence focuses on those aspects of your emotions that are most rewarding on the job. By being aware of your own emotional makeup, you can more easily determine how to make best use of your changing energy levels. But let's take a look at each component in some detail.

## I. Self-awareness: Sharpening Your Instincts

As I mentioned, self-awareness is the starting point. All else follows from this, including awareness of others' feelings. Without it, the communication channel between you and your customers becomes non-operative, for you can only reflect others' feelings if you yourself can recognize them, name them and have the capacity to feel them. Yet emotions are so complex that the naming process often remains vague at best. But some degree of categorizing is better than none.

Relax and sense the feelings flowing through you. One way of learning to become more aware of your own feelings is to take some quiet time and focus on the rhythm of your breathing and, if you can feel it, your heart rhythm as well. Next, determine if you feel more on the happy side or more on the unhappy side of the emotional scale. If you feel calm and relaxed, then consider yourself on the happy side.

On the other hand, if you feel agitated or uneasy, then examine that a bit further and see if it feels more like anger or more like sadness. Anger might feel tense and restless. Sadness might feel like no energy and the slight urge to want to weep or cry.

All feelings are some variation or combination of glad, bad, mad or sad. The happy, relaxed feelings go under the "glad" heading. Bad is an uneasy, uncomfortable feeling that fits under neither "mad" (anger) or "sad." If you can learn to identify these four categories of feelings, then you've got the basic components of all human emotion. Resentment is a combination of mad and sad, as is envy. Jealousy has a touch more sadness to it. Hopeful is mostly glad with a touch of sadness. Eager is mostly glad with a touch of mad. So you can use the four basic emotional building blocks to understand any of the most complex emotions.

Emotions are difficult to evaluate because they're more qualitative than quantitative. That's why highly analytical, objective types have difficulty with them. Most things that salespeople deal with can be measured in numbers — dollar value, units sold, frequency of calls, percent commission, etc. — but not emotions. Compared to digital mathematical processes, emotions are the result of highly complex, organic interplay among glands, hormones and brain activity. Just as we can distinguish positive from negative dollar amounts, so can we separate, happy from sad feelings. But that's where the similarity ends. Beyond that level of generality, it's hard to obtain agreement about exactly what you or another individual might be feeling.

However that doesn't mean you can afford to ignore your customers' feelings. As challenging as that is, an emotionally intelligent salesperson will use all the available "radar" to focus in on the heart-seeking process.

## II. Self-Management of Emotions: Controlling the Process

As long as you're emotionally in sync with your customer, the selling relationship remains alive. Once you've sought out your customer's heart feelings, then you can reflect such feelings in your own words and actions. The more closely you can reflect, the greater your chances of a successful sale.

I use the term "reflect" not to mean to mimic or copy, but rather to complement, or counterbalance, in an inquisitive, inquiring way. If your customer were to become angrily resistant, you wouldn't return the anger by becoming antagonistic, but rather reflect the anger by inquiring as to where the anger is aimed and then sympathizing with the frustration leading to the anger. Now both of you can work at overcoming that frustration together, as you form a closer bond with one another.

If your customer begins to withdraw and lose interest in your presentation, obviously you wouldn't reflect that by doing likewise. A complementary, inquisitive response might involve beginning to pack up your presentation materials or dropping your proposal mode and agreeing that a change in the tone of your interaction would be appropriate. "Not interested, huh?" you might ask. "At what point did I lose you, if you don't mind my asking?"

"Well, to be honest," your customer might say, "the problems I'm facing don't seem to be fixable by what you're proposing."

"Really?" you react. "Can you tell a bit more about that? I've been giving some thought to new application of my material and I might have something to learn." Hopefully, that'll put you back on track.

Point is, reflecting, as I'm using the term, has a drawing out function rather than closing off. Reflect to anger with sympathy, to boredom with curiosity — that's what I mean by complementary, filling in the missing pieces with inquisitive follow-through. The key is to acknowledge the emotion (anger, boredom) and then reflect with sympathy and curiosity as to the origins of your customers' feelings.

In response to your customers' anger you can inquire about its source, explore it together in a sympathetic manner, and then see if what you have to offer can rectify matters (now that you know more specifically what the challenge is.) Never, never, never get angry back at your customer. That's not what I mean by reflecting.

## III. Self-motivation: Yielding to Win

By becoming more aware of your inner feelings, you're in a better position to determine how you're at your best in the selling game. Selling involves many talents — speaking, listening, convincing, understanding, analyzing, planning, persisting, hand-holding. You're better at some than at others, and it varies with changing circumstances. By knowing yourself better, you can develop those aspects of yourself that serve you well in varying circumstances. Explore what works best for you and fine-tune those elements of your selling approach.

"Deferred gratification" is the term social scientists' use to refer to putting off what you like in order to get ahead in the long run. Putting your money in an income producing account instead of buying a new car is an obvious example.

A well-known study involving children and marshmallows has shown that those who could defer gratification, even for ten minutes, turned out to be more successful years later in terms of better grades, personal relationships, and self-confidence. The 4-year-old children were presented with a marshmallow and instructed that if they could hold off eating the marshmallow for ten minutes during which they were left alone, then they could have an extra marshmallow as a reward. Some were able to resist the temptation; others weren't. Those who did, turned out to be more successful when tested years later and were subsequently characterized as being emotionally intelligent.

Delayed gratification also comes into play in the process of reflecting your customers' feelings as described earlier. You may start out with your own private, personal feelings to which you have every right. However, the successful salesperson can go beyond personal, momentary needs and instead focus on the emotions or needs of the customer.

Although this involves delaying the gratification of your own momentary emotional self-involvement, the challenge of successfully focusing on the customers' needs and being able to bridge the gap between the two of you can, in and of itself, become quite gratifying at a professional level. The ability to successfully achieve this and to thoroughly enjoy the process is, I believe, one of the hallmarks of successful salespeople. The magical connection that super salespersons can create with their customers, making them feel prized and unique, is a talent that can definitely be acquired by those willing to explore the possibilities of an emotionally intelligent approach to sales. Here are the elements of acquiring this talent:

1. Listen first, speak later.
Before the heart-seeking missile can be set on course, it has to focus on its ultimate destination. By listening carefully before speaking, you can begin the process of connecting with your customers at a deeper level.

2. Read the unspoken.
In addition to the words you hear, become sensitive to the tone of voice and read the body language. If you pay attention to these unspoken signals, you'll be able to discern not only the mood of your customers but also their particular concerns that may very well connect to what you're offering them.

3. Say what you perceive.
As you begin to sense the issues of concern to your customers, describe them in a way that would make perfect sense to them, using their own terms of understanding. And so before you ever mention your product or service, your understanding of their concerns predisposes them to agree with you. Your aim is to put into words what you sense they're feeling but are unable to verbalize.

This is not easy and chances are you may very well be off target the first try or two. But if you can use their corrections as guidelines, you can hone in closer and closer to the issues as they see them. This process of closer approximations is the guts of the guidance system of your heart-seeking missile. By being open to making mistakes in your early tries and allowing your customers to correct you at each try, you eventually can get right to the heart of the matter in a way that will make your customers sit up and take notice.

4. Share your newly-forming perspective with warmth and caring.
Although what you're attempting is definitely a challenge, do it with a smile rather than a frown, and in a self-assured, confident and caring manner. Intend to be trustworthy, act accordingly and that's how you'll be perceived. Think warm and caring, act warm and caring, independent of whether you think your sale may or may not close.

5. Yield to win.
If your customers are going to buy, they'll do so because they feel understood and accepted. Only then are they most likely to become open to the possibility that what you have to offer may be what they need. In these days of intense over marketing, the hard sell is becoming obsolete. Only by really caring about your customers can you be assured of holding on to them. Only by putting them ahead of your need to sell will they thoroughly trust you. Only by giving up your need to control them, will they be most open to what you have to offer. Pushing no longer works. Yield, and let the close happen by itself. If you're truly sincere in wanting the best for your customers, then the whole sales enterprise takes on a new meaning.

You're no longer a salesperson. You've become a friend/partner. And your customers feel appreciated which, in truth, they really are.

To summarize the emotionally intelligent approach to sales:

1. Listen before speaking to fully understand your customers' perspective.

2. Before presenting your product or service, encourage your customers to lay the groundwork for you by giving you the big picture and political ramifications of their situation. You can then build on this information to clarify their needs and discuss how you can help them in terms that make sense to them.

3. Demonstrate full and genuine understanding of your customers' needs. Then slowly seek their agreement that what you have to offer can fit their needs.

4. Be warmly persuasive within that framework, never letting their needs be overridden by your need to make a sale. Keep the communication open and mutual, maintaining the rapport you've built.

5. Throughout all this, imagine yourself a friend who will do what's necessary to satisfy the client, becoming a networking partner rather than a pusher of your product or service.

Here is a clear-cut comparison between the old style of selling and the emotionally intelligent version:

| | *Old* | *Emotionally Intelligent* |
|---|---|---|
| *Selling Approach:* | All customers are alike. | Each customer is a unique individual. |
| *Connection:* | Customer is on other side of counter. | Customer is partner. |
| *Relationship:* | Emphasis on selling | Emphasis on consulting. |
| *Emotions:* | Ignored | Engaged. |
| *Focus:* | On closing | On customer's needs. |
| *Presentation:* | Canned | Informal flow of communication in order to "get in touch" with customer's real needs. |

The challenges for emotionally intelligent salespeople are great. They must be "in the moment" at each interaction yet aware of the eventual need to present what they're selling in the best light of the customer's perspective. They must act as a consultant in the customer's interest without completely losing sight of their sales purpose. They must be emotionally interactive yet not lose sight of the organized thinking necessary in offering what they are selling to the best of their ability. This is not a task for the lazy or the undisciplined. There is challenging work at hand, but the rewards are great.

Finally, here are the seven sterling qualities of successful, emotionally intelligent salespeople selling to corporate customers:

1. Inviting: Bringing out the best in your customers.
Accept each customer not as a potential sale but rather as a unique individual with concern for the needs that might (not will) be met by your product or service. Make each customer feel special for that uniqueness, treating such uniqueness with courtesy and respect.

2. Perceptive: Helping your customers understand their own needs in relation to what you offer.

Walk in your customers' shoes, sharing both their excitement as well as frustration, so their perspective becomes quite clear to you. This process may take its own sweet time — it can't be rushed.

3. Sincere: Avoiding deceit or hypocrisy.

If you exaggerate to the point of almost lying, you're as good (or bad) as a liar. As much as you champion what you're offering, be honest about its value and capabilities. Highlight the positive features, but be careful to stop short of bending the truth. Truth always breaks through the seams, no matter how well you package a lie, given sufficient time. As a salesperson with integrity, you'll be around a long time. Being honest and sincere wears best over time.

4. Descriptive: When the time is right, educating your customers as to the facts and details of what you have to offer.

This may be more relevant for beginners than for veterans, but be sure you're an expert at what you're offering. By the time you communicate all you need to communicate to your customers, make sure they're experts too. If they know virtually as much as you do about what you're offering, they're much more bound to be receptive. In all this, though, make sure your presentation is relevant to their needs as you fully understand them. Your challenge is to simplify the complex, making it germane to your customers' needs. Recognize your customers' priorities and put the focus clearly on them, guiding them to fruition.

5. Expressive: Allowing your enthusiasm to flow through.

Be open and forthright about the excitement and enthusiasm for what you are offering, especially as it pertains to your customers' needs. Draw in your customers by fine-tuning your focus on their unique circumstances. Be open to the overall values of their corporate culture and aim for a seamless connection between what you offer and what they need. Within these guidelines, allow your enthusiasm full throttle.

6. Supportive: Expressing full support for your customers' contribution to the success of their corporate entity.

Virtually all people enjoy contributing meaningfully to the success of the organizations they support. In the business setting that typically means contribution to overall corporate success. Often any single contribution seems so small that it's difficult to get a sense of its full impact. By fully understanding your customers' corporate culture, you can help in the process of appreciating how what you offer makes a meaningful contribution. Highlight the importance of the place that your product or service will have in contributing to overall success. Pledge your continuing interest to ensuring success as time goes by, both in terms of maintenance and support as well as emerging information on possible new applications.

7. Persuasive: With full understanding of your customers' perspectives, enjoying the opportunity to bring effective, long-lasting, bottom-line results to the table.

The more you can fully understand your customers' viewpoints, and the corporate culture in which they reside, the more precise and persuasive you can be about the effectiveness of what you offer. The more time you've invested in learning about the milieus in which your customers "live," the more competent you can be in persuading them that what you offer will survive the test of time. A sale that satisfies only the short term may be a final sale. A sale that improves your customers' standing in the company over time may be the beginning of a long and lasting relationship. This long-term view can be extremely persuasive.

By cultivating greater self-awareness of the elements of your emotional makeup, by managing your emotions to "reflect" those of your customers, and by motivating yourself to "yield" to your customers' perspectives, you can anticipate a substantial increase in your sales figures over time. Emotional intelligence has always been an essential part of successful selling. And, finally, we have the concept to spell it out clearly. The skills are there for anyone to learn. All it takes is awareness, self-discipline — and a decision to do it!

# Dr. David Ryback

Dr. David Ryback is a management consultant and speaker on personal and organizational success. His experience encompasses business management and government consulting, as well as teaching at Emory University's School of Business. His diverse client base includes the U.S. Department of Defense, government legal offices, financial institutions, manufacturers — both domestic and international, health care organizations, and national retail outlets. In Putting Emotional Intelligence to Work, Dr. Ryback brings many resources together to consolidate an approach to business that combines the practical with the thoughtful, emotional and intuitive. A new paradigm for leadership in the twenty-first century is clearly demonstrated.

You can reach David at David Ryback & Associates, 1534 N. Decatur Road, Suite 201, Atlanta, GA 30307 Phone (404) 377-3588.

# ★ 12 ★

# Sales Secrets You Are Not Supposed to Know

by **Gail Geary, J.D.**

I had always considered myself an intellectual, and certainly my position as corporate attorney specializing in contracts, trademarks, and new business start-ups verified this. And then one day I was faced with news of a corporate reorganization and (my) three choices: moving to Detroit as my boss's Senior Assistant; joining the other corporate attorneys in Baltimore; or going into sales (here) in Atlanta. Although the idea of "hard core" sales really turned me off, I chose to go into sales for a most intellectual reason — I was in love and knew that leaving Atlanta could mean missing the opportunity to marry Mr. Right.

My first year in sales coincided with my first year of marriage. I received training for both careers experientially, "in the school of hard knocks." It took me five months to make my first sale, and five months to locate a decent takeout restaurant; but in five years I had become the top sales person in a Fortune 500 insurance brokerage with over 17,000 employees. I believe that my legal background helped me challenge sacred cows and take a fresh approach to all sales situations and make the sales.

Today I speak to and train medium-to-large sales audiences, and I also have the pleasure of one-on-one coaching. Last month I helped a real estate broker with his networking skills. John wanted to be able to network with people in informal business and social situations without appearing pushy or manipulative. We designed an "ear-catching" self introduction: "Hello, I'm John Hensley," (What do you do?) "I help people realize their dream of home ownership. I specialize in beautifully renovated homes in the Virginia-Highlands neighborhood."

John happily reports two sales in progress as a result of our time spent together. I invite you to sit back, relax and join me as we share "Sales Secrets You Are Not Supposed to Know."

### *Sales Secret #1: Down the competition!*

I realize that "Down the competition" is politically incorrect because almost every sales training class will tell you not to "down the competition." Usually these classes are presented by sales trainers with limited sales success. The truth of the matter is that all successful sales people "down the competition" using their own sophisticated strategies.

One of my early mentors, Dick Hartung, was a successful producer (sales person) and a vice-president with Alexander & Alexander, a retail insurance brokerage. We had just presented an attractive commercial insurance package to a major carpet manufacturer in Dalton, Georgia, the carpet capital of the world. When Dick asked if the Chief Financial Officer wanted him to "bind the coverage," which meant close the deal, our client responded that he wanted to wait because he would be getting an alternative proposal on the following Thursday. Dick immediately secured a return appointment for that same day. On Thursday, Dick, intelligent and analytical as always, was able to compare our proposal to the competition's, pointing out several key differences. This was a case where "downing the competition" was appropriate and beneficial for everyone.

How often have you received the comment "We've got to take a look at another vendor too"? Have you ever asked to be present to assist in the subsequent selection process? Would this improve your competitive edge as it did for Dick and me?

I had the opportunity to "down the competition" by asking questions which caused my prospect to recognize a problem with the incumbent. I was trying to close a deal; the income from the insurance premium and underlying services alone would be worth in excess of $1.5 million to my company. In the course of my financial review of their program, I found that their current claims administrator appeared to have misappropriated funds. I asked the prospect questions which led them to "discover" the problem. We became the association's administrator, and the association recovered its money.

### Sales Secret #2: "No" means "yes."

Early in my career, I would ask for a sale and when I received a "no," felt dejected and rebuked. I didn't know that "no" could mean so many different things.

"No" can mean "Not at this time, but I'm open to the idea later."

"No" can mean "You have not yet convinced me of the benefits."

"No" can mean "I'm too busy to take your proposal seriously now."

We could probably come up with one hundred interpretations of "no." It is our challenge to find out what our prospect really means by asking appropriate and specific questions. Here is how I handled a recent "no."

I was calling on a major recycling company in Atlanta to promote my customer service program. The human resource director said that he used Dunn & Bradstreet for his corporate training and that he was happy where he was, which was a polite way of saying "no." Rather than going on the defensive, I secured an appointment to learn more about the client's business as well as the Dunn & Bradstreet programs. I learned that my prospective meeting planner liked the way the speaker related to the audience and the program content. Did this mean I was dead in the water? No way! I asked my prospect how he could improve on the program. He indicated that travel expenses were significant. I asked him about how customized the program was and he offered, "rather generic." I closed this sale by providing a more cost-effective, highly customized program. "No" didn't really mean "no."

You may be thinking of an example right now when "no" really meant "no." Maybe.

Last year my colleagues and I were courting a major automobile insurer with a sales program for their new agents. At one point, the prospect asked to be removed from our newsletter and further contact, but she accidentally remained on the list, and six months later we got the business. Why? The buyer had changed. In today's frequently downsized, reorganized environment, by your next contact your "no" influence may be gone.

I am personally coaching a sales representative of a private club who lost ten corporate athletic memberships to another club because she could not offer athletic memberships exclusively. She is working on re-titling and repackaging her product to meet the prospect's needs.

Frequently, "no" means that you need to repackage your product in the language the buyer can accept. "No" usually means "yes" and rarely means "no."

### Sales Secret #3: Be informal and personal in your conversation.

Many of today's sales speakers and trainers say to use formal titles and not get on a first name basis with your prospect until you are invited to do so, but they are propagating an outdated commandment. Clients today buy from people like themselves who are savvy, up to date communicators. So don't use Mr. or Mrs. or even Ms. unless the individual is of your grandparent's generation. Just as Amy Vanderbilt's 1952 decree that "When a woman is accompanied by a man, it is always assumed that he is the host, and he is expected to do the ordering (lunch is sometimes an exception) … the host catches the waiter's eye and requests the check" has changed, so has this custom of formally addressing prospective buyers. I have worked with sales groups from all industries who come to understand the importance of establishing immediate first-name connections with their prospects.

Another way to be "heads up" in your communication is to remember and use the prospect's pet phrases. Doing this requires good listening. In the last two years I can partially attribute two major speaking engagements to my use of adopted, pet phrases. I used "showstopper" to describe my speaking style to one meeting planner after I had heard her use the phrase three times. I used "heads up" to describe changes we were making in our program after I had heard "heads up" four times from my client.

Look for informal conversational clues and opportunities to reveal your adaptability and to achieve a "beyond business" basis. Ask questions of them and share yourself whenever you "feel" that they are in a responsive mood. I was working with a sales manager of an international financial services group. When I called her, she shared with me that she was "buried under with work." Having lived and worked in North Carolina I could relate not only to her situation but her choice of words and her accent, and I commiserated that I was also "buried under with work."

### *Sales Secret #4: Think negatively.*

As Senior Vice President and Director of Sales and Marketing, I was responsible for projecting our income and expenses for year end. If I had accepted these notoriously optimistic figures that my sales people presented to me, I would have been "run out of Dodge." To balance these optimistic sales projections, I designed a software program which not only accounted for their projected closing possibility but would also reduce their income projections by 50 percent and increase their expense projections by 25 percent. Even with these controls, we were still slightly over-projected on income.

A positive factor in my success was my negative approach preceding the sale. I would examine all of my buying influences: the economic buyer, the user, my coach, any other buying influences and ask myself, "Where are the holes? Who wants the incumbent to win? Whom have I failed to cultivate? What will go wrong in this equation? Will the market refuse to provide me with a quote? Will a new player enter the picture? What can go wrong?" When I identified the red flags, I would find solutions. I firmly believe that it is not what you do right that will cause you to win, but rather what you do wrong or fail to do which will cause you to lose.

When you ask a colleague or a prospect why he selected one vendor over another, he will always tell you what the loser didn't have or did wrong.  And so even in the heat of exhilaration of closing the sale, step back and ask yourself what will keep you from making the sale: what issue have you failed to address; and then take the necessary actions to fill in the gap. And especially whenever you fail to make a sale, analyze the reasons carefully and let the "no-sale" be a great learning experience.

One of my friends recently shared with me why she bought one used BMW convertible over another. One afternoon, a car broker brought over a gorgeous black convertible. After driving it, they went to have the car mechanically inspected. Over coffee, the broker volunteered that there would be 7% sales tax in her county, which would amount to $2100. She asked if she would have to pay sales tax if she bought from an individual, and he said no. Two weeks later she bought a burgundy BMW from an individual and paid no sales tax.

As she confided later, if this car broker had sold her on the car and then presented the sales tax at the closing, she would have bought his car. He gave her a reason to exclude him and she did.

### Sales Secret #5: _Radical_ honesty will save you time; reduce stress; and _radically_ increase your income.

I'm sure that I am not the only one raised to be extremely polite and to use euphemisms. For example, when I was a novice sales person I would present my proposal, and later phone my prospect asking if he had made his decision yet, and had any more questions, and when could I call him back? Wimpy approaches such as these only cause stress and cost time and money. This noncommittal situation can continue unresolved for years unless you get to the point and use radical honesty. Let's say that you have presented a proposal and answered all of the prospect's questions and objections, and in your best closing style, you say, "Is there any reason why we can't do business today?" The prospective buyer responds, "No, not really, but I want to talk to my sales manager. I will call you back next week." Of course, you get no call. What is the best way to deal with this situation? Use "radical honesty"; call the prospect back in about eight days and say, "I called you back to set a date to deliver and install your software package." This example is based on a real scenario with positive results. A conference call was set up the next day to include his sales manager, and the sale was closed.

Here is another case of radical honesty. One of my colleagues received a sales lead from his parent company that a university professor had requested information on his services. My friend tried voice mail because he could never talk to the professor in person. Using a very direct, honest approach, he called the professor and received voice mail again which he handled with the following message: "My time and your time are very important. I received a message from my company that you had requested information about my services. I am a fellow graduate of this university. Did you know this? I would like for you to call me back at... If I do not hear from you by Monday, I will know that you are not interested and I will not contact you again." He got a return call and an appointment on Monday. The sale is in progress.

Today's buyers receive hundreds of advertising messages daily. They send and receive an average of 178 messages, and receive an average of

14 unsolicited pieces of mail daily. That they are media-glutted and overwhelmed is an understatement. The average buyer responds one of two ways: by postponing making a decision, or by buying impulsively. If you fail to ask honest questions and get to the point, you can continue in a relationship of uncertainty for years, or
you can lose the sale to the buyer's impulse of the moment. Radical honesty provides you with a way to save time and emotional energy and close more sales.

From "Down the competition" to "'no'" means "'yes,'" all of the sales secrets I have shared with you are dramatically effective! I wish you great success in your sales career! Continue to slay sacred sales cows and explore fresh sales approaches as we participate in this exciting adventure!

## Gail Geary, J.D.

Gail is a gifted, dynamic speaker with a special ability to intuitively connect with her audience. Her extensive and varied business experience insures audience credibility. Some facts about Gail: she is an award winning speech and drama teacher; magna cum laude law school graduate and corporate attorney; top sales person out of 14,000 employees; Senior Vice President and Director of Sales and Marketing for a Fortune 500 insurance brokerage.

Gail specializes in sales and leadership programs which are highly interactive, enjoyable, and positively impact your bottom line. Her programs are available as full day workshops as well as keynote addresses. Audiences of all sizes relate to and benefit from Gail's experience and cutting edge program content.

You can reach Gail at Geary Communications, 220 River North Drive, Atlanta, GA 30328 Phone (770) 804-8449, Fax (770) 394-1848 or E-mail: gearycom@aol.com.

# ★ 13 ★
# You'll Never Be a Hot Dog If You Think Like a Weenie

by **Mike Stewart, CSP**

"The key to success," according to entrepreneur Walter Hailey, "is to do what you need to do, when you need to do it, whether you want to or not."

That may be the best advice for achieving success that I've ever heard. It embodies three elements that are critical to achievement — Goals, Timing, and Action. It presumes that you have clearly identified what needs to be done, that you have a sufficient amount of energy available to do it, and that you will apply that energy to the activities which will lead to the achievement of your goals. Want to, can do, and will do.

This concept is so universal and makes so much sense that it is common knowledge among many people who are sincerely seeking success. Why, then, are so many people talking about success and appear to be working very hard to attain it, yet so few are actually achieving it?

This is not about what to do in order to be successful. You probably already have some formula for success — Lord knows there are enough of them around. Somebody's "Seven Steps To Success," somebody else's "Architecture For Achievement," or still somebody else's "101 Ways To Win." The "how-to's" of success are endless. Most people don't need to learn more; they need to apply what they already know. The barrier to success I see with most people is not ignorance of what to do, it is making excuses why they can't do it.

## Excuses Allow Us To Transfer Blame And Responsibility

One of the excuses I hear all the time is, "If only…" "If only I knew what to say, I would make more calls on people I know who can help me get what I want." "If only I weren't so busy doing all these other things which are so critical right now, I would have time to update my resume." "If only I knew how to write a really good resume…" Sound familiar?

A friend of mine, who is a highly accomplished professional speaker, is as skilled on the platform as the top speakers in the profession, some of whom are literally earning over a million dollars a year. Yet she is barely making a living and her career is not even coming close to the level of success she is capable of. She told me recently, "Mike, I'm ready to go to the next level; I know it. All I need are the speaking engagements." We talked a while about what it takes to be successful in the speaking business and, specifically, the actions she needed to take to get more engagements. She confided in me that she had a list of influential people who could help her, but she just couldn't bring herself to call them. She chose, instead, to remain in her comfort zone (writing a new speech) rather than face the pain of doing the thing that would actually move her toward her goal (contacting people who could hire her to make speeches.) The fact is she was scared, which she acknowledged.

That is not an easy thing for most of us to admit. Instead of coming face to face with the fear that is blocking our success, many of us tend to find other explanations for our lack of achievement. This is especially true in professional sales organizations — can you believe that? It's true. Fear just isn't an acceptable alternative for most professional salespeople, including many sales managers. They always seem to find some other "explanation" (excuse) for failing to prospect for new business or close more sales. They make excuses such as: "Our prices are too high," "The competition is killing us," or, "The market is down."

Skip Bertman, head baseball coach at Louisiana State University, has spent his life coaching baseball. He has taken the LSU program to the pinnacle of success including two back-to-back NCAA National Championships in the last two years. Skip believes, "America's favorite pastime is not baseball; America's favorite pastime is the transfer of blame and responsibility."

How about you? Have you transferred blame and responsibility lately instead of initiating contacts with people who are necessary to your success? Transferring blame and responsibility is a simple way to avoid pain; it is also a sure-fire way to avoid success.

Success is rarely achieved in a vacuum. However you may define it, success is almost always a contact-dependent endeavor. You must initiate contact with other people upon whom your success depends. A person who wants a raise must initiate contact with her boss. People who need higher-paying jobs must initiate contact with potential employers who can hire them. Salespeople must initiate contact with customers. A new person in town must initiate contact with those he wishes to meet. Success is almost universally dependent upon initiating contact with other people. For many of us that is a scary proposition.

*But, to be successful, you must sell yourself. You don't have to be a superstar salesperson; you just have to be willing to initiate contact frequently and consistently with people who can help you get what you want. The fact is your success depends far more on your willingness to contact others than it does on your actual persuasion skills. You won't do a very good job of initiating such contact if you think like a weenie, so this is about helping you think like a winner.*

## The Biggest Barrier To Success Is Fear

I have worked with thousands of sales people, managers, and entrepreneurs over the years. The majority of them have toiled diligently for years to develop their professional abilities and interpersonal skills. Sadly, however, most of these highly competent professionals don't even begin to tap the potential they are capable of. Why is that? Because they make excuses instead of taking action.

Recently, a woman attending a seminar asked the speaker for his advice on how she could be more successful. He said, "Quit making excuses!" Good answer. And she agreed along with the rest of the audience who all nodded their heads knowingly at this universal wisdom. But I doubt seriously that this woman actually changed her behavior after the seminar. I know from hard, sometimes bitter, experience — both my own and the experiences of many of my clients — that making such a dramatic change in thinking and behavior is far, far easier said than done. We all love the security and safety of our comfort zones much too much to abandon them easily.

I would like to help you discover some insight into why it is so easy to make excuses instead of taking action and what you can do about it in order to be more successful.

## If There Is One Secret To Success, This May Be It

There aren't a lot of real secrets to success; in fact, most of what you need to know to be successful you learned a long time ago. But, here's something for you to think about. Nearly twenty-five years of extensive research into the phenomenon of sales Call Reluctance® by Behavioral Sciences Research Press reveals that the fear which blocks the success of many professional salespeople is the same fear that blocks the success of so many of the rest of us. *It is the fear of initiating contact with others to promote our selves and our own agendas.*

The truth is, there's a lot of pain in initiating and pursuing contact with others. I see it every single day in the sales departments of my corporate clients and in the faces of the participants in my programs and workshops. If professional salespeople who make a living selling tangible products to people who want and need to buy them are victimized by their fear of contact initiation, how much more difficult it truly is for the rest of us to sell ourselves successfully!

This research also confirms something else you might find interesting: the most successful salespeople share one thing in common. It isn't superior selling skills, a dynamic personality, extensive product knowledge, or years of experience, although those things all help. Top salespeople simply initiate and pursue more contacts with qualified buyers than other salespeople. They quit making excuses, decide what they want, break through their fear, and do what they need to do to be successful. Like my early mentor, Charlie Schiavo, used to say, "Do the thing you fear, and the death of fear is certain."

This is the stuff of an outstanding motivational speech. Positive messages! "You can do it! Attitude is everything! Go get 'em, Tiger!" (As a matter of fact, I've given a few of these talks myself.) This kind of motivation certainly has its place; positive self-talk and powerful affirmations unquestionably help us develop the thinking and actions of a winner. Self- motivation is sort of like eating or bathing – we have to do it every day, or we tend to run out of energy and our performance begins to smell pretty bad.

Lots of times, though, especially when we get too far outside our comfort zone and the pressure is on, this type of stimulation isn't enough nor does it last very long. Listening to motivational tapes, attending encouraging programs, or reading inspirational stories (like many of the ones in this book) may give you a motivational boost, and that's good, especially to keep you moving when you're on a roll.

Often, though, habituation becomes a problem. Habituation occurs when you must have a bigger motivational boost next time, and then an even bigger boost the time after that in order to move out of your comfort zone when the crunch is on and you feel pressure to do the thing you really fear. At some point, when your need for an increased jolt of feel good just doesn't work, you may even find yourself actually being de-motivated by these measures!

*When the crunch and the pressure are too strong, you may start thinking like a weenie, making excuses, complaining, whining, and blaming others. Then your success express gets side-tracked and you scrooch back down warm and safe in a reliable comfort zone, lick your wounds, and complete your avoidance behavior by involving yourself in some relatively unnecessary but personally comforting task.*

The ability to break out of our comfort zones and consistently do those things which are necessary to our success comes more from long-term programming of habitual positive thinking and action-taking than it does from short bursts of adrenaline-produced attitude adjustments. All of us have been programmed over time to respond to certain situations in specific ways. Unfortunately, the fear response to self-promotion is deeply ingrained in many of us. The good news is we can do something about it.

"Be careful who you let near your mind," says George Dudley, psychologist, researcher, and coauthor of the ground breaking best seller *Earning What You're Worth? The Psychology of Sales Call Reluctance*®. High achievers manage their own programming. Two weeks ago I was present during a question and answer session following an outstanding presentation by a well-known performance-development coach. He was asked if speaking more frequently would make him a better speaker. He responded very sharply that he was an outstanding speaker now and that no one would put anything less into his mind. Point well made, and he took the time to explain the point to his audience. He was the one handling his own positive programming and he refused to permit anyone to compromise it by injecting negatives of any sort into his thinking.

Much of what I have come to understand about achieving success is rooted in my relationship with George Dudley and his partner, Shannon Goodson, and the work they have done in the area of sales performance development. These lessons, learned mostly in the competitive cauldron of high-stakes professional selling, are applicable to almost anyone who must overcome the internal reluctance they feel when they must initiate contact with others to achieve success.

## Understand Three Critical-to-Success Factors

You can quit making excuses and take the actions that are required for you to achieve success much more effectively if you understand and manage the three primary elements that most strongly influence your actual outcomes. These elements, as we learned at the beginning of this chapter, are Want To, Can Do, and Will Do. Consider these as Goal Direction, Motivational Energy, and Applied Energy.

Think about some of the people you admire for the success they have achieved. Chances are they are highly motivated and clearly goal-directed. The real key to their success is their effectiveness in applying their energy to the accomplishment of their goals – instead of misdirecting it by making excuses to deal with their fear. If you identify the behavioral traits they consistently display, you will likely come up with words such as focussed, committed, and relentless. If they need to make twenty calls a day, four days a week, they make their eighty calls every single week without fail. In fact, they will often make as many as ninety to one hundred calls per week! They know exactly what they need to do, nothing seems to stop them, and they have more than enough energy to get the job done.

The behaviors and outcomes of your successful acquaintances are very different from the behaviors and outcomes of people you know who aren't so successful, aren't they? Do some of these less successful people remind you of a dog chasing its tail; full of energy but going in circles and never getting anything done that really matters? And don't some of them talk incessantly about all the things they are going to do to make it big, but never seem to get around to actually doing those things? Some others know precisely what they need to do, know exactly how to do it, and obviously want to do it in order to achieve the success they crave so deeply, but they just can't bring themselves to actually do it. Like my professional speaker friend I referred to earlier, they simply can not pick up the phone and make twenty calls a day, so they waste their precious energy on unproductive, but comfortable, avoidance activities.

These behaviors characterize three significant barriers that prevent many people from achieving the success they seek: lack of goal direction, low motivational energy, and misapplication of the energy they have available. Here are three qualifying questions you can ask yourself to help you overcome these barriers, stop making excuses, and start taking action to achieve your goals — along with two very important payoff questions that may cause you to reevaluate your success-seeking entirely. Answering these questions can change the way you think about achieving success, change the way you do business, and change your life.

## Qualifying Question # 1 — Am I Actively Pursuing Goals That Excite Me?

Conventional wisdom tells us to decide what we want, write our goals down, and be sure they are SMART: Specific, Measurable, Achievable, Realistic, and Time-framed. Here's the thing — you can't do a goal! You can only do the activities that result in the accomplishment of the goal.

If you are objectively measuring your accomplishments and find you are not achieving your goals on the time schedule you have established, take a look at the actions you are taking (not thinking about, but actually doing.) A very common mistake is trying to manage results — you can't manage results, you can only manage the processes that yield the results you desire! Trying to do a goal or manage a result is a fatal trap you can avoid by constantly reminding yourself that there are three dimensions to goal achievement:

Targets — the prioritized goals themselves. (Easy to do; lots of people have written goals.)

Incremental action steps required to reach each goal. (Harder; requires serious planning.)

Pursuit — Actually doing the action steps when they need to be done. (The hardest part.)

Goals that drive us to high achievement are the goals that excite and inspire us, such as winning a coveted promotion, living in a particular neighborhood, achieving a certain level of income, or even, perhaps, wearing a Rolex and driving a Mercedes. The activities which are required for us to achieve goals of that kind — activities such as asking for an appointment with a very important person or making a presentation to four hundred people — may cause us some distress or even frighten us terribly. It really is all right to feel challenged and uncomfortable if we want a goal badly enough. The key is deeply desiring the goal and feeling strong excitement and genuine satisfaction at the prospect of achieving it. If you have that desire and excitement, success is possible; without them, success may be very doubtful.

Dave Gardner said, "Success is getting what you want; happiness is wanting what you get." Take a few minutes to reevaluate your goals. Do you intensely desire them? Does the prospect of actually achieving them give you so much satisfaction that it keeps you awake at night visualizing them? Do they excite you so much you can hardly wait to get to work every morning? They should if you truly expect to attain the success you think you want.

## Qualifying Question # 2 — Am I Generating Enough Motivational Energy?

Have you ever noticed how a light bulb dims during a power outage? A similar thing happens with a flashlight; it may burn brightly when the batteries are new, but the light just fades away as the batteries run down.

A similar lack of energy can be a major barrier to success. If the activities required for you to reach your goals demand high voltage and long endurance, you must bring sufficient physical and emotional energy to the task. If your job requires 110 volts of energy and you are only generating 40 volts, your chances of success are dim. Similarly, if your energy only lasts five or six hours at a stretch it will be tough to succeed in a job requiring high performance eight or nine hours a day. The good news is, you can increase the amount of motivational energy you need to achieve your goals.

Chip Mayberry, a client of mine in the health and fitness industry designed a program to help me lose weight and increase my energy when I was enduring a period of extreme stress. The program involved a twenty-five minute strength training routine followed by a twenty-minute treadmill program three mornings a week. I also made some intelligent diet modifications. I lost nearly twenty-five pounds in less than four months and found that I could work three or four more hours a day without losing concentration. When a friend commented, "Boy, you've lost a *ton!*" all the early morning wake-ups didn't seem so bad and getting back on top of my goals really made the results worth the extra effort I had put forth. Feeling better, knowing I look better, and the excitement of being back on track continually inspires me to maintain my renewed lifestyle.

By reviewing your lifestyle, you may be able to boost your motivational energy level considerably. Here's a basic checklist to help you insure that you're bringing the maximum power you are capable of to the pursuit of your goals:

❑ Complete physical examination within the past year.
❑ Balanced, reduced-fat, controlled-calorie diet.
❑ At least 64 ounces of water every day.
❑ Physician-directed dietary supplements such as vitamins and fiber additives.
❑ Aerobic and strength training three times a week.
❑ Sufficient amount of sound sleep every night.
❑ Mind-body health exercises such as positive self-talk, meditation, and yoga. Spiritual affirmation and growth through your personal belief system.
❑ Maintain the same schedule every day including weekends.
❑ Moderate use of alcohol and tobacco.

### *And this all-important point*

❑ Goals that are truly anchored in your values and honestly represent what you passionately desire to achieve. Your goals are great motivators.

Marilyn Monroe said, "I just believe in doing the best I can with what I've got." Are you doing the best *you* can with what *you've* got?

## Qualifying Question # 3 — Is My Motivational Energy Going Toward The Achievement Of My Goals?

An electric light with a good bulb and plenty of electric power coming from the outlet still won't work if it has a short circuit in the cord — the short circuit will block the power and the light will flicker and fail. Where is your motivational energy going? Too often it may be short-circuited by fear and, instead of being used to perform the activities that lead to the achievement of your goals, your available energy will be consumed and wasted in fear-avoidance activities.

### The Physical Nature Of Fear

Wherever fear may originate, its symptoms are purely physical. This physical nature of fear can wipe out your energy and make you totally ineffective. Stories of major league pitchers throwing up before walking out to the mound are legendary. Visual television images of totally humiliated multimillionaire professional golfers completely falling apart before millions of viewers are heart wrenching. If you have ever had to speak before a group and felt the numbing terror of stage fright — or if you can simply imagine it – you can relate. The same thing is happening on a much smaller scale when you say to yourself, "That's enough calls for now. I think I'll get another cup of coffee."

Fear causes your mouth to go dry, your muscles to tense, your knees to weaken, and your blood to rush from your extremities into your internal organs. You may even begin to hyperventilate, and your cognitive powers may desert you completely. Not only can you not think about what you are supposed to say; you can't even remember your name. When you are so physically overwhelmed, it is usually too late for positive self-talk — the only thing your body is hearing is "fight or flight." No wonder people avoid situations that cause such stress!

But you can't avoid such situations completely if you're going to perform the anxiety-provoking activities that are critical to your success. Because fear is physical, word-based solutions (self-talk) alone are not usually successful in a crunch — cognitive redirection doesn't work when you're physically overwhelmed. In such situations, "mind over matter" just won't get it. Mechanical solutions (physical actions) which tell your body that you're okay — or which help you actually become okay — are usually far more effective than positive self-talk in such situations.

*It is much easier to act your way into positive thinking than it is to think your way into positive action. After my son, Mark, was diagnosed with cancer when he was twenty-six years old, he told me, "Dad, I'm scared to death, but if I act brave nobody can tell the difference — and neither can I." Nearly five years later he is an outstanding example of a person who continues to achieve great personal and business success despite a crippling, life-threatening disease. Mark thinks like a winner, not like a weenie. He doesn't intellectualize his challenges or let his fear immobilize him; he simply focuses his thoughts and his energy on taking positive action every single day to achieve that day's goal-directed activities. He does what he needs to do, when he needs to do it, whether he wants to or not. He refuses to be a victim. As a result, he has a great attitude and his life is truly rich in every sense of the word.*

### Three Techniques To Help You Overcome Fear

In cases where debilitating fear is severe enough to seriously threaten a motivated, goal-directed person's ability to do the things they need to do when they need to do them, scientific assessment and treatment may be called for. The SPQ*GOLD™ Call Reluctance® Scale, and the subsequent application of prescribed clinically-proven remedial techniques, is one solution which has helped many thousands of people overcome their fear and achieve their goals. Three of these techniques have near-universal application and can help you break through your fear, regain control, and do the things you need to do to be successful.

**I. RELAX.** Physical relaxation is a first and very important step in regaining control when you are feeling the effects of fear. *When you are afraid, your motivational energy is used up dealing with fear; when you are relaxed more of that energy is available for the pursuit of your goals.* Here are three techniques to help you relax. If you practice these, you will be able to relax literally on cue and regain control whenever you begin to feel the physical effects of fear limiting your performance.

1. *Relaxation Dialogue.* Sitting comfortably with both feet flat on the floor and your arms and hands comfortably loose, close your eyes and begin to breathe slowly and deeply from your diaphragm holding each breath for a few seconds. Focus on the soles of your feet and send them the mental message, "Relax." Send that same message to your ankles, then to your calves, your knees, your thighs, and so on until you feel your entire body relax. Perform this exercise for five or ten minutes, two or three times a day every day.

The more you practice this process, the faster, more completely, and more "automatically" you will be able to achieve a physical state of relaxed poise and confidence. I have watched professional speaker Karla Brandau, a friend of mine, follow a similar procedure before a speech. An amazing transformation occurred — one minute she was hurriedly finalizing the details of her appearance and the next minute she was relaxed, centered, and totally poised.

2. *Meditation.* When you begin to feel relaxed, completely clear your mind by focussing on one thought, or a single word, which has a positive meaning for you and which creates a feeling of well being within you. An example could be, "The Force is strong" or, if you prefer, "God is love." The Buddhist chant, "Om" ("auummm"), works well for some with or without religious significance. Focus on your key thought and let your mind go totally blank otherwise. Foreign thoughts will surely intrude, particularly when you are learning to meditate. Simply say something to yourself like, "That's okay," and gently push the intruder aside by focusing anew on your key thought.

As you practice and develop your ability to meditate, you will learn to deepen your state of relaxation and do so very quickly.

Many excellent relaxation and meditation tapes and CD's are available commercially. You may find such aids helpful in achieving a deep, peaceful state of relaxation and confidence during your daily relaxation/meditation sessions.

3. *Sensory Injection.* Select a pleasant fragrance that you rarely encounter, such as allspice or cedar, from a fragrance disc selection at a craft shop or notions store. A pleasing perfume you seldom come across works well, also. While you are in a state of relaxation slowly inhale the fragrance very deeply two or three times. Do this several times per session for five or six sessions. Renew it periodically. Afterwards, when you're feeling apprehensive about having to make a call to promote yourself, confront your boss, or do some other activity you fear, take a deep whiff of your selected fragrance. You will be amazed at the sudden feeling of relaxation and resolve you experience.

### An Instant Relaxation Technique

*When you are fearful, your blood rushes to your internal organs and your hands become cold and clammy. Hold a hot cup of coffee in the palms of your hands, or hold them under very warm water; as your hands warm up, they will signal your brain, "I'm okay" and you will immediately become more relaxed and less uptight.*

**II. ZAP YOUR NEGATIVE THOUGHTS.** Place a strong rubber band around your wrist. When a negative thought intrudes and you start to waver from the task at hand, snap the band — hard! Do this on top of your wrist, not on the tender skin underneath. This will interrupt your thoughts completely — except, maybe, "Ouch! That hurts!" Then, interject an affirming thought which reminds you of a positive experience you have had performing such tasks in the past. You will find you will be able to continue a bothersome task much longer. After a time, just looking at the rubber band will be enough to stop a negative thought instantly.

**III. GET MEDICAL HELP.** Your doctor can prescribe medication that will help you deal with your fear and perform needed tasks as consistently and frequently as you need to with a minimum of discomfort. Several years ago, during my corporate days, I was invited to speak at a meeting of the International Franchise Association. I asked a middle level manager on my staff to go with me and handle part of the presentation. He passed out — literally. He was so afraid of merely the prospect of speaking in public that he fainted right there on the spot! Today he enjoys a very successful hi-tech career built in large part on public speaking. He has been able to handle his stage fright over the years with medication prescribed by his doctor, and he still uses it today to control his anxiety before a speech.

## Payoff Questions — Who Will Change My Life?

Your life is going to change. Lee Trevino, the professional golfer, says, "If you want to make God laugh, tell Him your plans." There are some things you simply have no control over, which makes it even more crucial to control the things you can control. The payoff question is "Am I going to change my life to make it what I want it to be, or will I leave the changes up to happenstance and the will of others?" Consider this question very carefully. If it's going to be you, you must change yourself before you can change your life. So, if it is really going to be you, ask this follow up question, "Will my fear control me or do I have the goal direction, motivational energy, and self-management skills to overcome my fear and do the things I need to do, when I need to do them, whether I want to or not?"

As you reach for the stars, you must decide how you are going to answer these questions. When you do, be assured of this – your success will ultimately depend upon how willing you are to initiate and pursue contacts with other people to solicit their support in helping you achieve your goals. The solid concepts and proven techniques presented here will enable you to initiate those contacts more consistently and in sufficient numbers to insure that you achieve all the success you could ever desire.

**Suggested Reading:**

Earning What You're Worth? The Psychology Of Sales Call Reluctance®

GEORGE DUDLEY and SHANNON GOODSON, BEHAVIORAL SCIENCES RESEARCH PRESS, INC.

Your Maximum Mind

DR. HERBERT BENSON, TIMES BOOKS

Staying Motivated! by Mike Stewart, CSP. Contained in the anthology Chicken Soup For The Soul At Work

JACK CANFIELD, MARK VICTOR HANSEN, MAIDA ROGERSON, MARTIN RUTTE, & TIM CLAUSS HEALTH COMMUNICATIONS, INC.

# Mike Stewart, CSP

Mike Stewart, CSP speaks and writes on contemporary sales, management, and leadership issues. He is a leading expert on diagnosing and overcoming sales Call Reluctance®. Mike holds the prestigious Certified Speaking Professional designation from the National Speakers Association and is President of the Georgia Speakers Association. As a professional speaker, he has averaged more than 120 presentations per year since 1989.

His story, <u>Staying Motivated!</u>, appears in the New York Times best selling series <u>Chicken Soup For The Soul At Work</u> and he recently wrote <u>Sales Negotiations For Higher Profits</u> for the American Management Association. His textbook, <u>Professional Sales Skills</u>, is being used by the National Ready Mix Concrete Association for the certification of some 12,000 sales professionals.

Mike is President of Stewart & Stewart, Inc., a firm specializing in personal performance development. Clients he has worked with include Amoco, Chevron U.S.A., Ciba-Geigy, Delta Faucet Company, Fruit of the Loom, Gold Kist, Jiffy Lube International, Nikon, Rust-oleum Corporation, Shell Oil Company, Telecheck, The Prudential Insurance Company, United Parcel Service, and W.R. Grace & Company — plus the U.S. Department of Energy and hundreds of small business owners.

More detailed biographical information can be found in Marquis' <u>Who's Who in Finance and Industry</u>, <u>Who's Who in the Media and Communications</u>, and <u>Who's Who in the South and Southwest</u>.

Mike can be reached at Stewart & Stewart, Inc., 1140 Hammond Drive, Suite D4190, Atlanta, GA 30328 Phone 770-512-0022, Fax (770) 671-0023 or E-mail: <u>mstewart@mindspring.com</u>.

# ★ 14 ★

# Effective Strategies for Networking

by **Nancy Manson**

The term "networking" is used frequently from the board room to the social room. Why network? The benefits to networking are many. One of the most important is it is a way to achieve your goals. Most of us have big goals and aspirations to accomplish and networking provides the tool to make this happen.

In <u>Power Networking, 55 Secrets for Personal & Professional Success,</u> Donna Fisher and Sandy Vilas share the following information. Did you know that:

- A referral generates 80% more results than a cold call.
- Approximately 70% of all jobs are found through networking.
- Most people you meet have at least 250 contacts.
- Anyone you might want to meet or contact is only four to five people away from you.

Vast resources are available to you to help you achieve what you desire in life. Fisher and Vilas state that the secrets to success lie not in what you do but in how you do it and how well you network with others along the way.

Webster's <u>New World Dictionary</u> defines "networking" in the following way: *The developing of contacts or exchanging of information with others in an informal network, as to further a career.* Networking requires people skills we constantly cultivate and develop throughout our lifetime. Anyone can network at anytime anywhere. Networking is a powerful, invaluable technique for building mutually beneficial contacts.

Networking nurtures professional, personal, and social contacts by obtaining 1) information, 2) support, and 3) referrals in a spirit of sharing that goes beyond information or ideas. Effective networkers demonstrate this spirit by constantly sharing with others. They realize it is about building solid relationships over time. They understand the value of marketing their own product: themselves.

Some individuals feel networking is a game and they must learn the rules to play. Networking is much more than a game. We are in an era where so much rests on not just who you know, or what you know, but who knows you and will vouch for your credibility. It is key that you learn to master this skill whether you are in corporate or an entrepreneur. It is a method of effective communication of joint benefit. Smart networking is building relationships that are mutually supportive and empowering. You learn how to use resources that are available to you by sharing information, ideas, and contacts. Everyone benefits in smart networking. It is all about success, accomplishments, and having the confidence to work with others to get a favorable outcome. It requires operating from the abundance mentality realizing there is not lack, but enough to go around. Networkers must cultivate this mentality because networking is not about selling; it's about making contacts.

The first strategy of networking is *defining your support system.* Stop and think, who are the people in your network? Think about the people you interact with on a regular basis.

- Your family members
- Your neighbors
- Your accountant
- Your doctor/dentist
- Your friends
- Your spouse or significant other
- Your mechanic
- Your barber
- Your hairstylist
- Your boss
- Your minister
- Your co-workers
- Your lawyer
- Your children's friends' parents

All of the above know people that you can have access to because of your contact with them. Take time to sit down and list the names of the people that you can use as a reference. It will help you realize the connections you already have and areas you need to enhance. As you create this list, categorize in the area of personal affiliations, organizational/community affiliations, professional affiliations, and others.

Personal affiliations are those persons who know you on a one-on-one basis. Our network of family and friends fall in this area. We often discount this group when we start to network. Community/organizational affiliations are organizations you are involved in that may or may not be career-related. It may be volunteering at your church, synagogue, board of directors, foundations, political activities, fraternities/sororities, PTA, etc. Getting active on a committee creates involvement and a connection which is networking. Professional affiliations are those connections that lead to career advantages. Some of the professional contacts are coworkers, vendors, clients, competitors, and professional organizations. No matter what your goal and role in life, your ability to develop a strong, stable support system will be vital to your success. The other category is those unexpected chance meetings that occur on the airplane, in the grocery store, on the subway, and in the parking lot. These are opportunities that have the potential for enhancing your life. As you analyze all your networks, you will find a rich tapestry. A tapestry that once tapped into, can change the course of your life.

The second strategy for networking success is to *know yourself.* You must be keenly aware of your own needs and goals. Networking pro Alice Ostrower insists self-awareness and acceptance is the key to effective networking. "Each person has to be comfortable with himself or herself first." You must be able to communicate clearly what you need before others can help you. In order to accomplish that, you must know who you are and what you desire.

It is vital that you know what you have to offer and what you want to do with it. If you are not sure, set aside time now and do a serious inventory of who you are. It will require some soul-searching and may require getting some books to assist you in the process. What Color is Your Parachute? by Richard Nelson Bolles and Do What You Love, The Money Will Follow by Marsha Sinetar are two books that can provide you with valuable insight into who you are.

You should know your personal strengths and career goals. By knowing these, it makes you more effective at sharing your experiences and desires in networking situations. You must know things you like to do and things you are good at doing. It will be important to identify what type of work makes you the happiest. You must know clearly what your short term, intermediate, and long term goals are and determine strategies for achieving them. You see time will pass whether you do anything or not. By knowing what you want, you can effectively network to enrich your future goals. It will require hard work, follow up, commitment, a positive attitude, and the willingness to take action.

Here is a list of skills for you to use as you get started with your self-inventory.

| | | |
|---|---|---|
| Leadership | Accounting | Sales |
| Customer Service | Motivational | Marketing |
| Listening | Communication | Skills Negotiation |
| Training | Coaching | Organizational |
| Interpersonal | Computer Skills | Creativity |

Networking can be one of the most valuable assets of your career success. You must first know yourself to have well-adjusted relationships with others. This is not a difficult process. Doing this affords the opportunity to make changes and improve. Take the time to invest in the most important asset in your network — yourself.

> *Knowledgeable people know facts. Successful and prosperous people know people.* JOHN DEMARTINI

The third strategy for networking success is *the Three R's of Networking*. The first "R" stands for being *real*. How do we demonstrate that? Simply be who you are all the time. Get rid of the facades and be genuine. Be consistently sincere and willing to help others, not self-serving. We must learn to be ourselves no matter with whom we are talking. Don't try to be what you feel others expect you to be. It won't work and you will come across as pompous, phony, and insincere, which is the kiss of death in networking. Recognize that *real* can mean "Respecting Everyone's Authenticity in Life." Using this approach, there is no hidden agenda about what you want or who you are because the secrets to success lie not in what you do, but in how you do it and most importantly, how well you relate to others along the way.

The second "R" stands for establishing rapport. How do you go about developing this rapport? To establish rapport, you must build a strong line of communication. This requires greeting those you meet with a smile and making introductions. We must have an attitude of receptivity and interest in the person(s) we are talking with. Make sure you hear and repeat their name(s) in the conversation. This adds the personal touch. As always, use the name with moderation. The most important part of this conversation is to actively listen to what is being said and seek clarity. Make sure your eyes are focused on them instead of gazing around the room. Shifting eyes and heads show that you are a poor listener and tuned into your own station (AM, absorbed with myself.) Imagine telling a story to someone like this and afterwards having them respond with an unrelated story about themselves. It shows respect when we listen with our heart and ears. If we are to achieve any success through our networking efforts, we must learn to listen to what others say.

The third "R" stands for *relationships*. The goal of networking is to build relationships so that the exchange of ideas, information, resources, and opportunities can occur. We must work at building relationships that are mutually supportive and empowering. When you build relationships, everyone in your universe benefits. Building relationships ensures success, accomplishments, and confidence in working with others. It also facilitates connecting people for results. We must generate interest and responsiveness in maintaining our relationships. As you give more than you receive, watch how you are blessed with more than you need. Constantly approach people and ask what they are doing and how you can support them. Remember that you must continue to cultivate relationships. Think of a fishing net. It if has a hole, it doesn't work because all the knots are not doing their job. It takes all the knots to make the net work. This is true of our relationships, each of us represents a knot and *it takes all the knots to make the net work.*

The fourth strategy is *good listening skills.* As I've stated previously, poor listening skills impact your ability to network greatly. Developing the power to listen will increase your ability to make immediate connections, develop rapport quickly, establish trust, and build solid relationships that are very satisfying.

Listening is a core element in the communication process. It is through listening that we learn. In the communication process, we have a sender and a receiver and all the interference in the middle. The interference gets in the way of active listening. The interference or barriers may be some of the following:

- Preoccupation with something else
- Voice tone
- Dialect/Accent
- Personal dislike of the person
- Lack of interest in the topic

- Gender
- Race
- Ethnicity
- Speech that is too slow or too fast

The barriers/interference impact the way you listen. Some individuals pretend to listen when they are merely waiting to talk or thinking of their responses. How many times have you attended a networking function and met someone and the whole focus was on what you do? You walk away having gained nothing because you already know what you do. Instead, you want to focus on getting the other people to talk and learn about who they are. You then walk away with information added to your network. It may be information of value to you or someone else in your network. The information you received is useful in follow-up activity with the person. Remember information is power and information is gained through active listening.

*The person who listens has the power.* NANCY J. MANSON

Some people do selective listening. They come in and out of your conversation. They tend to do surface listening. They may not delve into comments made that require greater discussion. A lot of listening at this point is based on interest and "Do I need to know this?" Active listeners listen with eyes, ears, and heart. Their body language demonstrates attention. They nod their heads, ask questions for clarification, make notes, give you good eye contact, just to name a few of the nonverbal cues that say, "I care about what you have to say." Through active listening, you are able to help clients and customers by giving them leads and contacts. When you really listen, you find opportunities all around you to provide information to assist others. As you work to really listen, you must forget about yourself. To cultivate good listening skills, you must first ask yourself the following questions:

1) In what situations am I an effective listener?
2) In what area(s) of my life do I want to be a better listener?
3) What challenges must I overcome to be a better listener?
4) What benefits will be gained when I am a better listener?
5) What actions are required of me to enhance my listening ability?

The fifth strategy for effective networking is *identifying four important reasons for networking*. The first is information. We all have a vast amount of information that we have collected through our experiences. This information is as unique as we are. Just as you have a wealth of knowledge, so do others that you meet. Your goal should be to strive to be an expert on a topic, to set yourself apart from everyone else. As George Fraser, author of <u>Success Runs in Our Race</u> states, "networking for information includes seeking information, relative to job searching." As I mentioned earlier in the chapter, 70 percent of jobs are filled through networking. Most of my business has been attributed to the power of networking.

The second reason for effective networking is influence. George Fraser states that he translates influence to mean access to key people. Fraser goes on saying that the next best thing to knowing someone with the power is knowing someone who knows that person. Think of our fishing net again. The knots symbolize the relationship between two different people with mutual interests. The knots link them together. It is important to know those persons who are able to link you up with persons who can assist you in achieving your goals. Often as a result of volunteer efforts, you are able to connect with persons who can provide valuable insight to your success.

The third reason for effective networking is resources. At different stages of your career, you will need some of the following resources: advertising, marketing, products, or services. This is where human resources are important, especially organizations where there is limited funding. It is important to know where to go to get the resources to move the project further. Be considerate of the demands you place on people in your network.

The fourth reason for effective networking is personal reasons. I find it very rewarding to be involved in different organizations. The challenge is to not overextend yourself and learn how to say *no*. It is not just a matter of involvement but being committed to the organization, seeking to meet and know people who have similar motives with different backgrounds and skill sets. As we come together for the common goal, we learn to share and identify strengths to enhance our resources.

The sixth strategy for effective networking is *developing good business card tips*. Make sure your business card is easy, attractive, and informative. Don't give out cards that are torn, bent, etc.

Remember your business card is an extension of you. Don't get in the habit of the Three G's: 1) greet the person, 2) grab his/her hand, and 3) give him/her a card and move on. If you are going to give out a card, make sure that a connection has been established. Make sure your business cards are accessible and take more business cards than you will need. Develop a walking file cabinet for maintaining the business cards. It shows a sign of disorganization when a person asks for a card and you go through your handbag, your planner, and your pockets to come up empty. Or the other scenario, you give *someone else's* card. It is important to have one hand to give out cards and your other hand receiving the other person's card. Make notes on the cards of the people you meet as quickly as you can. This will be beneficial when you do your follow-up. Use good judgment when giving out business cards. You may choose not to give everyone you meet a card. The same is applicable to the other person. You may talk briefly and move on as a connection may not take place in that conversation. The last thing you want to do is give someone a card to find your card in the trash or on the floor. Remember, the exchange of business cards does not take the place of meaningful dialogue.

The seventh strategy for effective networking is *follow-up*. Once you have developed the skill, it becomes imperative that you follow-up with phone calls, note cards, breakfast/luncheon meetings, whatever is necessary to develop the relationship. Start a tickler file. It has been through active follow-up that I have created opportunities and you can do the same thing. Your ability to network depends on your willingness to step out of your comfort zone; but once you step out of your comfort zone, boundaries will disappear.

In summary, the seven strategies for effective networking are:
1) Develop a strong support system
2) Know yourself
3) Develop the Three R's of networking
4) Develop good listening skills
5) Understand your reasons for networking
6) Develop good business card techniques
7) FOLLOW-UP, FOLLOW-UP, FOLLOW-UP

> *A sure way for one to lift himself up is by helping
> to lift someone else.* BOOKER T. WASHINGTON

# Nancy Manson

Nancy Manson, a trainer for over 16 years with 12 of those in America's top training and personal development organizations, has coached senior executives. She is president of Manson Techniques, Inc., an Atlanta, Georgia, based speaking, training, and consulting company. Her theme is *Developing a Better You.* Nancy is a member of the National Speakers Association, the Georgia Speakers Association, Society of Human Resource Managers in Atlanta, and a charter member of the National Association of Women Business Owners — Atlanta chapter.

Nancy delivers high energy in her inspirational and informative seminars. She endears her audience with her professional and realistic presentation style. Nancy's areas of expertise include personal enrichment, communication skills, networking seminars, customer service, and motivational/inspirational keynotes. Her clients include AT&T, Center for Disease Control, The Atlanta Journal Constitution, Elite Staffing Services, Georgia Power, and SunTrust Bank.

You can reach Nancy at Manson Techniques, Inc., 110 Parliament Court, Fayetteville, GA 30215 Phone (770) 719-2425 or E-mail: njmanson@aol.com.

# ★ 15 ★

# The Inside Story

by **Fiona Page Hobbs**

This is the inside scoop on how the pieces of one's life story make us who we are. Finding one's value is a lifelong process. Sadly enough, many end up looking back and wondering what they have done that leaves their mark on the sands of time. Becoming blind at the age of forty-four put me in that place. I hope in sharing my life's journey will encourage other to piece their own stories together and find their strength to deal with the moment at hand. There are two sides to this story as there are to every story. First, I will share the personal pieces of my story which brought me to this place. Then you can flip the page to the story of the development of my professional life. If someone had asked, "If you had to lose your sight or hearing which would you rather it be?" What a thought. Nonetheless many have pondered that question. I actually recall being asked that question sometime before I lost my eyesight so suddenly. My answer was, "I could not bear the thought of being in total quiet, never to hear the ocean's roar, the rain on the roof, my grandchildren giggle, or music, the sounding board for all of our emotions. How terrible a darkness that would be." Yes, I thought of it as darkness. Yet I awaken shrouded in total darkness every day. Believe me, the adjustment wasn't as simple and is a constant challenge every day.

I was at once reminded of my love of the oral tradition, the richness of stories that touch us all. I had taught school for twenty-two years. My life was not over. I had a burning desire to share my beliefs on the power that story has to shape us. I chose to seize that opportunity while rehabilitating. I could still tell stories; I had spent five years honing my craft. There was no other option, but continue to speak, teach, and tell. I just had to figure out how to stay in the mainstream with my sighted colleagues.

My ability as a storyteller and a speaker grew as the strength of my family's stories were revealed to me. My mother was born with a crippling birth defect that required amputation and prostheses. I had watched my parents deal with this in their marriage. My mother had such grace and my father was the "wind beneath her wings," as the song says. When I thought back on her physical challenges, I assumed that I could do anything. I had taken my own mother's handicap for granted, all of my life. Now I was face to face with my own thinking, well, if she can do it surely I can too. My mother bowled me over with, "Fiona, I am not handicapped, you don't miss something that you never had." True, mine was much different; I was facing a loss. It was time to grieve. Could I cope as well?

We are never really ready for what is in store for us, even when we think we are. In this fast-paced world in which we live, we all seek acceptance and love. As young adults, we are so busy with this journey that we lose sight of our dreams and who we really are. Then in our middle years, the race is brought to a screeching halt. It is the time in our society that we experience the law of diminishing returns. Often we come face to face with our own mortality. If not that, we see ourselves differently; circumstances such as, a career change, a loss of a loved one, or a disability bring us to the chalk line. Time to get off this merry-go-round or use it as a springboard. As we come to grips with those challenges, we are brought to our knees. Next comes the reality of do we have what is takes to remove this barrier? Don't question; just deal with it. Our value is there; we only have to believe it. It is simple; we just have to put one foot in front of the other, consider the options, and give it our best shot. I spent time thinking about my life, and my family stories. It gave me hope.

In my first career, I learned how to juggle a job, and maintain a home, as a wife and mother. Now my mid-life crisis was financial ruin, my marriage of nineteen years was dissolving, and now blindness. Thank God it didn't come all at the same time!! I was fortunate to have many great opportunities in my career and my family life. There were rich rewards that made my life story. My memories could motivate me to reach and stretch and move beyond my situation. I have worked with young people inspiring them and motivating them to be all that they could be. I had encouraged them to stretch and grow, to reach for all they desired. Hard work and a belief in oneself were the building blocks, but the key is the ability to communicate. It was exciting because I was learning as I taught others.

People ask me, "How do you get out of bed in the morning knowing that you will not see the sunrise;" I in turn ask, "How do you face the day when everything seems to be preventing you from attaining your goals, and you feel so out of control?" We do not have the luxury of knowing the future any more than we can be assured that, when we leave home, we will safely return. As much as I have thought about giving up hope, I knew deep in my heart that I could not. I asked myself what made it possible for me to have such inner strength. Most of my insight came from my paternal grandfather's story. I can remember when I was ten greeting my grandfather at the train station on the day of his retirement. I could not understand the significance of the gold watch he held in his hand, nor the sadness in his eyes. It was not clear to me then, how he felt, but I certainly knew the moment was an important one. I recall how he wanted to move south where the weather was not so cold and he could enjoy the climate now that he didn't have to work as hard. No one told me, but I felt that Grandpa longed to do what my grandmother would not. Wasn't that what he had looked forward to? Unfortunately, he died two years later of pneumonia. I always blamed my grandmother for that.

No real reason for the blame except I saw one person who stood in the way of another's happiness. Today, I realize he allowed it to happen. Circumstances cannot be judged by outsiders. I was an outsider. I just thought it was important to reap rewards of your hard work. Now I know this situation is common. I believe it makes me more aware of what is important to me. Now, I asked myself, "How do I get there from here?"

Being blind only six months, I decided to challenge myself by making Easter dinner. My family thought I was reaching out just a bit too far, but knew they needed to stay out of my way. For the first course I prepared our family's favorite soup. We all sat down to eat and as I put the first spoonful into my mouth, I bit down on something rubbery. I held it up and exclaimed, "what is this?" "A rubberband!" laughed my son. How did **THAT** get there? Oh, well, I guess you could say that I was trying to stretch the soup. We all laughed. I was relieved to find out that I was the only one that got to taste that delectable tidbit.

My mother would always say, "God never gives you anything you can't handle." Honestly, sometimes I thought she was wrong. Is it not true that when a door closes to us, a window opens? Yes, if you believe it is so, it is so. When my Dad lost his job for the umpteenth time, he and my mother figured out a way to make a living for our family. They opened the front of Grandpa's old grocery store. Antiquated as it was, they supplied it with a soft ice cream machine and a hot dog steamer. Now they were restaurant owners! When they had to borrow money to expand, Mama commented wistfully, "We should have held onto the land in Atlanta (it was developed into a fine shopping center), we could have been rich." But she always laughed because being rich, she knew wasn't what life was all about. Instead they worked hard to turn that hot dog stand into a fine family-style eatery. Their pleasure and pride in the entrepreneurship would become their legacy to their children and grandchildren.

In high school, I worked for my father in that restaurant. I know my family enticed me with fancy titles and the practical idea that living at home would save me money. I missed a little fun and the opportunity to get into mischief, but now I realize that I learned much about valuing myself. I still had a lot of fun. I felt that I had natural abilities to entertain and secretly wanted to become an actress. I yearned to attend a top drama school, but I was scared and without the necessary funds. I now realize it must not have been important enough for me to take the risk or make the sacrifice. Each of these growth experiences molded and shaped inner strengths that I never knew were there, until I needed them. I have since used that energy in my work teaching young people and in my professional speaking business.

Looking back on the first fifty years of my life, I see half a century that has had its ups and downs. I recall many times walking the malls longing for the material goods that flashed before me — always thinking that if I had a little more money all would be well, wishing for something more. Advertising has truly done a number on us. It has made us want more. We do not know what that "more" is or where it ends. I find my cravings have changed. I want love, peace, balance, and, most of all, acceptance of the moment — yes, to be satisfied with me. To do that I have had to learn to trust the moment, have faith in my inner self, and seek the company of those who want to make a difference, as I do. I want to participate that means get out there and do something.

This world is full of lonely people. We all fear loneliness. To overcome that we have to reach the point of self-acceptance. Believing that doing something is better than standing still and doing nothing is a start. Learning to trust your gut or intuition and moving ahead means a step forward. This is not about blindness. Everyone doesn't need to be blind to face this self-discovery. Thank God! Everyone should expect to face fears, insecurities, and their inner selves at some point in life. When the unexpected happens, there was no place to go but up. The bottom is not a pretty sight. Many of us have been in situations where we thought it was easier to end it all, rather than face our lives as they are. I experienced that feeling early on in my blindness.

Every morning I would climb the stairs to my office. I had no sooner reached the top when realized I had forgotten a paper I had been working on. Heading back down to retrieve it, I missed the step, tumbling down all the way to the bottom. As I sat on the floor, I began to cry. I felt so hopeless. This turn that my life had taken was too much to bear. A few moments later I said to myself, "Hey, hold on a minute, I have too much to live for and I began counting my blessings — devoted family and friends and a career which I would still be able to enjoy. I tapped into the inner reserves that I had stock piled all these years. It's amazing how much I had of what I needed. I wanted more! What I had to do was to pick myself up and put trust in my ability to overcome. I know that incident gave me the power and the courage to face the future. It was a dark day, but the sun always has a way of breaking through, as it did for me that day.

I have always been a people person and recognized the value of friendships. This attitude helped me face my most difficult challenge, letting go of some of my independence. I had no choice but to allow others to be my eyes in certain areas of my daily life. Trust became a big factor in my ability to function day to day. It was important for me to accept their help. It was a way for them to feel that lending a helping hand would make a difference. This assistance filled a need in each of our lives. We all want to feel valued, accepted, and loved. These important ideals are the fuel we need to keep going.

Positive companions, humor, and music... anything uplifting was my desire. I spent time reading and gathering information, just as you are with this book. Listening to others helped me to tap into my inner reserves and believe that I could move forward. I wanted to be able to look back on my life knowing that I attempted to accomplish the things that were important to me. If I can energize others to think and act beyond themselves, to risk failure when skirting the issue would be easier, then I will feel satisfied that I made a difference in this world.

When I became blind, I had not a clue what lay ahead. I soon discovered the power of story as I moved in the circles of those who enjoyed folk and homespun tales. I began to understand that our stories are what make the world go round and cross all barriers aiding us in the value of relating with one another.

Relating and valuing one another can be especially important in our business dealings. A professional friend of mine relayed this story to me. A large automaker hired him to advise them on how to generate more sales and better relate to their customers. First and foremost, he told them put your business aside and take time to listen to them. Show them that they are of value to you by connecting with them, through eye contact, facial expression, and body language. These are all ways in which you can positively relate to them that you care and value them and their business. You will gain loyal, satisfied customers, and your business will thrive.

One of my favorite stories takes into account all the important virtues that will give us inspiration to face our obstacles and enjoy our successes. As a young man Alexander Graham Bell was always busy trying to invent things that would be of significance to the world around him. We all know how talented and successful he turned out to be, but he, too, was plagued with self doubt. When he got the idea for a machine that would be able to telegraph the human voice, he needed reassurance that the idea was not a crazy one. He decided to go to Washington, D.C., to seek the council of his good friend, Joseph Henry, then Director of the Smithsonian Museum. As he revealed his ideas to Henry, Alexander seemed to have a doubting tone in his voice and expressed that he felt his lack of knowledge of electricity would stand in the way of the telegraphing machine. Henry, and eternal optimist, told Bell he must have confidence in his abilities and cited for him all the other marvelous things he had accomplished. He told Graham that he had to put his fears aside, tap into the power of his ideas, and follow it through. Needless to say, we are all grateful for the convenience and the human contact that this invention has brought to all our lives.

**Turn the page to find the other side of the story...**

Each year on the first day of classes, I would write on the chalkboard, "Today is the first day of the rest of your life… make the most of it!" My students and I would discuss how the slate would be wiped clean, everyone had a fresh start. Encouragement and fresh ideas were my wares. I was selling success.

Initially, we have to know in our heart that failure isn't an option. Success begins with believing in ourselves. To achieve that confidence, I told the students that they had to believe what they had to say was of value. It might start with, "I KNOW I AM RIGHT!" Then a short while later needs to come the proof of their conviction and the subsequent action that they plan to take. The success of this method depends upon their credibility to themselves and to others.

- Be prepared. Arm yourself with information, statistics and referrals. In other words, do your homework!

- Keep a journal. Even though I cannot see what I write, the simple act of jotting something down helps me to mentally store it for future reference.

- Remember to write things down on a realistic To Do list. When I taught, I was constantly keeping a variety of lists. Week after week, I would never make it to the bottom of any of those lists. Carry over chores will drag you down and defeat your motivation to move forward. That defeating feeling breeds insecurity and frustration, it was important for me to feel that I had accomplished **something**. To do that I had to develop rewards and incentives for myself.

- The most valuable tool I acquired was how to simplify my life. It is a great stress reducer. Ask yourself: What is really important to achieve my goal? Does what you do, say, save, or plan have any validity; does it fit the big picture or are you lost in a muddle? Have you lost sight of your goals?

- Short cuts are divine! They provide you with lost time to enjoy in other areas of your life. Learning how to balance your time can be as difficult as trying to balance a pencil on its point! There are many excellent books on the market devoted to time management; take advantage of the great ideas and suggestions they offer that are tailored to your personality and profession.

- Value your customers and be aware of their needs. Provide special treatment with honesty and fairness. My parents managed a business for over forty years and always gave the credit for their success to their customers. Other business people would seek advice from my parents; their words of wisdom were always the same: treat people as you would like to be treated — a tried and true idea.

- Organize yourself by categorizing your thoughts and ideas into groups. Set your goals, both personal and professional. These goals, both short and long term, will overlap giving you a grasp of your life's big picture.

- Analyze your competition. Familiarize yourself with their successes and determine your gameplan to gain more of a market share. Talk to people who have been customers of these competitors to determine their level of satisfaction with the services that were provided to them. Your success will be determined by how much you know and how well you can perform in the marketplace.

In 1987 I began speaking to educators across the county, introducing them to my educational storytelling techniques. I knew my middle school teaching days were over due to my blindness, and that I had to take my career in a different direction. My love of storytelling and motivational speaking prepared me to invest myself in this area full-time. Learning to network to discover my worth, how to market myself, negotiate a contract, and what my target audience was to be were all hurdles I had to face. My enthusiasm for entertaining people and sharing my personal story as well as those of others propelled me into the area of networking. I realized how important it was to identify my potential audience would be, and where they were coming from. My goal as a teacher was to attain a special connection with my students, it would be no different with future audiences. That connection was the key to people understanding my message and buying into the changes that I was promoting. To make a difference is to accept that change is inevitable I was living proof of that; so let's make the best of it.

Deciding on your value requires considering many factors. Sometimes though only your intuition can tell you how to establish your own. Of course, if you are right on the money, you will be in demand but not without doing your homework. Then there's the problem of how much to invest, the old adage "It takes money to make money" was staring me right in the face. In life there are no guarantees. Taking a risk is the first step in which the rewards or failures are considered valuable learning experiences.

Open your eyes, look, around you, listen to your customers, identify your competitors and take time to analyze. As you plan, ponder the following questions:

Can you state a code of ethics?
Can you give examples of follow-through?
Have you simplified all you can?
Are you clear on what you are worth?
Can you express your worth and support that figure with facts?
Have you provided that insurance of success by finding an effective way to tag your memory?

The following acronym will be helpful:

### TEST YOUR POWER

**T** is for **tag** it: Keep your thoughts and strategies organized. Find the time management strategy that works for you.

**E** is for: A firm code of **ethics**.

**S** is for: **simplify**. Remember K.I.S.S... keep it simple.

**T** is for: **take time** to value yourself and keep focused.

**Y** is for: **you** are the one responsible, for yourself and those you entrust responsibility to.

**O** is for: **opportunity** that comes to those who wait and plan to be ready when it does.

**U** is for: **utilize** others' skills and talents; delegate.

**R** is for: **respect**, for yourself and others.

**P** is for: **power**. There is power in believing in your own inner strength.

**O** is for: **obstacles** that must be used as stepping stones to march forward and up.

**W** is for: a **win-win** attitude makes the difference and gets better results.

**E** is for: **energize**. Keep healthy and in balance in order to lead with confidence.

**R** is for: **rigors** that will drag you down; but each time you fail, make it a growth experience to learn from.

## Fiona Page-Hobbs

Fiona Page-Hobbs is a speaker, storyteller and author with a masters degree in education. In 1987 the U.S. Department of Education awarded her the Christa McAuliff Fellowship for her program, *Storytelling as a Teaching Tool*. Over the next three years she conducted seminars and workshops for educators introducing them to her innovative educational concepts. She is associated with Young Audiences, Inc., Georgia Council for the Arts and is a member of both the National Speakers Association and the Georgia Speakers Association. The last eight years have been spent writing and presenting humorous, inspirational and motivational programs to professional business organizations, hospitals, churches and schools throughout the eastern U.S. Recently her storytelling skills were the subject of an article in Southern Living Magazine, *Got the World by the Tale*.

You can reach Fiona at Fiona Page, Inc., 10625 Stonefield Landing, Duluth, GA 30097-2030 Phone (770) 497-8807, Fax (770) 814-0771, or E-mail: page@negia.net.

# ★ 16 ★

# No Doze Prose

by **Steve Cohn**

I've often heard people say "I would be so successful if only I could catch their attention!"

Yes, first you've got to catch their attention. Then you've got to keep their attention. Communicate through *No Doze Prose*, and you will do just that.

Today, we're communicating through the written word in prodigious amount. Hundreds — thousands of written messages are crossing our desks each year.

And we're not reading them.

A middle manager in one of my *No Doze Prose* seminars told me he received 920 E-mail messages during the five days he was gone for vacation.

Nine hundred twenty E-mails!

I asked him, "What did you do with them?" He told me he used the "delete" button a lot.

The people who sent him those memos didn't consider that possibility. They thought he was reading their messages!

HA!

The late president and publisher of Forbes magazine, Malcolm Forbes, wrote in the late 1970s that he received more than 1,000 pieces of correspondence per month. That's more than 12,000 pieces a year.

Forbes wrote this before the advent of E-mail, and before the advent of "put it on paper so you can cover your —."

We are getting more messages than Forbes got 20 years ago, and they're not being read. In fact, many of our written letters, memos, proposals, reports, announcements, press releases, and requests are putting people to sleep.

## Don't Put the Reader to Sleep

Have you ever gotten a letter that sounds like this?

"As per your request, dated September 4, with respect to the requested appointment in my office for September 29, I regretfully must inform you that the designated date is at this time unavailable for such a meeting. Due to unforeseen circumstances beyond our control, a recent breakdown in the building infrastructure has resulted in our office walls being less than satisfactory for the purpose which they were originally constructed. A crew of certified construction professionals will be occupying the premises on September 29 in order that we may have this situation corrected. I would like to report, however, that I would be able to schedule a meeting with you on October 5 or 6, if that is satisfactory for you. I look forward to discussing our mutual concerns on that date. Thank you.

Sincerely,

Boris Blowhard
CEO

Zzzzzzzzzzzzzzzzzzzzzzzzzzz...

This letter puts us to sleep. With *No Doze Prose*, the letter would have sounded like this:

"I'm sorry to say I won't be able to meet with you on September 29. A construction crew will be fixing the walls of my office on that day.

However, I'm free on October 5th and 6th. Please call me to let me know if you are available on either of those dates. I look forward to seeing you. Thanks."

In this chapter, I'm going to show you how to get people to read your written communication. I'll show you how to keep them reading after they start, despite interruptions. I'll show you how to write *No Doze Prose*.

The time we're wasting writing things that people don't read wouldn't be so bad if we had enough time to begin with!

**The Death Bin**

We're busy! And when people get correspondence that doesn't catch their attention immediately, they say something like this:

"Hmmm… I know this is important, and I should read it but I'll finish it later. I'll just put it… right… here."

And the reader puts it on one of the corners of the desk. I call that corner… THE DEATH BIN.

THE DEATH BIN. It's where documents go to die.

This is how they die: Joe gets a document from Gloria. Gloria writes "As per our conversation last week, I am attempting to ascertain whether you are cognizant of the dilemmas I find myself with on the Cooper account."

Joe, about to fall asleep, puts the document in THE DEATH BIN for later reading. To wake up, he decides to get a cup of coffee. On the way, he runs into Gloria in the hallway. Gloria says "Joe, did you get my note?"

Joe hesitantly says "yes," but then asks Gloria to explain it again. She says:

"I wanted to ask you: Did you know I was having problems with Larry Cooper and his account?"

Joe and Gloria discuss the situation and come to a conclusion. Joe goes back to his desk. A week later, Joe decides to clean his desk, finds Gloria's memo, realizes he took care of it, and tosses it in the trash.

It was dead before it had a chance to do what it was intended to do.

If Gloria had started her letter, "Did you know I was having problems with Larry Cooper and his account?" Joe might have read it and taken care of the situation before Gloria confronted him in the hallway.

**Business Speak vs. No Doze Prose**

Joe might have read the memo because it was written in *No Doze Prose*. Most of us write in business speak.

> Business speak is formal!
> Business speak is impressive!
> Business speak uses big words!
> Business speak has no personality!
>
> Business speak is BORING!!!

We all learned to be formal when writing for business. We learned to use words to impress people with our vocabulary, and we learned to take out any hint of personality from our correspondence.

Forget everything you ever learned about business writing. The world has changed. The business world has changed. We have changed.

We need to make our documents attention-grabbing, expressive, clearly written, friendly, and something people are going to want to read. We need to keep our documents out of THE DEATH BIN.

The best way to do this is to use No Doze Prose when writing. *No Doze Prose* is what we use when speaking with each other. It is more to the point, uses words with fewer syllables, is friendly, and doesn't try to impress anybody. It doesn't go into long-winded explanations written to fulfill a subconscious memory of Mrs. Brown, your seventh grade teacher.

Remember seventh grade? We came back to school and the teacher said, "Write a composition with the title 'What I Did on My Summer Vacation.' And make it 700 words."

About a half-hour later, we would be counting, "301... 302... 303..."

I did it, too! And I loved writing!

What do you think we were concentrating on? Our creativity, or the number of words? Is it any wonder we look at business documents and decide they're not long enough?

With *No Doze Prose*, we finish writing when we've said what we need to say. And we say it in a way that allows the reader to understand our message completely and quickly.

**Write for the Ear**

People used to write for the eye. Fifty years ago, 90% of the information we received was through the written word. We read a newspaper every morning and sometimes read another newspaper in the afternoon. Three-quarters of the business information we got from out-of-town clients and offices was written because long-distance telephone calls were too expensive. Little was communicated to the ear.

All of this has changed. For any of us born after 1940, our world has been shaped through oral communication. Television and radio have become the source for 70% of the news and information we get.

When I started writing radio news, I was taught to write as if I was speaking to somebody face to face. In television and radio, information is transmitted to be absorbed quickly, as in conversation.

The most important information must be given right up front, just as it would be if a friend had big news to tell.

Today, we have gotten used to information written for the ear. If you don't believe me, compare the writing in newspapers and magazines today to those of just 20 years ago. Staid, conservative newspapers such as the <u>Wall Street Journal</u> are writing in a more active, expressive style than ever before. If this "newspaper of business" can cut down on the formality, so can we.

*No Doze Prose* is written for the ear. It is active, casual, and expressive. It is information we can listen to and digest in a matter of seconds.

So, the first step in getting the attention of the person who is reading the document is to write for the ear. Get to the point quickly; use active voice; cut down on the big words; be concise.

## Know What You Want To Write

Once we've accepted the idea that *No Doze Prose* gets a lot more attention than business speak, we can get down to the nitty-gritty of writing. The first step in good writing is knowing what we want to write.

Of course, that takes preparation. It means actually thinking about what we want to write before putting anything down on paper.

Ask yourself: Why am I writing? What is my purpose? What do I hope to achieve by writing this document?

If we can't answer these questions, maybe we shouldn't be writing.

Every document has got to have a purpose! We want to achieve something with our writing, or else why would we be writing?

Every document should have one clear central idea. It should be trying to achieve one overall goal. If the document has two central ideas, there should be two documents. If that is not possible, make sure the two ideas are clearly separated.

Know what you want to accomplish. Then quickly get to your point so that the reader knows why he or she is taking the time to read the document.

## Get to the Point

Remember, we're busy. When we get right to the point in the first paragraph, the reader can decide whether to read your document or put it into THE DEATH BIN. The first line should sound like this:

"Dear Mr. McGillicudy,

I am interested in talking to you about your $100,000 project. Please call me to set up a meeting where we can discuss this further."

This sentence gets right to the point. McGillicudy now knows that I am interested in his project and knows what I want him to do. He can take action.

Let's say McGillicudy offered the same project to five people and waited for their responses. If I sent that letter and Bill sent the following letter, who do you think would catch his attention?

"Dear Mr. McGillicudy,

It was very nice seeing you the other day at the Chamber of Commerce meeting downtown. The city always looks so lovely at this time of year, with the trees blossoming, the birds singing, and spring in the air.

As per our conversation, I would like to speak to you about the project you mentioned. It sounds quite intriguing to me. I have always wanted to work with a company that produces products such as yours and believe this would be a great challenge. I would like to know more.

Perhaps we can meet at some time to discuss this further. Please call me at your convenience to set up an appointment. I look forward to speaking with you."

Don't beat around the bush. Get right to the point.

**Talk to the Reader**

Let's say you're getting married. You run into your friend Cindy. You've got to tell her the good news. Would you say, "Cindy, I am talking to you today to tell you that I will be getting married. The nuptials will be taking place on October 14, approximately three months from now. I would greatly appreciate it if you would attend and help celebrate this momentous occasion. Please advise me of your intentions. I look forward to seeing you."

Do people talk that way?

If you were getting married and wanted to tell Cindy about it, you would probably say, "Cindy! Guess what? Paul and I are getting married on October 14! Just three months from now! I would really love it if you would come. Will you?"

I'll admit it. This statement is a little too casual to put in a letter. And the chances are, you wouldn't discuss marriage in a business letter. But if it were in a business letter, it could be written this way:

"Dear Cindy,
I have some great news. Paul and I are getting married on October 14, just three months from now. I'd be thrilled if you would share that day with us. Please let me know if you'll be there. I can't wait to see you."

This letter sounds like a person wrote it.

If a co-worker, Tom, came into your office, sat across from you and told you of the huge project he was working on, would you say, "Tom, please contact me if I can be of assistance?" Would he say "Thank you. Your cooperation is greatly appreciated?"

No. You would probably say, "Tom, let me know if I can help in any way," and Tom would say, "Thanks, I'd appreciate it."

We can write our business correspondence the same way.

Nobody is asking you to throw all formality and structure out the window. Structure is fine! Boredom is not.

Write your documents as if you're talking to somebody, not as if you were talking at them.

Read your document aloud before you send it. If it doesn't sound like something you would say, rewrite it.

### Write it For the Reader

It never ceases to amaze me how many documents I get that have nothing to do with me. They're written to me, and they have information I might be able to use, but nothing else about the letter or offer is geared towards me.

In order to make our readers want to read our documents, we need to write for our readers. Know who the reader is. Once we know that information, we can make our points, requests, or anything else in terms of the benefit to the reader.

I hate to say this, but most of us don't care what you think, what you've done, what you want, or anything else about you!

As a reader, I want to know what those things will do for ME!

ME, ME, ME, ME, ME!

Information in business documents should be written in terms of how it will affect the person reading the document, or how it will affect the person's company or department.

Suppose you work as a paper pusher for Big Conglomerate Insurance, Inc. You make about $45,000 a year and last year got a raise of 2 percent. Coming back from lunch, you find a memo on your desk.

"To:      All employees
From:   John Curruthers IV, Executive Vice-President, Finance
Re:      Company Performance

I am pleased to announce today that Big Conglomerate Insurance, Inc. had a 35 percent increase in sales in the year just ended. These sales figures solidify our hold on the number one position in the insurance industry.

Congratulations to all who contributed to this effort."

What does that memo mean to you? Nothing. You pick it up and throw it in the trash. Or you make it into a paper airplane.

Now, if the memo had said "Because of this performance, we are giving everybody a 6 percent raise in pay," you might have taken the memo, tacked it to your bulletin board and used it as a reminder of what a great company you work for.

## Ask Questions About the Reader

What do we want to know about our readers?

- ❑ Education
- ❑ Position
- ❑ Knowledge base
- ❑ Technical background
- ❑ Attitude toward the proposal
- ❑ Experience
- ❑ Inside or outside the company
- ❑ What they need
- ❑ What they want
- ❑ Male or female
- ❑ Age
- ❑ and more

The more we know about our readers, the better the chances of making them want to read what we wrote.

## Make it well organized

Every good business letter should have a beginning, a middle, and an end. It sounds simple enough. Yet we all get letters that start in the middle.

The beginning of the letter should tell the reader the purpose. Sure, we can also use the beginning to introduce ourselves or say thank you, but 90 percent of the time, the purpose will open the letter.

The middle should include background, facts, figures, backup information that supports the point made in the beginning. If there are instructions, procedures, or steps to be given, this is where they go. Many people believe that the middle is also where we bury bad news. Yes, but only if it's inconsequential.

If the bad news has great consequence or meaning to the reader or the reader's company, put it right up front. This is especially true in safety, regulatory, or financial issues. Don't risk somebody's not seeing important bad news or treating it lightly just because it was buried in the middle.

Also, we should put good news right up front. If we've got good news, we should want to tell the world.

The end should include the summary. There's an old theory on letter-writing: tell them what you're going to tell them (beginning), then tell them (middle), and then tell them what you told them (end). They will get the point.

The end can also include next steps ("I will meet you next Tuesday at Houston's restaurant." "Please send me the package by next Thursday"), and a thank you.

Make your document well organized and clear. Make it understandable. Don't make people try to figure it out.

**Give Your Document Visual Impact**

The greatest invention in the history of writing was the printing press. The second greatest invention was the Word Processor.

Word Processors have changed the face (literally!) of business writing. When I talk about getting people to want to read our writing, I am not only talking about using words.

We can give our documents visual impact. We can make our documents so attractive that nobody will ever put them in THE DEATH BIN.

Here are some ways to give your document visual impact:

Headings — Headings help take the reader through the document. We not only want to catch the reader's attention, but we want to make sure he or she keeps reading once he or she starts. We all get interruptions, so we need to give the reader a reason to keep reading.

Headings help the reader know where to go. As a reader, you've been following my headings ("Don't Put the Reader to Sleep," "The Death Bin," "Write It for the Reader," etc.) throughout this chapter.

- Bulleted and Numbered lists — We use numbered lists when writing a list in sequence, or to let the reader know that a certain number of things are being offered, i.e., "I have these questions for you:

  1) Are you enjoying this chapter?
  2) Are you learning anything?
  3) Do you want to know more?"

These questions are not written in a particular order, but let the reader know there are only three questions to deal with.

Bullets are used for any other lists.

Short paragraphs. Short paragraphs create "white space." The eye loves white space.

White space makes the reader more relaxed when reading the document.

Indentations. Indentations create more "white space" and let the reader know quickly when a new paragraph has begun.

Graphics. When we talk about graphics, we're not talking about clip art. We're talking about graphs, charts, maps, tables, etc. Some people are more visual than others. Know the reader. If the reader likes visuals, give the reader visuals to make the point.

**Bold**, <u>Underline</u>, *Italics*, ALL CAPS, **different fonts**, and point sizes. All of these things are used for emphasis. **Bold**, <u>underline</u>, and <u>ALL CAPS</u> are used for a strong emphasis. Italics are used for a softer emphasis and different fonts and points sizes are used to attract the reader's eye to a word or place in the document.

### Don't Try To Impress People

You have a message to send. Whatever your message is, do it in a clear, understandable way. If you don't, you'll confuse the reader.

And when you confuse, you lose.

There are one million words in the English language. There are also one million geniuses in the United States. Using large words doesn't make us geniuses or make us sound like geniuses.

Abraham Lincoln was a genius. We all remember his Gettysburg Address. The Gettysburg Address had 272 words, 196 of which were one syllable.

Do we remember any of Lincoln's other speeches? Probably not, but we remember that one because it had short words throughout.

When Martin Luther King, Jr. spoke before hundreds of thousands of people at the March of Washington in 1963, he could have shown them what a genius he was by using big words.

He could have addressed the crowd and said, "I have a nocturnal illusion!"

A nocturnal illusion. An illusion that comes at night. A dream.

He said, "I have a dream." We all remember it. Four words, four syllables.

Use simple words and simple sentences. Keep it simple and concise. Keep it short. Cut out the extra words.

The other day, I read a letter that said, "I was sorry to learn that you were disappointed with our service."

I was sorry to learn? In other words, "If I hadn't learned that you were disappointed, I wouldn't have to write this stupid customer service letter!"

The customer doesn't care that the writer was sorry to learn that you were disappointed." The customer would feel better if the writer wrote, "I am sorry you were disappointed." It addresses the customer's need and takes out three useless words.

## Use Active Voice

Which is stronger? "You did a great job," or "A great job was done by you?"

The former is an active voice statement. In an active voice statement, the subject is doing the action. In a passive voice statement, the action is being done to the subject.

Studies have shown that people are 12 times more likely to read, absorb, enjoy, and act on correspondence that is written in active voice. It is strong, active, exciting, interest-grabbing writing.

## Be Courteous

There is never any excuse in business writing for being nasty or negative. Even if people write negative documents to us, we shouldn't be nasty to them.

Watch the use of negative words. Watch the conversation killers like worthless, wrong, uncalled for, must, unacceptable, terrible, and false. There is no response to these words when used in a letter or conversation. When someone says "You're worthless!" we can't respond "I'll be a little less worthless next time." We're either worthless or we're not.

Try not to use accusatory phrases like the mistake that you made, surely you must have known, you neglected to, and if you actually did. These words will start fights. Guaranteed.

## Make Sure it's Correct and Complete

Is the document complete? Does it contain everything it should contain? Ask these questions before sending the document to the reader. If some information is missing because we couldn't get it, we need to say so. It is better to let the reader know the information is not there and that we did make an honest attempt to get it.

Is it correct? One mistake can put the rest of the document in doubt. After all, if one thing was wrong, why should they believe the other things in the document?

When I was a news reporter, I was told, "check your facts. And after you check them, check again." It's good advice.

## Have Fun with Your Writing!

It's really too bad most people hate writing. Because it can be so much fun.

Use **humor**. Throw in *italics* and **bold**. Write like you speak. Use contractions. Be a person. Make them feel like they're listening to YOU, not some business writing computer.

Most of us know how to have fun in our lives. Use the same concepts to have fun with your writing. I'm not saying fill your business documents with jokes, or be cute or flippant. I'm asking that you have some fun with it.

Have a sense of humor. Don't be dry. If you give the reader the information he or she wants and needs, it doesn't have to be done in a boring way to be taken seriously.

Bore them, and your document will end up in THE DEATH BIN.

Remember, get their attention. Then keep it.

When you write *No Doze Prose*, your documents will be read. They will catch people's attention and keep that attention through the document.

People will pay attention to you and what you have to say. Enjoy your success!

# Steve Cohn

Steve Cohn is a speaker, trainer, and writer who has been communicating professionally for nearly 20 years. His business writing course, *No Doze Prose* has been given at public and corporate seminars throughout the United States. His keynote program, *Absolutely Delightful Dreamers*, encourages people to focus on their dreams and make them come true. As a writer and journalist, Steve worked for such organizations as NBC, United Press International, the Associated Press, and many newspapers and radio stations.

You can reach Steve at Absolutely Delightful Dreamers, 560 Summer Breeze Court, Alpharetta, GA 30202 Phone (770) 667-3042, Fax (770) 667-3142 or E-mail: addreamers@aol.com.

# ★ 17 ★
# Winning Strategies for Working with Your Personal Computer
## Do It the Doar Way — The Practical Approach to Technology

by **Denise Doar**

## Introduction

Remember your first time with a PC? Mine occurred in September 1992. I was working at IBM. The Training Division had experienced a summer of radical changes, where the internal and external customer training divisions were merged and the first of several downsizings was beginning. A new president from outside the division had been appointed over two well-respected directors and was totally reorganizing everything. I was on the marketing staff for Customer Education and had spent two years putting together executive presentations, developing marketing plans, and managing an 800 number that handled education questions and enrollments.

My manager, Stan, asked me into his office. He shut the door — highly unusual. He had my attention!  Now Stan was the best manager I had during my career at IBM. He was a rare combination of logic and acute business sense, packaged with genuine caring about others and creativity. Stan's immediate boss, Byrd, was one of the directors. He had a reputation as a "mad dog" at IBM. Sure, he had a loud bark and bite, but Byrd was the most brilliant individual I have ever met.

In his logical manner, Stan stated, "There's a new management position being created in Barry's group. It's a non-traditional position with high exposure. Byrd and I were discussing candidates, and your name came up. We think you'd be a good fit, if you're interested."

"What's the position?" I asked.

"Manager of Technology. It's a promotion, not a lateral, for you. The team's mission is to review emerging technologies for adult training potential and make recommendations as to which technologies should be acquired or developed for our instructors. They've got a couple of projects in the works and a prototype under development. Part of the staff is here in Atlanta, the rest is up in New York. It's past time a decision was made about the prototype."

"What are the pros and cons?"

"The upside is that it's a significant promotion while downsizing and laterals are occurring. And, you'd get a broader business perspective with R&D, finances and non-sales and marketing people. The downside is that it's not a traditional career path."

I took the job. The team's credentials were impressive. Two had built their own PC's and written their own software. Another was an avid ham radio fan who had built his own equipment. Another could repair anything with a small Phillips screwdriver and a toolkit. Another was an expert at leveraging IBM's purchasing systems. The techno-nerd "propeller-blade-to-body" ratio was extremely high. My credentials? Sales and marketing, with "interesting ideas." And, oh yes, I owned a VCR... which I couldn't program.

Fast forward two weeks. Jim McMichael, who could be the techno-nerd's poster model, brought a laptop PC into my office. He's a tall, slender, soft-spoken man who thinks before he speaks. His responses are thoughtful and deliberate. He is not a man to be rushed.

"What's that?" I ask.

"A PC." Jim is a man of few words. Sometimes I think he thinks I'm an idiot.

"I know that... why are you bringing it in here?"

"You need it." By this time, I can use a few more of his precious words.

"Why?"

"You're the Manager of Technology. You should be using technology."

I pause. He's got a point there. "Can I get E-mail on this?" Remember, it's 1992. The only way I got my E-mail was to come into the office and use the terminal there.

"Yes."

Okay, I bite. "How?"

Jim pushes up his glasses and says, "I'm loaning you these five manuals for you to read. And, here's a list of courses you need to enroll in."

Long pause. Jim does his staff work and is thorough. "Can you show me how to get my E-mail?"

Fast forward nine months. I'm still using the PC. I'm still getting E-mail. I still haven't gone to class nor opened a manual. I still haven't learned anything new.

And I'm no different than many of you. You know you should learn to use your PC more effectively, but you don't have the time nor the inclination. The pain of not doing so has not surpassed the pain of doing. When it does, we learn enough to get by.

What the techno-nerds of the world forget is that, for all of us business people, our PC is a tool, just like our telephone. And just because we're not techno-nerds doesn't mean that we're stupid. We just need help with the hardware and software so that we can apply our thoughtware to do our jobs more effectively.

In this chapter, we'll discuss how you can use your PC to be more productive with less stress. Each section contains a practical "Do" and a "Don't" for different areas, such as purchasing equipment. Some of the ideas may not be applicable to you at this point of your relationship with your PC. Take and use what works for you.

> *Success is a journey, not a destination.* BEN SWEETLAND

| *Do buy the best you can afford* | *Don't be seduced* |
| --- | --- |

Before you buy a PC, get out a pencil and paper and write down why you are buying it. Is it for the children's homework, for work at home convenience, for a home business, or because "everyone has one"? Next, write down everything you *need* to do on the PC. If you do not know what you need to do, ask the family member who will be using the PC what he/she needs to do on the PC. ***This is not want to do, but what you need to do.*** Then, write down everything you *want* to do. If you do not know what you want to do, ask your friends, your business associates, your significant other, and your children. You'll get lots of opinions! You now have a list stating why you are buying, what you need to have, and what is nice to have.

Now comes an important step. Think about your friends and decide which techno-nerd you can trust to help you with the buying decision.

This person must understand why you are buying, be fluent in geek language, be able to translate into plain English, have some sense of financial reality, and possess a sense of humor so that you can both laugh together over the buying process when it's over. Your neighbor's son who recently graduated from college is not who you need. Neither is your significant other, unless you enjoy confrontation.

Armed with the list and your trusted techno-nerd friend, buy the biggest and the fastest PC you can afford. Remember the old adage, "You can never be too rich or too thin?" Well, you can never have too much memory or too much hard drive. Buy more than you think you'll need. Trust me, a year from now it won't seem like all that much.

Other essentials include the fastest modem and CD-ROM available. A modem allows you to hook up your PC to a telephone line. You will be sending E-mail and surfing the Internet, so you need a fast modem to connect to the outside world. Speed saves time and reduces the irritation associated with waiting. So, unless you enjoy standing in line at the grocery store, buy the fastest modem that is available at the computer store. In the past, software packages and clipart graphics were distributed on diskettes. Now, most software and graphics are distributed on CD-ROM, so you need a CD-ROM drive. Again, the faster the CD-ROM drive, the less time you will wait.

Do not be seduced into buying equipment you do not need. For example, do you really need a scanner? If you cannot come up with a better reason for buying a scanner than to scan family photos into your PC, save your money or put those dollars into software or more memory. You do not need to buy a digital camera unless you have the need to add your own photos to files you are creating. You do not need an extra large monitor unless you plan to spend several hours a day in front of the monitor.

One of the most seductive items in the toy category is the color deskjet printer. Yes, they are inexpensive and the price is still dropping. But a color deskjet printer will not look nearly as professional as a laser printer. If you can buy only one printer, spend your money on the laser printer. This is especially true if you plan to use the printer for business documents.

Do not buy a laptop unless you really *need* (not want) portability. You will pay a premium for the privilege of portability. If you plan to use your PC for business and you travel extensively, you might want to consider a laptop. If you travel to clients during the day, but return to a home office, you may not need a laptop. Or you may want to purchase a fully-equipped desktop system and a less robust laptop.

> *Computers are useless. They only give you answers.*
> PABLO PICASSO

| Do focus on the fundamentals | Don't forget to practice |
| --- | --- |

Remember the first time you tried a new sport, like golf or tennis? For me, it was tennis. My family is decidedly non-athletic. We children learned to swim young because my mother could not swim and is afraid of water, but that is the only exercise we did. Until I was in college, my idea of exercise was turning the pages of a book. In college I discovered dance, aerobics and yoga, and began exercising regularly. When I moved to Atlanta, I needed a place to exercise and I wanted to meet people. My husband at that time suggested I join a golf or tennis club where I could meet people and learn a sport that would be applicable in a business environment. I had no clue how to play tennis, but the players were graceful, they wore sharp clothes, and they didn't seem to sweat a lot. Besides, golf took too long. Little did I know...

For my first tennis lesson, I wore a new white pleated tennis skirt, a green and white short-sleeved blouse and a white ribbon around my ponytail. I looked like a dark-haired, slightly overweight Chrissy Everett. It was late August in Atlanta, with high humidity. The instructor, I called her Miss Vicki, was barely 21, barely 100 pounds, and barely dressed. She began with the basics of the forehand and backhand, feeding me balls from the baseline. Miss Vicki quickly discovered that I was not ready for baseline work and showed me how to hold the racquet, swing and run — all foreign concepts for me. She ran me a lot. I finished that first lesson with a torn blouse, a skinned knee and an outfit drenched in sweat.

I had high interest and motivation, but zero skills to build on. I had to learn to anticipate where the ball would go, run, position my body and my racquet, watch the ball, swing and follow through, and run. Did

I mention run? I hate that part! For a long time I was engrossed in learning each step of the mechanics. Nothing felt natural, and nothing flowed from one step to the next. Intellectually, I understood the concepts and understood the steps, but I did not have the body knowledge to execute without conscious thinking. Then one day it clicked. I ran, nailed a forehand right into Miss Vicki's stomach, and ran back into position. It felt good!

Learning to use the PC is a lot like learning to play tennis. Instead of learning the rules of the game and how to hit a forehand, follow through, volley, and run, you need to learn the following fundamentals of PCS:

- Keyboarding — basic typing skills plus how to use keys specific to the PC, such as the Insert key and Tab key.
- Mousing" — how to operate the mouse with one hand efficiently. Many new applications use the secondary (or right button if you are right-handed) mouse button for shortcuts. The secondary mouse button is easier to use if you are operating your mouse with one hand.
- Selection skills and shortcuts — The Doar Way's Golden Rule of PCS is "Select first, then do." Selection skills and alternatives to click and drag are basic PC skills, like learning the alphabet is a basic skill for reading.
- Copy and paste — a basic skill for sharing information across applications.
- Internet search — an emerging skill today, and a crucial skill to finding information in the next few years.

Like learning the fundamentals of tennis, learning the fundamentals of PCS will feel awkward at first. You must make a conscious effort to master the mechanics. You must consciously concentrate on performing each step. Later, with practice, you will be able to execute these fundamentals unconsciously and with grace.

Did your mother tell you that, "Practice makes perfect"? A sobering statistic is that adult learners lose 50% of a new skill within 48 hours if they do not practice. Not only must you learn the new skill, you must make a conscious effort to practice it within the first 48 hours of learning. In other words, "use it or lose it."

Does this mean you must plan a two-hour practice session? Absolutely not! When you learn a new skill, take fifteen seconds to think about how you could use that skill later today or tomorrow ***doing work that you already plan on doing.*** In other words, you are incorporating your practice session into your real life activities. And jot down in your planner or on your to do list a few key words that will remind you to use that new skill when you begin the work. Another way to practice is to spend ten or fifteen minutes reviewing your notes, reading online help or a manual about that new skill. This method is typically not as effective as actually performing the new skill, but it is certainly better than not practicing at all.

> *I am convinced that it is of primordial importance to learn more every year than the year before. After all, what is education but a process by which a person begins to learn how to learn?*
>
> PETER USTINOV
>
> *Practice makes perfect.* UNKNOWN

| Do learn one high-impact product | Don't try to know it all |
| --- | --- |

Where are you on the PC knowledge scale? Are you a novice, a know-better, or a nerd? A ***novice*** is up and running but can perform only the most basic tasks. For example, the novice knows how to start the system, open the word processing program, and type a letter. The novice has limited knowledge about shortcuts or more advanced tasks, such as creating a mass mailing. A ***know-better*** can perform intermediate tasks, such as performing a mass mailing or creating a chart, and has a working knowledge of the packages he or she uses. A know-better "knows better" because he or she has been burned in the past. The know-betters have lost crucial files that weren't backed up, have been victims of viruses, have accidentally deleted files or formatted their hard drive, or taken hours to perform tasks that could have been done in minutes. The know-better knows when to ask for help. Meanwhile, a ***nerd*** considers the PC a new toy, and work on the PC as play. The nerd is that person at your office that you go to for help. A typical response is, "Yeah, go do this, this and this. Check back with me if you got any questions." Or, "Let me play around with it." A few hours later, the nerd is back with the solution to your technical problem. Nerds play with their PC's at home. They sit down for a few minutes, look up and the entire family has gone to bed.

If you're not a nerd, the fastest way to increase your PC skill level is to focus on one product. If you work with a word processor, a spreadsheet, a presentation package, a contact manager, a money manager, E-mail and an Internet browser, pick the package that you use the most or that will make the most impact for you personally or professionally. Then invest the time to learn this one product well. Take a class, read the online help, read manuals, pick your techno-nerd friends' brains, and practice. You will reap ongoing benefits.

First, you'll be an expert at this product and be able to create complex, attractive files quickly. That will save you time. Second, others will recognize you as an expert and seek your advice. The old adage, "knowledge is power" holds true. And third, learning one product gives you transferable skills for learning the next product. If the product you have chosen to learn is part of a suite of products, like Microsoft Office or Lotus Office, many of the functions you have learned to perform in the first product will function almost identically in another package within the suite.

> *A computer program does what you tell it to do, not what you want it to do.*
> UNKNOWN

| Do practice "safe" computing | Don't ignore your geek friends |
| --- | --- |

I left corporate America in the summer of 1993 and spent the fall learning to use a PC. For over a year I practiced "semi-safe" computing, which means I wasn't really safe at all. I backed up my crucial files when I thought about it, never checked for viruses, and never backed up my hard drive. Fall 1994 I became a *know-better* about safe computing when I purchased my first laptop.

Business had grown to the point where I needed a laptop for client presentations and classes. My business partner had a source for PC's through one of our clients. A laptop was available with the features we wanted at a lower price than we anticipated, so we purchased the used laptop.

I remember that laptop well. It was leading edge, not bleeding edge. It was an IBM ThinkPad, with Windows, Microsoft Office, fax software, and a few games. On the surface it was just what I needed. Unbeknownst to me, it also had a nasty virus.

How does a PC catch a virus? By practicing *unsafe* computing. That means unprotected contact with another PC. How does my PC have unprotected contact with another PC? By touching something that another PC has touched without protection. The most common ways of getting infected are by sharing a diskette without protection or downloading a file from another computer without protection.

How did I find out about the virus? Just like viruses with people, viruses on a PC may not be readily apparent. Often it takes time for the viruses to make itself felt. Alas, that was what happened to me. About two weeks after I purchased the PC, I had my first incident. I created a file in Word, then saved and closed the file. A few minutes later, I tried to open the file and got the message "file not found."

Well, I thought I was tired and had just keyed the wrong file name. I keyed the name a second time, and got the same nasty message. By now, I'm getting annoyed at the computer. I entered it a third time. (I can be perseverant! Actually, perseverant is an euphemism. My mother called it pigheaded.) Sure enough, it wasn't operator problem, it was a PC problem.

How did I learn this was a virus? Painfully. I called the person from whom we purchased the PC, explained the problem and my perspective about buying defective merchandise. I gritted my teeth while I was talked down to and listened to her suggestions. I tried what she suggested. No luck. I called again. I got another suggestion. No luck. I called again (remember, I'm persistent). By this time, she's getting testy. She called a modern-day witch doctor, a heavy duty techno-nerd, who ran a virus scan and determined that the PC had a virus. In the two-week time span that it took to resolve this problem, I hooked up to a client's network several times. Luckily for me, I did not infect my client! However, it

takes drastic measures to cure a virus. My hard drive was reformatted.
I lost almost three weeks of work, and a lot of time.

What do you need to do to practice "safe computing?" You need to
do three things:

1. Backup your files
2. Protect yourself from viruses
3. Shut down before power down

What is a backup? Making a backup is saving a copy of your files to
diskette, tape, or another drive. That way, if you accidentally delete a file
or something nasty happens to your PC, you have a backup copy you can
use. Backup your files often. How often? As with money, it pays to
"save early and save often." Backup your files as often as you can stand
the pain of not losing a file. If you have a crucial file that you spent
several hours updating, you probably want to backup that file
immediately after updating. If you have not made changes to your files,
you do not need to backup.

Protect yourself from viruses by buying and using a virus protection
software package. Virus protection packages allow you to scan a
diskette, selected files, or your entire PC for viruses. If a virus is found,
it is disabled and your PC is cured.

Why do you need to shut down your applications before you power
off your PC? If you repeatedly power off your PC without shutting
down your applications, your PC may become confused as to what
software is installed and began to create unnecessary files in order to
ensure a successful startup. Eventually, your machine may run slower
and you may even begin to lose software or files. Always close your
files, then close your software applications, then power down your PC.

Nurture your friendships with techno-nerds. Not only do you hear
interesting perspectives on life in general and computer use in particular,
you also may receive valuable free tips on computing. A geek friend can
save you time, money, and headaches. They will tell you what games are
really cool, when to buy or not buy a hot software package and
timesaving shortcuts. They can steer you clear of potential pitfalls in
using a software package. You may even surprise yourself as to how
much geek talk you can actually understand.

> Do you know the difference between education and experience? Education is when you read the fine print; experience is what you get when you don't.
>
> PETE SEEGER
>
> Experience is the best of schoolmasters, only the school fees are heavy.
>
> THOMAS CARLYLE

| Do get wired | Don't automate everything |

Everyone seems to be talking about the Internet. Magazines and newspapers seem to be full of articles about the Information Highway, our friends and business associates are talking about the going online, and business cards and letterhead contains E-mail addresses.

What is the Internet? It is a global "network of networks" consisting of computer networks at businesses, educational institutions and government agencies. This connection of computers allows us to send and receive electronic mail, send and receive files, and research databases for information on virtually any topic. The Internet concept was developed in the late 1960s by the Department of Defense in order to protect the government's computer networks during an enemy attack. Today, the Internet is being used for recreational and commercial purposes as well.

If you read magazines or watch TV, you may think that everyone is "surfing the net" regularly. Perception is not reality. Although Internet usage is growing at an exponential rate, current surveys show that less than 10% of the PC owner population receives information through the Internet (The Net, May 1997.)

The most popular application available through the Internet is electronic mail, or E-mail. E-mail is similar to Voicemail. E-mail gives you the ability to communicate with your friends, family, or business associates at any time by typing a note. The note is delivered to the recipient's mailbox, and the recipient can review and respond to the message at his or her convenience. E-mail mailing lists are used to communicate with a group of people interested in a particular topic.

Newsgroups are similar to E-mail in that you can conduct ongoing conversations about your interest with other like-minded people.

The World Wide Web helps you find information on virtually any subject in minutes. The Web consists of electronic pages, similar to the pages of a book, that display text, pictures, video, and sound. When you access a Web page, you begin reading that section of the book. Specific phrases or pictures within the page will link you to other pages related to the topic.

What if you do not know the address of a web page for a specific topic? Internet search programs examine the entire Web for pages that match your interest area. Using Internet search capabilities is an emerging skill today that will be a crucial skill to finding information in the next few years.

As in all things in life, a little common sense goes a long way. Just because you have a computer available to you doesn't mean you need to automate everything. I may choose to use a paper calendar and phone directory instead of keeping my calendar and phone numbers in a PC. Even though my PC has telephone and faxing capabilities, I may choose to use a separate telephone and fax machine.

Use your PC to automate repetitive work. Spreadsheets can automate repetitive mathematical tasks such as preparing expense reports, calculating sales commissions, and preparing budgets. And, the math will be correct regardless of how many times you're interrupted! Word processors can automate customer mailings and quickly create a table of contents and indexes for large reports.

Not only will you free yourself from drudgery, as a bonus you may also receive additional information just by automating. For example, although I like numbers and money, I hate to balance my checkbook. It's boring to perform the math and irritating when it doesn't balance the first time through. However, a program like Quicken will quickly balance your checkbook and give you additional information concerning your spending habits through reports and graphs. Sometimes it's more information than you want.

Invest the time to create and use forms and templates. Suppose you create a custom template incorporating your company's colors and logo. You use this template to create your presentations. Since all your slides were created using the custom template, they have the same professional look. When a client calls requiring a customized presentation tomorrow morning, you can quickly pull slides from multiple presentations and add a client specific cover slide and summary slide.

> *In man-machine symbiosis, it is man who must adjust.*
> *The machine can't.*
> ALAN J. PERLIS

## Conclusion

| | |
|---|---|
| Do buy the best you can afford | Don't be seduced |
| Do focus on the fundamentals | Don't forget to practice |
| Do learn one high impact product | Don't try to know it all |
| Do practice "safe" computing | Don't ignore your geek friends |
| Do get wired | Don't automate everything |

> *Life is what we make it, always has been, always will be.* GRANDMA MOSES
>
> *Life is what happens to you while you're making other plans.*
> BETTY TALMADGE
>
> *The important thing is not to stop questioning.*
> ALBERT EINSTEIN

# Denise Doar

Denise Doar is an entertaining speaker and seminar leader with extensive experiences in sales and training. Her company, Doar Barnwell & Associates, specializes in computer technology training and consulting for sales representatives and management. Her practical, need to know approach assists people in more effectively utilizing their personal computers. Her clients include IBM, Hewlett-Packard, Dun & Bradstreet Information Services, Sales Technologies, Aurum Software, AMP, Kawasaki Loaders, Volvo Construction Equipment, Roche Pharmaceuticals, and Allamerica Financial Services.

Denise is an active member of the National Speakers Association and Georgia Speakers Association. She holds magna cum laude degrees of Bachelor of Arts in Mathematics and Bachelor of Music in Performance from the University of Tennessee at Chattanooga.

You can reach Denise at Doar Barnwell & Associates, 220 Renaissance Parkway, Suite 1105, Atlanta, GA 30308 Phone (404) 892-4961, Fax (404) 874-3351 or E-mail: DeniseDoar@aol.com.

# ★ 18 ★

# Life Is Daily, So Is Success!

by **Meg Croot**

Life is daily. Each day as we rise and join the proverbial rat race, we follow routines of living that become habits. Day after day, these habits become the fabric of our existence. Thus, we live. Our habits and routines determine the quality and direction of our daily living. When we follow patterns that include a balance of work and play, give and take, laughter and tears, we experience success in all aspects of our being.

When the balance is shaken and uneven, we experience frustration and obstacles to fulfilled living. We feel the full impact of the fact that life is daily. It becomes difficult to stay on course and continue learning and growing personally and professionally. Stress and burnout get in the way of the inner drive and motivation needed to make progress.

Yet, when a comfortable balance is achieved, our energy level is high, we feel creative and inspired. We are able to live in the present, maximizing our resources and feel satisfied at the end of the day. The fact that life is daily gives us something to look forward to and anticipate with vigor.

The irony is that it's in the mundane, the routine, that we find our greatest triumphs. Over the course of time, day by day, dreams are born, plans are laid and slowly, methodically, we take baby steps toward the achievement of our goals. If life is daily, therein lies a truth; life is daily, so is success.

In <u>Illusions</u>, Richard Bach writes that you teach best what you most need to learn. In July of 1991, I experienced a melt down of energy and a complete burnout. I'd been working in the resort industry for 10 years, helping other people relax and enjoy vacations, when I realized that I had

not had a full day off in 15 months, and even worse, I had lost any sort of balance of work and play. All work and no play had indeed, made me a very dull girl. Professionally,
I was realizing many goals, yet personally, I was miserable and unhappy. The time had come to make some changes. With a background in Leisure Education and Recreation, I didn't have to look too far for a solution. The answer I discovered was that the better job I did incorporating fun and play in my schedule, the better job I did at work. When I was less burned out, I was more creative, productive, and enthusiastic.

In the words of a born recreation director and coach, there are success rules for the game of life. We don't choose how we are born or when we die; but each day, we have the opportunity to make up the rules about how we'll spend our time. The rules we play by, the strategies we follow, enable us to win at balancing and overcoming burnout.

## Burnout – Plague of the 90's

Today's world is busier. We are consumed by a sense of urgency. Frantic living makes us feel fried and fretful. We fret about the amount of responsibilities and pressures placed upon us. We are frazzled by a lack of energy and lack of time to fit everything into 24 hours. There seems to be less time to do the things we want to do. Dreams fade into the background of a mural of demands.

Burnout is evidenced by the fact that you are no longer able to deal with conflicts or manage your reactions to stress. Just thinking about getting up is exhausting. There is a pervasive feeling of not wanting to go to work, not wanting to take care of chores and not even having the energy to enjoy leisure and hobbies. Millions are affected by this plague of the 90's. In fact, fatigue is among the top five reasons people visit the doctor!

By definition, burnout is mental and physical exhaustion. If energy and motivation make up the battery in our bodies, burnout is the drain of daily life and excessive demands that exhausts our batteries' resources. Fortunately, our batteries are rechargeable and not disposable. Different people can tolerate different levels of demands and stressors. It's important to recognize that hard work doesn't cause burnout. In fact, hard work with a purpose can be a tremendous energizer. It's the lack of enthusiasm and direction that is indicative of burnout.

The progression of my burnout began with good intentions. Conscientious and eager to please, I worked hard to be excellent at my job. My high standards were not only noticed by my mangers, but also rewarded. The bar got higher and higher and pretty soon, even back flips over the top were met with a lukewarm response. So, naturally, I pushed harder than ever to prove myself. If I could only work harder and produce more, I believed the rewards would come my way. Small stresses and annoyances seemed to bombard me. <u>Everyone</u> got on my last nerve and was out to sabotage my success. Each day, I got up and began to go through the motions in a fretful way. Tasks gnawed at my already low energy supply. My patience was worn away by the time I arrived at work. The way my morning cup of coffee tasted rubbed me the wrong way. My co-workers irritated me nonstop. I worried continuously about things that would never happen.

One soft summer night, as I sat miserable at a 4th of July barbecue, I scowled as people passed me by. Even when someone offered a smile of encouragement and friendship, I turned my head to look over my shoulder to see what they were smiling at. Surely, it could not have been me. I saw others enjoying themselves and I wondered how I, *a Social Director, provider of leisure experiences to thousands of vacationers, Recreation Manager, past president of Resort and Commercial Recreation Association,* could have forgotten how to play! I had become the ugliest of all persons — busy, grouchy, alone and burned out.

## Five Reasons We Are Burned Out

Why does everyone feel so burned out today? Ask the question and most people will admit to having been burned out or even feeling being burned out right now. It's the problem dujour, this plague of the decade that you even hear about children experiencing.

**#1. Life is hard and life is fast.** We get used to the pace of hard and fast being the norm. Our daily lives include a good dose of media glutted with bad news. Every night we can select from a plethora of violent disaster movies and TV focused on the sensational and horrible. "Specials" like the World's Scariest Police Chases followed by World's Scariest Shootouts are available for our viewing pleasure. With the Internet, we can get bad news up to the minute 24 hours a day.

There is a lot to worry about. We worry about our finances and about social security running out before we can claim it back. We worry about crime and the state of the environment. We worry about natural disasters and the weather. We worry about our job security and how to achieve our dreams. We even worry about silly things like being fashionable or forgetting someone's birthday. Even knowing that most of what we worry over never happens, is beyond our control or trivial, doesn't stop us worrying.

Technology has made our lives busier, but not necessarily better. We are starting to consider that microwave ovens and fax machines are too slow. We are connected by cell phones, pagers, E-mail, and the web. There is a sense of urgency that time is running out. We need to get it fast or be left behind. This results in a tremendous sense of never being caught up, never being fast enough to do it all. All of this technology makes us accessible to pretty much anyone at anytime. News Flash — you don't have to be available all the time to everybody. No one is indispensable.

**#2 Do as I say, not as I do.** Somewhere along the way, we got the idea that eating healthy and keeping fit was OK for everybody else. As for ourselves, we'll get to it tomorrow or when we have time. Bad nutrition and a lack of exercise contribute to the feeling of fatigue that sends so many to see the doctor with complaints of lethargy and various aches and pains.

**# 3 Winning is Everything.** A great value is placed on being number one. As children, we could enjoy playing and trying new things without the pressure of mastery. Then one day, when we finished school and got a real job, it became important to grow up, be an adult, and at all costs, be the best at whatever we tried. Society doesn't place much value (and gives no publicity) to those who are number two or even worse — the dreaded average!

**#4 The Control Factor.** Having either too much or not enough control will contribute to burnout. A sense that control belongs to others, such as in situations where there is downsizing in formerly secure positions and companies, brings a huge amount of stress that is very hard to manage. Even in secure positions, many workers feel a lack of completion or closure on projects. A common gripe is being "micro-managed" by someone who wants to control not only the results, but also the process.

Burnout is equally evident in individuals who want to have total control over every detail of their lives. A perfectionist is especially prone to feeling burned out. The over attention to getting everything perfect often means that a project or idea is never launched. This is frustrating and eliminates the sense of accomplishment we all need to recharge our batteries.

**#5 We Forgot Recess.** Since settling in the colonies, Pilgrims managed to eliminate 50 holidays that were enjoyed by the English since Medieval Times. This hard-nosed work ethic has woven itself into management's expectations of today's employees. We have less leisure in 1996 (16 hours per week) than we did in 1972 (26 hours per week). At best, most of us only enjoy one or two weeks of vacation a year.

Lee Iacocca once said, "I'm constantly amazed by the number of people who can't seem to control their own schedules. Over the years, I've had many executives come to me and say with pride, 'Boy, last year I worked so hard that I didn't take any vacation.' It's actually nothing to be proud of. I always feel like responding, 'You dummy! You mean to tell me that you can take responsibility for an $80 million dollar project and you can't plan two weeks out of the year to go off with your family and have some fun?'"

Even when we do get a vacation, think about how hard it is to relax! Do you take the kind of vacations that are so over-organized and over-planned that you need a vacation when you get back from vacation to recover? I frequently work with hotels and resorts on strategies for helping guests have a memorable vacation experience. This need is driven by the fact that so many people have forgotten how fun recesses and vacations can be. The very idea of recess is about having free time, unfettered by a schedule or too many expectations.

## Burnout Busters, SmileMakers and TeamBuilders

The strategies for preventing and zapping burnout are available to us to start using today. In fact, it takes a commitment of a little time every day to insure that burnout doesn't become a factor in your life. It's important to know the difference between stress and burnout. Stress is not the same as burnout. Everyone experiences changing circumstances, pressure and a lack of control. This creates stress. Stress cannot be managed; in fact, stress management is a myth. The only thing you can manage is your reaction to stress; and, if you're burned out (mentally and physically exhausted) you don't stand a chance when you're up against stress.

Burnout Busters and SmileMakers are most effective when used daily. Just like you should eat at least five to seven fruits or vegetables a day, I recommend that you incorporate at least five to seven Burnout Busters and three SmileMakers a day. If life is daily, then we must employ ways to keep physically and emotionally energized.

Burnout Busters are the things you do for yourself that help you make the most of each moment of the day. You are fully able to live and enjoy when you feel good inside and out. In order to keep burnout at bay, incorporate these basics:

Start and end each day quietly with a few minutes of reflection, meditation, and prayer. Think in terms of what you have accomplished and what you are thankful for. Look ahead and prepare yourself for what you must do in the next 24 hours. Always dream a little about your goals and wildest imaginings of personal and professional success.

The Surgeon General has proclaimed "no more couch potatoes!" Get up and get moving. Walk, run, skip, jump rope, aerobicize, pump, swim, hike, bike, blade, ski, board, float, dance, stretch, shoot, swing, ride, slide, glide, motor, bend, plant, clean, lift, rake, pedal, row – you get the idea! Discover a verb and make it a part of your daily routine.

All this activity works up an appetite! Eat right; you know the rules. And drink water instead of soda, tea, or coffee. Your body will thank you and pay you back a thousand-fold.

Give up the idea that you need to be accessible to everybody all the time. When I gave up a pager and cell phone, I eliminated about 70% of the stress I had to manage my reaction to every day. I will never again put myself in a position where I can be disturbed at whim by an obnoxious beeping. Don't you deserve the same?

Have recess. The origin of the word "leisure" is from the French *leisur*. It means to permit. Permit yourself to play. You can play at your desk or play at home. You can play in your car when you pop in a book on tape. This is not the same as exercise, which is more like an obligation. Take a little time every day to permit yourself to do things that feel good. Recreation is for refreshing, relaxing and reenergizing ourselves. By recreating ourselves, we stimulate our creativity. You've experienced this — how many times have you gotten your best ideas in the shower or on the golf course — did you ever make the connection? Our brains come up with solutions and ideas only when we free them up or permit them to stop thinking about work and worries.

Another good reason to play is that it releases endomorphines which are natural feel good chemicals and pain reducers. And if you engage in adventure or extreme sports, your brain releases phenylethylamine which is the same hormone that is released when you first fall in love!

They say that variety is the spice of life, but it is not just a spice, but an essential element. So I say change is the salt of life. Vary your routine and responsibilities. Sometimes it's good to change your focus. At age 32, Ben Franklin wasn't happy with the way his life was going. He made a list of 12 life goals including to be a better father and husband and to be financially independent. By changing his focus, Ben Franklin was able to achieve more in his lifetime than many of us ever imagine.

Have patience and faith. Patience is the ability to wait. Faith is the ability to wait with confidence. When you let them, things work out the way they are meant to unfold. Trust the natural progression of life and success will follow. When you are doing all the right things, success will find you where you are, and so will happiness.

SmileMakers are the things we do or experience that surprise and delight us. They are the joy of life; and, when you are aware of each minute of the day, you will be amazed at how abundant SmileMakers are. Not only do they happen to you, but when you are the reason for a smile on anothers' face, it will bounce back to your face. My theory is that, if you give at least three smiles a day, you will receive at least that many in return.

What makes you smile is very personal and holds individual meaning. Being a SmileMaker doesn't take a lot of time, you'll find a multitude of chances to do it in the course of the day. Being a SmileMaker is about giving to others. Your imagination and creativity for being a SmileMaker has no limits; but, if you need help getting started, here are a few ideas:

Give really excellent service
Let a baby take a nap in your arms
Overtip a waiter who took good care of you
E-mail a "quote of the day" to a client
Read a story to a child
Just say "hi" to a stranger
Be gracious in traffic
Take your dog to the local nursing home
Write a thank you note to your parents
Leave a vase of cut flowers somewhere unusual — like a gas
station restroom
Listen to someone who is annoying, but wants to talk

Not only do we burn out as individuals, but it happens at work too. It has been noted that we praise those who balance, but reward people who work themselves to death. One of the best ways to prevent burnout at work and increase chances for success is to create a strong team environment. Many hands make for a light load whether it's moving bricks or designing software.

Good managers are those who know how to keep burnout out of the work place. This begins with the basics. A team-oriented manager will remove obstacles and supply the resources necessary for productive work. Vary routines and responsibilities. Make it fun to deliver results at work. Create work teams with varied types of people — mix it up a little and set aside traditional roles. People are more than their job descriptions. Don't be afraid to let them show you how good they can be. To avoid team burnout, a good manager will make sure that these guidelines are followed:

*Don't expect perfection, but emphasize excellence.*
Recognize good work.
Avoid ambiguity — make sure everyone knows what is expected of him.
Be reasonable about workloads.
Eliminate bureaucracy as much as possible — it makes employees feel powerless; it de-motivates and kills the spirit and soul of the team.

Good employees manage their managers. They know how to avoid letting anyone put the monkey on their backs! Take frequent mini breaks during the day and encourage your co-workers to do the same. Create an office environment that stimulates your imagination and creativity. Make sure that your work and your employees' work inspire passion. Figure out ways to share the drudgery and share the really challenging projects too. Have a zero tolerance policy toward gossiping and badmouthing other departments or managers. Trade things you don't enjoy doing for tasks you relish.

TeamBuilding is one of the most effective ways available to flatten out the organization chart and put everyone on the same playing field. By teambuilding, I mean using recreation, adventure, challenges, and activities to provide experiential learning focused on specific objectives like leadership skills, communication, trust and risk taking. This provides the opportunity to break down barriers and build up rapport among teams while having fun.

Not long ago, I did a program for a chemicals company whose meeting theme was "Extending the Boundaries of Excellence." We formed teams of six or seven and gave each team four big sheets of cardboard and two rolls of duct tape. In one hour, the teams were charged with designing and building a boat that would float then competed in a mini regatta. The experience paralleled work projects. In the beginning there was confusion and doubt — "Who is on my team and where's my stuff?" As work progressed, some team members became bored with the process and less involved, just as can happen with real work projects. As the deadline approached, everyone jumped in with a sense of urgency and excitement. After the regatta and awards, we asked teams questions like how did you feel about the project; what worked well; what obstacles did you overcome; and what would you do differently? The point that everyone took home was that through innovation, hard work, perseverance, and belief in the team, they could actually build a boat that floats from little more than cardboard and duct tape!

## The Last Minute

My own story has a happy ending, or rather, beginning as I learned to eliminate burnout in my life. The beginning of the end of burnout came when I took the first step toward taking control of my professional life and goals. My father gave me the best advice, "Don't let the pressure get on top of you and hold you down — get on top of it and let it lift up." Once I changed my attitude and got on top of the pressure, I was able to see over the stress and look toward a future. My vision of a future included doing work I enjoyed, having time to spend with my family, and meeting someone with whom I could share the adventures of daily life.

Once I knew what happiness and success meant to me, I knew how to recognize it. Too often, people aren't able to recognize or enjoy happiness. I think of the quote that defines happiness as a butterfly that will light upon one who sits still. One day my two-year-old nephew was playing on the porch. Suddenly, a blood curdling scream split the air! I raced out, imagining a bee sting, splinter, or cut requiring stitches. The actual cause of alarm was a small butterfly darting around his head. Since he had never actually met a butterfly, he didn't realize it was a nice thing! How often has your own happiness scared you and been the cause for undue alarm?

The next step for me was doing the things every day that would lead me toward success. I left my job — gradually; and, realizing that I was best at managing projects, communicating, facilitating teams and creating, I made up my own job description and became a recreation and leisure consultant, speaker, and trainer. I learned to fill my plate less and prioritize what mattered to me by defining what I liked to do best and least.

I started taking yoga and learned to breathe and reflect. On a whim, I adopted a puppy that taught me to focus on needs other than my own. My puppy turned out to be a very special dog and eventually, I joined a pet therapy volunteer organization with her. I chauffeur her to the hospice, nursing home, and disabled children's school where she shares the gift of unconditional love and acceptance. Vacation became a word that meant something to me rather than work (as in working to make someone else's vacation fun!) On one of my first real vacations, I made a friend who became a very attentive tour guide during a visit to England. He did such a good job with being a guide on my holiday, I decided to let him be my tour guide every day. We married just three short years after my crash and burnout summer!

For me, happy endings are actually an ongoing pursuit and daily challenge to balance and maintain a burnout-free lifestyle. Being free of burnout means feeling motivated to do the little stuff every day that contributes to success. Being free of burnout also helps us enjoy each minute of the day. A favorite quote of mine is "If it weren't for the last minute, nothing would ever get done!" Beyond the time management message in the quote, consider it on a different level. If you knew that your last minute was imminent, how differently would you spend your time? What would be important to accomplish? Whom would you choose to spend the time with? What worries would you forget? Whom would you say, "I love you" to?

Tennessee Williams wrote, "Life is all memory, except for the one present moment that goes by you so quick you hardly catch it going." Make the most of the moment, enjoy the memories and you'll be successful in your daily life.

# Meg Croot

Meg McLeroy Croot, owner of Creative Recommendations, Inc. is an internationally known speaker and consultant in the field of Recreation and Leisure Education. She has provide creative recommendations to clients such as The Walt Disney World Dolphin Hotel, Sun International, Wyndham Hotels, The Family Channel, Boca Raton Resort and Club, Chrysler, GE Capital and Sandy Lane Resort and Club. For these clients, Meg has designed themed recreation, team building events, service strategy workshops and hundreds of programs that enthuse, educate and entertain. By involving individuals and groups, Meg has the ability to enhance experiences and inspire through creative and dynamic presentations.

You can contact Meg at Creative Recommendations, Inc., 1310 Land O'Lakes Dr., Roswell, GA 30075 Phone (770) 645-2862, Fax (770) 645-2869 or E-mail: mcroot99@aol.com.

# ★ 19 ★

# Make This Your Best Year Yet!

by **Doug Smart**

My friend Mike lives in Metairie, Louisiana. He owns a lawn mower and bicycle shop. It's a neighborhood business, but Mike has had it for years and he does very well. A particular customer comes in two or three times a year and always asks for a *discount*. Mike is a good businessman and smiles, but it really bugs him. After awhile Mike had to know, "Why do you keep asking me for a discount? I have good prices. You must agree. You keep coming back." The man smiled a sheepish grin and said, "Forgive me. I don't mean to be obnoxious about this. It's just that, no matter where I shop, I always ask for a discount." "Do you get it?" Mike wanted to know. "Sometimes," he replied, "about 10% of the time I get a discount." Mike was amazed.

Does that mean you or I can walk into Sears, ask for a discount, and expect to get it? Sometimes. The clerk might look at us as if we just fell off Jupiter, but don't be surprised to hear, "Well, okay. I'm empowered. At least that's what they tell me. I can make decisions. Come with me. We'll ring it up." And presto! It works! You know the old wisdom, *You don't ask, you don't get.* Let me ask you something. In order for you to reach the stars, isn't asking *self-asking* vital to getting?

Here's a quick true/false quiz:

---

### *In Order to Reach Your Success Stars...*

| | | |
|---|---|---|
| T | F | **You have to ask yourself to be open to new information.** |
| T | F | **You have to ask other people to believe in you.** |
| T | F | **You have to ask yourself to believe in yourself.** |
| T | F | **You want to cultivate a deep appreciation for what you already have.** |
| T | F | **You have to ask yourself to try new ideas.** |
| T | F | **You need a renewable resource for your personal energy** |

---

The answers to all are *True*. Asking yourself to be strong in these personal areas boosts your personal energy (your *rocket fuel*, which we will call the *RF*).

When President John F. Kennedy asked the American people to accept his vision of a man on the moon by the end of the decade, he was really asking for the energy that comes from commitment to a goal. He did not ask if it was possible (which is a good thing because the answer would have been *impossible*. At that time the scientific community did not even have 15% of the information needed to accomplish the goal.) He just asked us to *believe* that his vision was possible. From the energy of that belief came the *RF* to do the impossible.

You and I regulate our *RF* every day through the constant stream of conversations in our head. On a typical day we talk to ourselves approximately 10,000 times! However, here is a bad news tip: unfortunately, for many of us, most of those 10,000 conversations are negative. As adults, sometimes we are P.O.W. (Prisoners of Our Wishes). We get so bogged down in the impossibility of our challenges we drain off our *RF* and what is left is diluted and polluted. Our rocket does not rise to the clouds much less the stars. What can we do?

I am a motivator, keynoter, consultant, author, and entrepreneur. After making almost 1000 presentations to organizations from Walmart's home office to Cape Canaveral's NASA Kennedy Space

Center (hey, I work with *real* rocket scientists!), I have observed first hand that the people who are having their best year yet are the ones who maintain a high energy level. They do it by <u>asking themselves to be energetic</u>! Huh? They are manufacturing their own RF, and you can, too, with a unique formula for success.

### *10-20-30-40-50 Formula for Success*

**It's a smart idea to read for 10 minutes every morning.** We become what we think about. Start your day by reading something inspirational, motivational, or *how to*. I call it taking mega vitamins for the brain. For example: my passions are in personal development, growing my businesses, and gardening. I usually start my day by reading an inspirational book, a computer magazine, or a gardening catalog. Those first few golden minutes of the day tend to frame the day. You know how this happens. It is like when you wake up to a song on the radio; its beat establishes a tone for your morning that you just can't clear out of your head for a while.

Many people tell me newspapers are important, but they stopped reading them early in the morning; they save them for later. I intentionally refrain from watching television at the start of the day, too.

**Spend 20 minutes a day around positive, motivated, optimistic, upbeat people.** They are your instant energy source; and, if you can't find some, go rent some! Check out motivational tapes from your training library.

Denis Waitley, in <u>The Psychology of Winning</u>, says "We become the people around us." You and I want to embrace the company of people who are good for us. We want to be around people who have the energy and enthusiasm for life of a nine-year-old. Christine, our nine-year-old neighbor, came across the street and asked, "Can I catch bugs in your garden?" "Sure, Christine," I replied, "but why don't you catch the bugs in *your* garden?" "Because my daddy sprays," she informed me, "and he says you don't. Last night he told Mom the big ones must still be coming from *your* side." I still chuckle when I think about it. Isn't that openness refreshing? Doesn't it feel good to be around adults who still have that frankness, optimism, and energy? Don't we need to be around people who speak their minds and don't play politics or wear masks? Go find them because life does not necessarily bring them to us. Have you noticed that if you do not go find the good ones, the bad ones fill the void?

Other people add to or deplete our *RF*. You know how you feel around people who gripe and moan about how life is unfair and work stinks. Nobody really understands them. Depressed and de-energized come to mind because they contaminate our *RF*. On the other hand, when you are around upbeat people who volunteer for new assignments, put in the extra hours, and assist others in reaching their goals you feel renewed and re-energized. Your *RF* is pure and increasing in volume. Spend 20 minutes a day around optimistic people and feel their energy and charisma arc into you. Enjoy them, let them flourish in you, and arc your spare *RF* over to somebody else.

**Say 30 positive things about yourself to yourself every day.** On a typical day we say 10,000 things to ourselves. Make at least 30 positive self-statements to build a still of self-generating *RF*.

I believe each of us has special talents. And I believe these talents are gifts from God. But the gifts are like brand new computers still in the box. It's up to us to take the computers out of the box, plug them in, and learn the software. If we skip any of these steps, we run the risk of going to our graves without realizing our talents.

If you were in my audience and I held up a copy of *The Cat in the Hat* by Dr. Suess and asked if you recognized the book, would you? Typically 90% of adults do. And have you ever bought a copy? Typically 75% say yes. Dr. Suess knew the importance of believing in his talents, but life can be so cruel. The first 27 publishers basically looked at his first book, then looked at him and said, so you think people will buy this for their kids? No, they won't. This will scare their kids! This is weird. You are pretty weird. You give me the creeps. Get out of here! The first 27 publishers were very unkind to Dr. Suess. Publisher 28, though, basically said, you really believe this is something kids *need to read*. I don't know. No one has ever done this before. We'll print a few copies and see. Maybe a niche will develop. The Cat in the Hat has touched 90% of the lives in the audience to the point that 75% have done business with it; yet, the finest brains in publishing — the experts — saw only one word on the cover of the manuscript: *loser*. What word is on your cover? Do you believe in your talents so deeply that people can "see" them when they see you? Or do you obediently acquiesce to the judgment of the "experts" who might overlook your gifts and diminish your *RF*?

To help yourself believe in your talents, say 30 positive statements to yourself about yourself every day. These positive statements are not phony and made-up. They are declarations of truth about yourself. There is one person you can never lie to; that person is *you*. As long as you *know* that what you are saying is true, then it is truth. Personally, I had a challenge coming up with 30 positive statements about myself. It took me several weeks to make a list I believed in! To give you an idea of what your list might look like, here are my first five:

I like myself.
I am a good husband, father, son, brother, uncle, friend.
I improve people's lives through sharing information
and experiences.
I am a motivational and inspirational speaker.
I am optimistic and enthusiastic.

There are close to six billion people on earth. Out of that astronomical number, your fingerprints and DNA are unique to you. Something else is unique to you: no one on earth has your one-of-a-kind combination of education, experiences, beliefs, values, talents, gifts, culture, and skills. You are special and *we need you*. To illustrate: there is an outcry over the destruction of the Amazon rain forest in Brazil. Why? It is feared that some species of birds, insects, and trees are becoming extinct before we have a chance to study them. So? Consider that those living entities have an immune system that has been fighting infection and disease for thousands of years. A particular species of the bird might have the unique combination of enzymes that we need to unlock the cure for cancer in humans. Of course, that bird does not understand or appreciate its uniqueness. Yet its disappearance is a loss that in some way impacts every one of us. We need that bird. What about you? If you don't believe in your talents and you disappear without realizing your gifts, there is a loss that impacts every one of us. Do you believe in your talents like Dr. Suess and self-manufacture your forward-thrusting energy or do you cave into the "experts" who might not appreciate your uniqueness? Speaking selfishly, *we need you!* Why? Our society is changing at hyper-speed; *YOU* may possess keys to our successful future. And like a little bird in the Amazon rain forest, *you do not realize the impact you can have on the rest of us.* To keep your *RF* in full supply, to recognize your gifts and to multiply those gifts bountifully for the rest of us, say 30 positive things about yourself to yourself every day.

As you reach for the stars, **say *thank you* 40 times a day**. Zig Ziglar calls this "the attitude of gratitude" because it really is good right now. You and I have low energy people on our team who don't appreciate how well they have it — and they won't appreciate it until they lose it!

I was standing on the curb outside the Fayetteville, Arkansas, airport while I waited for the hotel shuttle to pick me up. A bright red car screeched to a halt just a few yards past me and a man, obviously in a hurry, jumped out the second it stopped. Without looking, he swung hard to shut the car door. Like an errant batter who missed the ball he totally missed the door. He froze. His face distorted into a look of total disgust. He grabbed the car door at the top and slammed it shut. Then with a sour look, he stomped past me into the airport. I was just standing there waiting for a ride, but I felt impacted by him. I could not help feeling sorry for whomever it was he came to meet — like they needed a shot of him in their lives right then!

Compare that incident to this. My plane landed in Dallas, Texas, at noon on a very hot day. I belong to a rental car club and so I do not have to stand in line and wait; shiny new cars are conveniently lined up with keys in the ignitions and paperwork on the front seats. I choose any car I wish and a guard checks me out at the exit. That particular day, I look around and see the exit and I notice there isn't any guard house. There is no one to check my paperwork. "They sure are trusting in Dallas!" I can't help but think. I choose a beautiful new car and prepare to drive away. As I near the exit I see a car parked at the curb and someone in uniform inside. The motor is running; the air conditioning is on. The guard is keeping cool by using the car as an office. That has to make for a challenging day! As I approach, a young woman with a beautiful smile ( I guess her to be in her early twenties) emerges from the car. I roll down my window; and, as I pass the papers to her, I remark, "Sure is hot." Maybe because she is smiling or maybe because I'm a Mr. Nice Guy, I add, "it must be difficult working in a car all day." "It's not so bad," she replies. And then after a pause she adds, "I'm working 16 hours today." "Sixteen hours! How come?" I ask. "I'm working a double shift. Since they don't have a guard house, they can't keep anybody. I don't mind. So they always call me and I say yes." There was another pause and she said, "They are paying me time and a half." As she hands my papers back to me and I feel my air conditioning rushing out my open window into the broiling Texas heat, I offer, "Well, I bet you will be glad when they build a guard house." Her beautiful smile widens and she leans so far forward that she sticks her head in my window and whispers, "Mister, I hope they never build it! And don't you recommend they build one, either!"

To me, happy people are successful people. And happy people have a thankful attitude. There is much to be thankful for and to be happy about right now. Enjoy life. You know, there is a funny quirk in human nature; after ten years passes, we tend to label a period of time as *the good old days*. Research shows that even if we did not enjoy that period while it was happening, we tend to look back with a fondness and a bit of longing; for example, can you hear your best friend saying, "The kids were so little then"? "I hated that old car, but I miss it now." "I was ten years younger then." "We didn't have much more than a phone, a desk and just the two of us. It's a wonder we survived." "We sure did some crazy things." The good news is, your life is running now. Why waste ten years before appreciating what is happening? Enjoy  the journey as you reach for the stars and feel energized by appreciating the opportunity.

**Try 50 new things every month.** Doesn't that sound obnoxious? To put it in perspective that is not even two a day! And just keep it simple. For example, go to work by a different route so that your brain cells can get fired up by playing with different visuals. Choose something to eat for lunch that you do not normally eat. Write your to do list in green ink and mark off completions in purple. Go browse in some of those little stores you never go into. Volunteer your next four Saturdays to work in a homeless shelter (and take your children with you.)

Why bother? Doing 50 new things a month will help you get very comfortable with the rhythm of change. To make this your best year yet, you will have to let go of some comfortable habits because they hold you back. For example, instead of reading the newspaper first thing in the morning, grab a "how to" book in your hobby interest and read for 10 minutes. Instead of waiting until you are *in the mood* to start a major project, tell yourself that you will block out 30 minutes today to get a portion of it going. Instead of leaving your job at the end of the day with a discouraged feeling of "I'll just deal with this stuff again tomorrow," use the last 15 minutes to plan and prioritize your next day. Instead of leaving the game early so you can beat the traffic, stay and enjoy every moment and then have fun observing the world around you — so it takes *an extra 20 minutes(!)* to get home; big deal; refuse to waste your energy on feeling aggravated.

Here's another reason to embrace change in a personal and continual way. Even if you were not on a confirmed journey to find greater success in your life, you would have to make big changes anyhow. Why? The Information Age is upon us.

The Information Age is actually a sweeping, worldwide revolution that is shaking up people's careers — in many cases shaking up people's lives as evidenced by how our jobs keep changing. And all around us we see corporate mergers, downsizing, restructuring, government and military functions that are now outsourced to private industry, and new growth industries that explode into our lives like fresh adolescent volcanoes. To put it in perspective: the last big worldwide movement was the Industrial Age. It lasted approximately 200 years. We are at the *start* of the Information Age. There is nothing on the horizon to foretell its slowing down, much less its end. Likely, we will live the rest of our lives *only at the start* of the Information Age. But you and I have people around us who think they are going to wait this thing out! They are choosing not to participate in the changes. Say a prayer for them because they are as doomed as dinosaurs. The world is moving at a fast clip and has waning patience for people who choose not to keep up. The people who will survive and thrive in this environment are the ones who embrace change in a personal way. And one method for doing this is to experiment with 50 new things a month so that you are personally comfortable with the rhythm of change.

Do not forget to try fresh new changes in your relationships, either. I spoke at a leadership workshop in Brattleboro, Vermont, and I instructed the audience in the value of using this *10-20-30-40-50 Formula for Success* to be the type of leader that others *want* to be around. A tall, good looking young man (I guess about age 25) with a broad smile, approached me at the break and said, "Thank you!" His energy was contagious, so I beamed, "You're welcome!" There was a pause and I felt compelled to add, "Thanks for what?" "You just gave me my wife's birthday present. And I am so excited I can't stand it." "Birthday present? What do you mean?" I asked. "Tomorrow is her birthday. We have been married for four years. We don't have a lot of money and I love her so much. I really wanted this to be the special birthday. I didn't know what I was gonna do. But when you said, 'try 50 new things a month, about two a day' that gave me an idea! Tomorrow, when she opens her card, I am going to have already written in it, 'I love you so much that every day for the next 30 days I am going to dream up a fresh new way to tell you just how much I love you.'" Ahhhh. Isn't that romantic? What a nice guy. I suspect that most of the readers of this book would prefer that gift to something from the shelf in a store.

Let me ask you. Do you have somebody in your life you love more than anything in the world? What are you doing about it? You know, we could go stop cars on your street and everyone would have a trunkload of *intentions*. That makes the market value for *intentions* exactly zero. What are you *doing* about it? I commend to you, for the next 30 days you dream up one fresh new way every day just to say "I love you." Watch what happens to the quality of the relationship. Watch what happens to the quality of your *RF*. Best of all, watch what happens to the quality of life! Denis Waitley says we become the people around us. But guess who the people around us are busy becoming. *You and me.* We have to be people worth becoming. How to do that? We're lucky. There are lots of ways you and I can become stronger, better, higher energy people. One method is this *10-20-30-40-50 Formula for Success.*

To keep your supply of *RF* abundant, make two copies of the following formula. Put one on your mirror at home and the other in your work space.

### Making This My Best Year Yet!

For 10 minutes each morning, I'll read something inspirational, motivational, or "how to" to raise my energy and launch my day with an optimistic perspective.

I'll spend 20 minutes a day around motivated, upbeat, positive people. I become the people around me. I enjoy and absorb some of their electricity and I'll pass it on.

I'll say 30 positive things about myself to myself daily. I become what I think about and these 30 positive self-affirmations will steer the quality of my life.

I'll say thank you 40 times a day. I choose to enjoy life while it is happening with an attitude of gratitude.

I'll try 50 new things a month. That's less than two a day. Embracing change daily builds my career, drops stress, and increases the fun of living!

As my friend Mike says, "If you don't ask, you don't get." As you head for the stars, one question to ask yourself, "Do I have enough rocket fuel?" You know the answer is *yes* if you use the tools for generating your supply. Let this Success Formula serve as a renewable resource for your personal energy. Have fun on your journey. And to make the trip even more satisfying, be sure to take other people to the stars with you!

# Doug Smart

Doug Smart is a speaker, consultant, entrepreneur and author of two books on achieving personal success. As president of Doug Smart Seminars, he conducts programs tailored to helping business professionals in industry, education, healthcare, sales and government increase personal productivity and organizational ability — while reducing stress! Using ideas gained while working with over 900 groups in six years, his insight is unique and up to the minute. He has spoken for organizations as diverse as AT&T, IBM, University of Illinois, Columbia/HCA, Hospitality Sales and Marketing Association, and the U.S. Dept. of Education.

Doug keeps current with membership in the National Speakers Association and Meeting Professionals International. He is a past president of New Orleans Toastmasters.

You can contact Doug at Doug Smart Seminars, PO Box 768024, Roswell, GA 30076 Phone (770) 587-9784 or (800) 299-3737, Fax: (770) 587-1050 or E-mail: DougSmart.Seminars@worldnet.att.net

# ★ 20 ★

# From One to Another

by **Austin McGonigle, CSP**

Whenever my two teenage daughters and I visit my mother, we inevitably review the many photo albums from years past. Some of the photographs go back to the early part of the century and include a passport photo of my mother when she emigrated from County Mayo, Ireland. She was a beautiful sixteen-year-old who decided to take a risk and build a life in a foreign land, a land of opportunity.

The albums provide a chronology of my mother's life — a life dedicated to raising her sons and being the best wife she could be to my father. Her success is evidenced by the many happy and talented children, grandchildren, and great-grandchild her life has caused. She passed on her wit and wisdom to her children, who have passed it on to their children.

My daughters and nieces and nephews are all part of the legacy that Joe and Nora McGonigle created. My parents had three sons who have had six children. All are doing well and are making a positive difference with the people in their lives. The next generation is represented by Michael McGonigle who, after one year of life, has already made a significant impact on those around him. The legacy continues.

My dad passed away many years ago and mom is 86 years old but their legacy will live on from one to another to another. Success is living life, learning its many lessons, and passing it on. To me, happiness is seeing in other people that which has been passed on.

Observing my children do well in their academics, extracurricular activities, and social interactions is rewarding. Seeing their behaviors and knowing that I and their mother had positive influences on them is thrilling. The role of parent is the most important role in life. It shapes the future.

I do not claim to be a role model for ideal parenting. I am extremely thankful that I have been blessed with the children I have. My understanding of what my parental role is has helped me be a good parent. It is my strong belief that parents should consistently help their children make decisions that are good for them. It is my observation that many parents help their children make decisions that are good for the parents or, even worse, make decisions for them.

**Yes, success is passing it on from one to another.**

We do not have to be parents to be successful passing it on. We have the opportunity in our various societal roles to pass it on. As I was writing this chapter, my home telephone rang and a female voice asked to speak to "Mr. or Mrs. McGoogagal." This was a definite sign that I was receiving a telemarketing call early on a Saturday morning.

I answered, "This is Mr. McGonigle." She said, "How are you today?" I mentioned to her that I teach telephone skills and suggested that she eliminate the phrase "how are you today?" since it usually causes a negative reaction from the person being called. She then asked me "Where do you do your grocery shopping?" I said, "Publix." She next asked "How much do you spend a week?" I answered, "$75.00." She then told me that I would not be a good candidate for the bulk food purchasing plan she was selling. I agreed with her, but before she hung up she thanked me for the telemarketing tip and said "I am not going to say how are you today anymore."

**Sometimes it is a very small pass.**

Having been a professional speaker, trainer, and consultant over the past 15 years has afforded me the opportunity to make a living by passing it on to another. It is rewarding to know that my words and suggestions make a difference in other people's lives.

Last year I spoke at INC's Customer Service Conference in Seattle. The title of my presentation was *The Most Important Company That You'll Ever Work For, I INC*. This talk stresses the responsibility of developing our own careers and having the confidence to face the changes corporate downsizing, mergers, and acquisitions can cause. The talk was well received, the applause was loud and strong but the real thrill of that talk for me came months later.

I received a letter thanking me for my talk in Seattle. My message that day helped a man make the decision to resign from his company and start his own business. He explained that he had been unhappy in his job for many years and the stress of knowing he should be doing something else was negatively affecting his personal life. My message that day simply helped him make a decision that has turned out to be good for him. I believe it also helped his former employer. I like to refer to that story as *Waking Up in Seattle*; movie rights are pending.

### Sometimes we don't know who is receiving the pass.

Fifteen years ago I met a remarkable young woman named Anita Kemp. She was the wife of a friend who was one of our salespeople. She was employed as a flight attendant and was an aerobics instructor in her spare time. She loved people and had a real zest for life. I remember telling her that she had a great future in sales and had the potential to be the best. She doubted her potential career in sales because she did not have a college degree. I told her that academic success had little to do with future success in business.

She took one of our public sales seminars and absorbed the information like a sponge. She has been successful in four different industries as a true professional salesperson. Anita has consistently earned a six-figure income and is now one of the most successful residential real estate agents in the country. She also remarried and is now Anita Best. It was quite prophetic when I told her she would be the best, in more ways than I anticipated.

### Sometimes you know you're passing it to the best.

In 1983 and 1984 I had the opportunity to speak to a business fraternity at Georgia Southern College, Pi Sigma Epsilon. It is sponsored by Sales and Marketing Executives International. There was a student named Jeff Almond who, particularly motivated by my message, was re-energized and decided to apply his talents. His story is remarkable.

He worked hard and got his degree. He obtained a sales position in the printing business and excelled. With the confidence of his successes, he has had an outstanding career and is now Vice President and General Manager of The Woodman Company, the major manufacturer of packaging equipment for the snack food industry.

Over the past seven years I have consulted and trained for The Woodman Company and marveled at how Jeff has grown as a person and manager of people. All of his sales people are significantly older and many are more experienced yet they all have admiration and respect for Jeff and his leadership abilities.

## Sometimes the receiver becomes the passer.

One of my dearest friends is a woman named Elizabeth Bill. She is a special person who has been very successful for many years in the hotel business. She is a true professional but that is not what I am amazed at.

Elizabeth does something that very few people can do. She spends many volunteer hours at hospices and assists so many people with her compassion and love. She passes on her wisdom not only for the benefit of the terminally ill but for their families.

## Sometimes it is more difficult to pass it on.

In 1984 there was a recent graduate of University of North Carolina who came to Atlanta to start her career. A mutual friend referred her to me and wonderful things happened for us both. I met Ellie for a three-hour cup of coffee and knew she was a winner. She took a job with a long distance telephone reseller but would contact me about once a month to say hello. She was meant to be a trainer and was starting to realize it.

She developed into an excellent trainer and manager for my company. I cried when she left because her husband had been relocated. I cheered for her when she got her masters degree in training and development from Wake Forest. I have watched with pride as she keeps achieving in this wonderful profession of developing people. She also has had two children along the way.

In December, I will be working with Ellie Johnson as we deliver a program together for a mutual client. I anticipate the teacher will be learning from the student.

## You know a winner will pass it on.

Hal Griswold, a former client and friend, has fathered and raised nine children. He told me the following story and I have told it many times since.

When Hal was eleven years old, he was riding with his dad in the family car on a hot summer day. They saw a car with a flat tire on the side of the road and decided to stop to see if they could help.

It was a man and his wife and three small children. They were hundreds of miles from their home and had a long journey ahead of them. There was no spare and they didn't have enough money to purchase a new tire.

Hal and his father drove the family to a service station bought cold drinks for them and purchased a new tire. They all drove back to the family's car and put the new tire on the car. The father of the family was thankful and emotional and offered to mail Hal's father the money for the tire. Hal's vivid memory of what his father said to the man was, "No need to repay me. Someday, simply pass on a similar gesture to someone else."

The experience for Hal was significant one and has served him well over the years. Thanks Hal, for passing on to me your cherished *pass it on* story. I have passed it on to many people since you shared that memory of your dad with me.

**Sometimes it passes from generation to generation.**

As I live my life, I am conscious of the fact that I am leaving a legacy and that legacy consists of what I pass on to others. What I pass on to my children and their children is my main legacy. What I say as a speaker and what I write as a writer is also my legacy.

It is the multiplication of what is passed on that has a huge impact on our society.

Success is passing and receiving and passing. Pass it on from one to another.

# Austin McGonigle, CSP

Austin McGonigle, CSP, is America's Thought Provoker. As president of Success Cycle, Inc., he has had a powerful impact on thousands of individuals from hundreds of companies and associations. His expertise is centered in sales, motivation and customer service. Austin challenges his audiences with humor and real life experiences to minimize their fears and reach unprecedented levels of personal success. Austin simply gets results.

Austin is a member of the National Speakers Association and has been recognized as a Certified Speaking Professional.

You can reach Austin at Success Cycle, Inc., PO Box 724905, Atlanta, GA, 31139-1905 Phone (770) 436-0600 or Fax (770) 432-2130.

# ★ Resource List ★

*Karla Brandau*
LIFE POWER DYNAMICS

PO Box 450802
Atlanta, GA 31145-0802
(770) 923-0883, Fax (770) 931-2530
E-mail: Karla@kbrandau.com

*June Cline*
COURT JESTERS CLUB

935-A Cobb Place Blvd.
Kennesaw, GA 30144
(770) 423-7278, Fax (770) 423-7279
E-mail: junejester@aol.com

*Steve Cohn*
ABSOLUTELY DELIGHTFUL
DREAMERS

560 Summer Breeze Court
Alpharetta, GA 30202
(770) 667-3042, Fax (770) 667-3142
E-mail: addreamers@aol.com

*Meg Croot*
CREATIVE RECOMMENDATIONS,
INC.

1310 Land O'Lakes Dr.
Roswell, GA 30075
(770) 645-2862, Fax (770) 645-2869
E-mail: mcroot99@aol.com.

*Denise Doar*
DOAR BARNWELL
& ASSOCIATES

220 Renaissance Parkway, Suite 1105
Atlanta, GA 30308
(404) 892-4961, Fax (404) 874-3351
E-mail: DeniseDoar@aol.com

*Shirley Garrett, Ed.D.*
SHIRLEY D. GARRETT

PO Box 1195
Carrollton, GA 30117
(770) 836-1926, Fax (770) 834-9969
E-mail: drshirl@mindspring.com

*Gail Geary, J.D.*
GEARY COMMUNICATIONS

220 River North Drive
Atlanta, GA 30328
(770) 804-8449, Fax (770) 394-1848
E-mail: gearycom@aol.com

*D.J. Harrington*
Phone Logic, Inc.

2820 Andover Way
Woodstock, GA 30189
(770) 924-4400, Fax (770) 516-7797
or (800) 352-5252

*Arthur (Mano)*
*Manoharan, M.D.*

2006 Azalea Circle
Decatur, GA 30033
(404) 325-0592

*Nancy Manson, MS, PHR*
Manson Techniques, Inc.

110 Parliament Court
Fayetteville, GA 30215
(770) 719-2425, Fax (770) 719-2425
E-mail: njmanson@aol.com

*Myra McElhaney*
McElhaney & Associates

8531 Birch Hollow Dr.
Roswell, GA 30076
(770) 664-4553, Fax (770) 752-0817
E-mail: pmcelhaney@aol.com

*Austin McGonigle, CSP*
Success Cycle, Inc.

PO Box 724905
Atlanta, GA 31139-1905
(770) 436-0600, Fax (770) 432-2130

*Vicki McManus*
Fortune Practice
Management

5579-B Chamblee Dunwoody Road,
Suite 207
Atlanta, GA 30338
(770) 512-0341, (888) 347-4785
Fax (770) 512-0341

*Fiona Page-Hobbs*
Fiona Page, Inc.

10625 Stonefield Landing
Duluth, GA 30097-2030
(770) 497-8807, Fax (770) 814-0771
E-mail: page@negia.net

*Dr. David Ryback*
DAVID RYBACK &
ASSOCIATES

1534 N. Decatur Rd., Suite 201
Atlanta, GA 30307
(404) 377-3588
E-mail: docryback@aol.com

*Jean Houston Shore*
BUSINESS RESOURCE GROUP

408 Vivian Way
Woodstock, GA 30188-1654
(770) 924-4436, Fax (770) 924-1128
E-mail: shorebrg@aol.com

*Doug Smart*
DOUG SMART SEMINARS

PO Box 768024
Roswell, GA 30076
(770) 587-9784, Fax (770) 587-1050
(800) 299-3737
E-mail: DougSmart.Seminars@worldnet.att.net

*Marcia Steele*
STEELE SUCCESS, INC.

11250 Quailbrook Chase
Duluth, GA 30155
(770) 813-9767, Fax (770) 813-9864
E-mail: success@discom.net

*Mike Stewart, CSP*
STEWART & STEWART, INC.

1140 Hammond Dr., Suite D4190
Atlanta, GA 30328
(770) 512-0022, Fax (770) 671-0023
(800) 422-5252
E-mail: mstewart@mindspring.com

*Patti Wood, CSP*
COMMUNICATION DYNAMICS

2343 Hunting Valley Dr.
Decatur, GA 30033
(404) 371-8228, Fax (404) 370-0141
(888) 4PattiW *or* (888) 472-8849